SHAPING A NEW INTERNATIONAL FINANCIAL SYSTEM

This is a first-rate piece of work which contributes significantly to our understanding of the current state and future prospects for stability and order in the international financial system. The editors should be congratulated for bringing together such a wide range of scholarly and bureaucratic experts and for bringing such high standards of academic excellence to bear on the project. This is an excellent volume which will make a critical contribution to the debate over how and why the international financial structure might be transformed.

- Dr. Michael K. Hawes, The J. William Fulbright Distinguished Chair in International and Area Studies, University of California at Berkeley

This is a timely and interesting collection on the future of the global financial order by a group of real experts in the field. It is difficult to imagine a more distinguished cast list. The book reads well and will be received with gratitude by scholars of international political economy as a rare example of the cross-fertilisation that is possible between policy-makers and academics.

- Andrew Williams, University of Kent, UK

The G8 and Global Governance Series

The G8 and Global Governance Series explores the issues, the institutions and the strategies of participants in the G8 network of global governance, as they address the challenges of shaping global order in the new millennium. Intensifying globalization is moving many once domestic issues into the international arena, requiring constant international co-operation, and demanding new collective leadership to direct the galaxy of multilateral institutions created in 1945. In response, the Group of Eight, composed of the world's major market democracies, including Russia and the European Union, is emerging as the effective source of global governance in the new era. This series focuses on the new issues at the centre of global governance, from finance, investment, and trade, through transnational threats to human security, to traditional political and security challenges. It examines the often invisible network of G8 and G7 institutions as they operate within and outside established international organizations to generate desired outcomes. It analyzes how individual G7 members and other international actors, including multinational firms and those from civil society, devise and implement strategies to secure their preferred global order.

Also in the series

Hanging In There
The G7 and G8 Summit in Maturity and Renewal
Nicholas Bayne
ISBN 0 7546 1185 X

The G7/G8 System
Evolution, role and documentation
Peter I. Hajnal
ISBN 1 84014 776 8

The G8's Role in the New Millennium
Edited by Michael R. Hodges, John J. Kirton and Joseph P. Daniels
ISBN 1 84014 774 1

Shaping a New International Financial System

Challenges of governance in a globalizing world

Edited by
KARL KAISER
Deutschen Gesellschaft für Ausvartige Politik
and University of Bonn

JOHN J. KIRTON
University of Toronto

JOSEPH P. DANIELS
Marquette University

Ashgate

Aldershot • Burlington USA • Singapore • Sydney

Published by
Ashgate Publishing Ltd
Gower House
Croft Road
Aldershot
Hants GU11 3HR
England

Ashgate Publishing Company
131 Main Street
Burlington
Vermont 05401
USA

Ashgate website: http://www.ashgate.com

British Library Cataloguing in Publication Data
Shaping a new international financial system : challenges
of governance in a globalizing world. - (The G8 and global
governance)
1. Group of Seven - Influence - Congresses 2. International
economic relations - Congresses
I. Kaiser, Karl II. Kirton, John J. III. Daniels, Joseph P.
337.1

Library of Congress Control Number: 00-132590

ISBN 0 7546 1412 3

Printed in Great Britain by Antony Rowe Ltd.

Contents

List of Figures

List of Tables

List of Contributors

Sir Nicholas Bayne, KCMG, is a Visiting Fellow at the International Relations Department of the London School of Economics and Political Science. As a British diplomat, he was High Commissioner to Canada, 1992-1996, Economic Director at the FCO, 1998-1992, and Ambassador to the OECD, 1985-1988. He is co-author, with Robert Putnam, of *Hanging Together: Cooperation and Conflict in the Seven Power Summits.*

Dr. Joseph P. Daniels is the Director of the Institute for Global Economic Affairs and Associate Professor of International Economics at Marquette University, Milwaukee, Wisconsin. As a Canadian-US Fulbright Research Scholar, he was Visiting Professor of Economics and International Relations, University of Toronto in 1997-98. An established scholar on the G7 Summit process, he has published widely on international economic policy processes.

Dr. Olivier Davanne is Scientific Advisor to the Conseil d'Analyse Economique (CAE) and Associate Professor at the University Paris-Dauphine. Before joining the CAE, he held various senior positions both in the private and in the public sector. He has also served as Senior Economic Advisor to the French minister in charge of labour and social affairs policies, as Co-director of European Economic Research with Goldman Sachs, and held various positions in the French Ministry of Finance.

Dr. Curzio Giannini is Deputy Head of the International Relations Department at the Banca d'Italia, where he previously served in the Research Department. He has been a member of several international groups, including the G-10 Committee on Payment and Settlement Systems, the G-10 *Ad Hoc* Working Group on the Resolution of Sovereign Liquidity Crises, established after the 1994-95 Mexican crisis, and has written widely on monetary policy, financial intermediation, and international financial institutions.

Dr. Pierre Jacquet is Deputy Director of the French Institute of International Relations (IFRI) in Paris and Chief Editor of IFRI's quarterly review *Politique Etrangère*. He teaches economics at Ecole Polytechnique and is also Professor of international economics and Head of the Department of Economics and Social Sciences at Ecole nationale des ponts et chaussées. He is widely published in the fields of globalization, international monetary and financial issues, the coordination of economic policies, trade policies and negotiations, and European integration.

Dr. Karl Kaiser is Otto Wolff-Director of the Research Institute of the German Society for Foreign Affairs in Berlin and Professor of Political Sciences at the University of Bonn. He has taught at Harvard University, where he returned several times as Visiting Professor, as well as at the Universities of Bonn, Johns Hopkins (Bologna), Saarbruecken, and Cologne. He published numerous books in the fields of German foreign policy, transatlantic relations, European integration and international affairs.

Dr. John J. Kirton is Director of the G8 Research Group, Associate Professor of Political Science, Research Associate of the Centre for International Studies and Fellow of Trinity College at the University of Toronto. He has advised the Canadian Government on G7 participation and international trade and sustainable development, and has written widely on G7 summitry. He is co-editor of The G8's Role in the new Millennium.

Takashi Kiuchi is Economic Advisor of the Long-Term Credit Bank of Japan (LTCB). He has been a guest scholar at the Brookings Institution, and a member of the Faculty of Economics at Yokohama National University. He served as an advisor on governmental committees on numerous occasions and authored many articles and scholarly works.

Dr. Alan M. Rugman is Thames Water Fellow in Strategic Management at Templeton College, University of Oxford. Previously he was Professor of International Business at the University of Toronto 1987-1998, Dalhousie University 1979-1987 and the University of Winnipeg 1970-1978. He has also been a visiting professor at Columbia Business School, London Business School, Harvard University, U.C.L.A., M.I.T., Warwick Business School and the University of Paris-La Sorbonne, and has published over 200 articles dealing with the economic, managerial and strategic aspects of multinational enterprises and with trade and investment policy.

Dr. George M. von Furstenberg is a titled Professor at Indiana University in Bloomington. He spent several years of work at the International Monetary Fund as Division Chief, and at various U.S. government agencies, such as the Department of Housing and Urban Development, the President's Council of

Economic Advisers, and the Department of State. He has also been a resident fellow, economist, or adviser at both the Brookings Institution and the American Enterprise Institute, as well as the first holder of the Bissell-Fulbright Professorship in Canadian-American Relations at the Centre for International Studies. Based on his extensive scholarly contribution, he has been selected by his peers to serve as associate editor of the *Review of Economics and Statistics* published by Harvard University, editorial advisory board of *Open Economies Review*, and is currently president-elect and program chair of the North American Economics and Finance Association.

Dr. Norbert Walter Managing Director, Deutsche Bank Research, and Chief Economist, Deutsche Bank Group. While Professor and Director at the renowned Kiel Institute for World Economics, he was consultant for German Economic policymakers. He has also served as Lecturer at the Christian Albrechts University, and John McCloy Distinguished Research Fellow and resident scholar at the American Institute For Contemporary German Studies in Washington DC. He is the author of What Would Erhard Do Today, More Market - Less Intervention, and On the New Wealth of the Nation.

Dr. Duncan Wood is Professor of International Relations and Director of the Canadian Studies Program at the Instituto Technologica Autonoma de Mexico in Mexico City. A specialist in international political economy, he received his Ph.D from Queen's University in Canada. He is the author of forthcoming works on approaches to international political economy, and the role of the G7 in banking regulation and supervision.

Preface

This book is the first in a set of studies, published in "The G8 and Global Governance" series, of the way in which the G7/8, related international institutions, and relevant international organisations shape international order in regard to the major issues that confront the global community in the opening years of the twenty-first century. It is appropriate that international finance should be the subject of the first such study. The challenge of redesigning the international financial system in the wake of the 15 August 1971 breakdown of the Bretton Woods system of fixed but adjustable exchange rates was one of the major shocks that catalysed the creation of the G7 in November 1975. It was also the subject of the G7's first major achievement at that Summit, and an area of considerable accomplishment at subsequent Summits, such as those in 1986 and 1995. Moreover, the severity of the Asian-turned-global financial crisis of 1997-99, and the concomitant effort to reconstruct a new international financial system appropriate for a rapidly globalising world have dramatically illustrated the essential contribution, and the shortcoming, of the G7 as a centre of global governance in the new era.

This book deals with the role of the G7 in both crisis response and system reconstruction, and with the wisdom and the impact of the G7's efforts in both spheres. It is the product, most immediately, of the papers presented at a conference held in Bonn, Germany, on 14 June 1999, immediately following the meeting of G7 Finance Ministers in Frankfurt, and immediately before the opening of the G7 and G8 summits themselves in Cologne on 18 June. The conference, sponsored jointly by the G8 Research Group based at the University of Toronto and the Deutschen Gesellschaft für Ausvartige politik (DGAP), took as its theme "Strengthening the International Financial System: The Role of the G7/G8". It assembled eight leading scholars and analysts of the G7 and the international financial system, one from each G7 country, and an audience of 150 knowledgeable individuals from the scholarly, nongovernmental organisations (NGOs), government, business, and NGO communities to explore the central issues surrounding this topic.

This volume contains the extensively revised papers presented at the conference, supplemented by selected contributions from an academic symposium held on 17 June 1999 and co-sponsored by the G8 Research

Group and the Institute of Economic Policy at the University of Cologne. Yet its chapters also contain the results of long years of research, analysis, and reflection by many leading scholars and practitioners who have grappled with the key issues confronting the international financial system from within and without.

This volume is, therefore, able to explore its subject from several vantage points. This volume contains contributions from those based in virtually all of the G7 member countries. The contributors come from the disciplines of economics, political science, and management studies, from the universities, leading research institutes, central banks, and private banking, and in some cases have had experience with the core intergovernmental institution in the field - the International Monetary Fund (IMF). They thus bring a wide variety of perspectives, analytic approaches, and judgements to bear on the central issues at hand.

Given the rich diversity contained within these chapters, no effort has been made to embrace all in a single theoretical tradition, interpretive framework, or concluding consensus. Rather, the volume begins with a review of the G7's contribution to managing and reforming the international financial systems, and offers divergent views in each of the three sections that follow: the response to the financial crisis, the construction of a new system, and the broader issues that the attempt at crisis response and system reconstruction exposed.

Assembling such a volume had left us with a large legacy of gratitude to those who contributed in many different ways to this enterprise. Our first debt is to those members of the G8 Research Group's Professional Advisory Council who either served as speakers and contributors or who provided advice and support in the conference design: Sir Nicholas Bayne, George von Furstenberg, Alan Rugman, and Robert Fauver.

We owe much to our partners at the Deutschen Gesellschaft für Ausvartige politik for joining us in this important project. This debt begins with Dr. Joachim Krause, who first saw the promise in this venture, and who served as the lead contact and organiser. We are grateful to the German Confederation of Trade and Industry for making their facilities available to us for the conference, to the Office of the Chancellor in the Government of Germany for fostering critical connections, and to the Canadian Embassy in Germany, and its ambassador Gaetan Lavertu, for facilitating this joint venture in Canadian-German and pan-G7 intellectual co-operation. We also acknowledge the contribution of Professor Wilfred von Bredow of Marburg University, who first put us in contact with his colleagues at the DGAP.

We are most grateful to those organisations that provide the material resources, both financial and in kind, to make this conference and the associated program of the G8 Research Group possible. Our financial sponsors include the Canadian Department of Foreign Affairs and International Trade, that saw the potential of this project at the critical formal stage, the Siemens Corporation, which generously provided the matching funds that enabled us to assemble our distinguished group of international speakers, and the City of Toronto, which had hosted the G7 Summit in 1988 and understood the significance of the event. Our in-kind sponsors, for the conference, and for the innovative webcasting program through which it was broadcast to the world, were eCollege.com, Media One, Hewlett Packard, Sony, Kodak, the German Government host broadcaster for the Cologne Summit, Canada's National Post, and the Washington Times. Together they joined with the G8 Research Group to produce, using the conference program and other material, the world's largest online classroom ever, engaging close to 5,000 students from over 60 countries around the world.

We are also grateful to the Social Science Federation of Canada, for sponsoring a special symposium in early June in Sherbrooke and Lennoxville, Quebec, on the theme of globalization. This provided an opportunity for some of the authors in this volume to present early versions of their papers and otherwise test out their ideas. We further appreciate the initiative of Professor Tony Porter of McMaster University in organising a panel on this subject for the annual meeting of the International Studies Association in March 2000 in Los Angeles, so that the dialogue on this important subject can continue and expand.

We owe a special word of thanks to Paul Jacobelli, whose dedication, initiative, persistence, and skill were vital in drawing together the sponsorship consortium that made this conference, and thus this volume possible.

We are further grateful to the members of the G8 Research Group, and particularly those who were able to join us for the conference and the Summit in Cologne. While all contributed in so many ways, we must thank in particular Gillian Bannister, the G8 Research Group's Director of Communications, for promoting the conference, Madeline Koch for taking on essential editorial tasks, and Ivan Savic and Gina Stephens for helping see the manuscript through to completion.

Within the University of Toronto, we are grateful for the continuing support of our colleagues at the Centre for International Studies: Professor Louis Pauly, its director, who oversees our research activities, and Professor Peter Hajnal, who assumed the onerous but vital task of securing the anonymous referees who reviewed our draft manuscript and collectively approved it for publication. We owe much to the incisive criticisms of those four reviewers. At Trinity College, we acknowledge the critical support of Provost Tom Delworth, Bursar Geoffrey Seaborn, Head Librarian Linda Corman, and Professor Robert Bothwell, Co-ordinator of the International Relations Program. At the Department of Political Science, Professor Robert Vipond, the Chair, and Professors Ronald Deibert and Ronald Biener have provided constant encouragement. At the University of Toronto Library, Chief Librarian Carole Moore, Internet Director Sian Miekle, and Project Manager Marc Lalonde have been indispensable. And at the Office of Public Affairs, Cheryl Sullivan has cheerfully and effectively assisted us with publicity and promotion.

Perhaps our greatest gratitude is reserved for our series editor, Kirstin Howgate, and her colleagues at Ashgate. It was Kirstin who had the vision to launch this series, to see the virtue in a set of works on the major issues that confront the international community in the twenty-first century, to ensure a smooth adoption and publication of the manuscript, and to support the series in so many ways.

Finally, we acknowledge the patience and support of our families as we laboured to convert raw drafts into publish text. It is with great pleasure and thanks that we dedicate it to them.

Karl Kaiser, John J. Kirton and Joseph P. Daniels, 2000

Introduction

1 Shaping a New International Financial System: Contributions and Challenges

KARL KAISER, JOHN J. KIRTON, AND JOSEPH P. DANIELS

Introduction: The Crisis and the Challenge

As the 1990s unfolded, citizens of the international community seemed destined to bid farewell to a turbulent twentieth century with a celebration of the end of the European cold war, the global spread of market democracies in its wake, and the buoyant prosperity and expanding freedoms they brought. Instead, the century closed with the global community engulfed in an unprecedentedly severe financial crisis that devastated many of the world's most rapidly growing economies, threatened the world's most mature and powerful countries, and called into question the mechanisms and very model of a globalised international economy and community.

The floating of the Thai baht on 2 July 1997 catalysed a contagious sequence of financial meltdowns. Over the subsequent year these devastated not only Thailand but also Indonesia, the world's fourth most populous country, and Organisation for Economic Co-operation and Development (OECD) member South Korea, imperiled such traditional bastions of stable growth as Malaysia, Hong Kong, and the People's Republic of China, and helped plunge the world's second largest economy, Japan, into deeper recession. On 17 August 1997, the crisis spread to Europe, when, three weeks after the latest infusion of financial support from the International Monetary Fund (IMF), the Group of Eight (G8)'s newest member Russia was forced to devalue its currency and default on its loans. Within a month, the global panic unleashed by the Russian default battered other G8 countries such as Canada, and threatened to paralyse the financial system of the world's most powerful and superbly performing economy, the United States. As 1998 moved into 1999 it was the America's which were afflicted, as Brazil faced a major run on its reserves and a sharp recession as a result. As Group of Seven (G7) and G8 leaders gathered in Cologne, Germany, in June 1999 for their 25th annual

Summit, a precarious calm prevailed, although strains in Argentina, and later South Korea, kept everyone in a state of nervous vigilance. The focus had shifted from the miracle to the meltdown of emerging economies in Asia and elsewhere, from the magic to the mania of the marketplace, from accolades to anxieties about globalisation, and from the vigour to the vulnerability of the leading industrial democracies and the international institutions they had constructed to govern global finance.

The G7 countries themselves escaped, if by the narrowest of margins, the most devastating effects of the crisis. But for the many countries who did not, the destruction it brought surpassed that of the great depression of the 1930s. Moreover, the speed with which it spread, the broad scope of the countries it swept up in its grasp, and the wide number of individuals within them whose life prospects were destroyed, gave it a unique character. The failure of the world's leading national authorities, international institutions, or market actors to foresee its outbreak, predict its course, or confidently contain its cumulative devastation reinforced the collective realisation that the international financial economy of the twenty-first century was very different in kind than that which had proceeded it. The crisis also made obvious that, in an interdependent world economy, more than mere openness to foreign capital and a free investment climate was necessary to guarantee a stable evolution, but that many conditions for the development of market economies in the developed world, which had been vital but generally overlooked, were of equal importance, such as the rule of law, regulations concerning the reliability of balance sheets, bankruptcy law, or rules forbidding corruption. It further bred a conviction that a fundamentally new architecture for its international governance had to be constructed if an open international financial system was to continue, and be controlled in ways that benefited all.

The challenge of creating that new architecture unleashed a series of intense debates over several fundamental and interrelated questions. What was the real cause of the Asian financial crisis and the contagion which brought it with such force to most regions of the world, and to many, but not all, of the countries within them? How best could the crisis be contained and who should take the lead, and bear the burden, in so doing? Was there a truly globalised rather than regionalised international economy, and to what degree and in what ways was it different than that which had proceeded it? Was a new architecture required to govern it, or merely a set of improvements and additions for the plumbing and the metres that regulated and monitored it? What principles and processes should guide the renovation effort, and what new procedures and mechanisms should be put in place? And who, within international institutions, national governments, private markets, civil society, and citizens of an ever more connected global community, should guide and govern the emerging market system?

These debates still rage in intellectual circles. But long before they will have come to command a consensus, indeed from the very early stages of the crisis, leaders of the international community equipped with only tentative answers and fragile confidence have been forced to confront the crisis and begin constructing an architecture that could cope with it, contain it, and vastly reduce the chances that it would return. In doing so they had to invent and institute a structure that would meet the needs of an increasingly globalised financial system and the aspirations of those throughout the world well beyond the financial community who were so profoundly affected by it. It was an effort that mobilised the energies and enthusiasm of many. But at the very centre of the effort were the deliberations, debates, directions, and decisions of the Group of Seven leading industrial democracies.

The Approach

This book explores the effort to contain the global financial crisis that erupted in 1997, to construct a new international financial system in its wake, and formalise the role in this process of the G7, its international institutional colleagues and competitors, and its member governments and financial communities. It embraces all of the fundamental questions unleashed by the crisis that still dominate analytical and policy debates. Yet its focus is on how well the crisis response and reconstruction effort, importantly shaped and guided by the G7, has proceeded as the new century begins.

This collection thus has three central purposes. First and foremost, it critically assesses efforts thus far to construct a new, strengthened international financial system to meet the needs of the global economy and community in the rapidly globalising world of the twenty-first century. Secondly, it challenges core elements of the epistemic consensus underlying this effort by subjecting the premises and principles of the emerging edifice to a hard analysis of their economic logic, market impact, and political feasibility. Thirdly, it offers suggestions about which directions to avoid, and which to pursue as the project to construct a strengthened international financial system moves into the decisive final stages required for its completion.

To meet these objectives, this collection assembles the analyses of leading experts from the scholarly and policy world. It embraces the talents of those within government, private sector finance, and the academic/research community. Its analysis is firmly grounded in the economics of international finance, and supplemented by the insights of political science and management studies. It includes experts from Europe, North America and Asia, and from all G7 member countries, as well as a view from the world outside. In many cases the insights of these authors have been shaped by their direct experience, in the past or present, in shaping and managing the international financial system. But in all cases they bring to bear outstanding academic and analytic credentials and the critical distance that flows from them.

No effort has been made to impose a common analytical or interpretive framework to guide these contributions. Each has been guided by the dual discipline of focussing on fundamental issues in the effort to shape a strengthened financial system, and to do so in a critical spirit guided by an independent analysis of underlying premises and processes. As a result, this collection reflects the diversity of the debate and points to new directions for advance, as each author addresses the core issues from a distinctive vantage point.

The Core Issues

Taken together, these analyses address the five core issues at the heart of the contemporary debate over shaping a strengthened international financial system. These deal with why the crisis came, how well the existing system responded, what more is needed now, which sector should bear the burden, and who should take the lead.

The first concerns the causes of the crisis and contagion and whether it has now been finally contained. How different was it from panics, manias, and depressions past? With the insights generated by the Mexican peso devaluation of December 20, 1994, the collapse of Barings Bank in the spring of 1995, and the focus of the G7 on international financial system reform at their 1995 Halifax Summit, could it have been anticipated and prevented? Was the crisis fundamentally the result of a collection of policy and institutional defects within particular countries, if at broadly similar stages of development, or was the crisis essentially driven by the dynamics of a newly globalised international system and the inadequacies of the principles, procedures, and institutions for its governance? Has enough now been done to contain and conclude the crisis, or is there merely a current respite until it resumes in its next stage?

The second core issue, flowing directly from the first, is how and how well the international community has coped with the challenges of crisis response and system strengthening thus far. Is the challenge one of calling for incremental reform, deeper reconstruction, or historic replacement with a very new system of principles practices, processes, and set of institutions? Whether the challenge be one of architecture or plumbing, is the project proceeding quickly enough? And is it unfolding in the correct direction, with an overall coherence and adequate allowance for experimentation, and subsequent mid-course correction?

The third core issue focusses on the particular critical defects of the old system and the best design for the new mechanisms to be added in response. What is the best weighting and mix of mechanisms for transparency, surveillance, precautionary lending, and international standstill or bankruptcy procedures? What are the best forms, procedures, and sequence of introduction and use for each? Is it necessary to move into broader domains, such as control of international financial and capital flows, greater exchange rate management, fixity, or even currency unification, and the rules for international liberalisation or foreign direct investment? How does one guard against consequences such as moral hazard?

The fourth issue is the relative responsibility and role - past and prospective, positive and normative - of international institutions, national governments, and private sector market players in the design and operation of the new system. How much and how should the principle of private sector burden sharing be instituted? What volume and form of additional public sector resources are required and where should they come from and be controlled? And what place do other civil society actors and their concerns have in the new architecture?

The fifth issue is the past, present, and prospective role of the G7, its governments, the financial community and citizens, in providing leadership and guidance in the construction and governance of the new system. Is it the United States alone or the G7 as a collective that has been, and remains the necessary centre of leadership and guidance? What has been the role, and what role should broader processes such as the new Group of 22 (G22) and now Group of Twenty (G20) and Financial Stability Forum (FSF) or the established IMF, World Bank, International Organisation of Securities Control Organisations (IOSCO) and other bodies play? And what is the best practical formula for involving those outside the existing centres of international financial governance, so that the necessary expertise, legitimacy, surveillance, and sanctions can be secured?

The Analyses

To address these core issues, it is necessary to explore in turn earlier efforts to shape and strengthen the international financial system, the actual crises of 1997-99, the specific issues at the heart of current effort to construct a new system, and the broader array of issues closely related to the process. Thus, Part I considers past successes and failures through the current crisis, from its origins in Asia, through its impact on emerging and G7 economies around the world, and the response of the G7 and its members at containment and control.

Chapter 2 begins with an analysis of efforts during the past quarter century to reform the international financial system, and the role of the G7 in this enterprise. In examining "The G7 Summit's Contribution: Past, Present, and Prospective", Nicholas Bayne identifies four earlier defining moments when the world, and the G7, confronted as a central challenge the task of altering in basic ways a financial system under severe stress. The first was the crisis over the global exchange rate regime that served as very *raison d'être* for the birth of the G7 summit as an economic institution - the breakdown of the Bretton Woods system of fixed exchange rates in 1971, the failure of the IMF and existing processes to construct a durable, widely accepted alternative, and the decision of the first Summit at Rambouillet, France in 1975 to institute a new system of managed floating. The second was the commercial bank debt crisis precipitated by Mexico's *de facto* default at the IMF meetings in Toronto in 1982, and the work of G7 summits from Versailles in 1982 to Paris in 1989 to arrive finally, in the form of the Brady Plan, at a solution. The third episode, debt relief for the world's poorest countries, began with the "Toronto terms" for relief at the 1998 Summit and continued through to the Cologne debt initiative of 1999. The final quest for the G7 has been its effort to cope with speculative financial crises, starting at Halifax in 1995 and continuing to the present day.

From this analysis flow five conclusions. The first is the unique opportunity the Summit offers G7 leaders to resolve issues that have defied solution at lower levels. The second is the need for advance preparation so leaders can use their time most effectively, while the third is the need to keep up the high level pressure until commitments are forged and implemented. The fourth is the need to move beyond the informal leadership of the G7 to integrate the new arrangements into formal organisations and give them legal force. The fifth is the indispensable need for the G7 to lead, but also through their own example, explanation, and sensitivity to the desires of outsiders, to secure a broader acceptance for their actions.

In Chapter 3, "The Asian Crisis and its Implications", Takashi Kiuchi looks, from a Japanese perspective, at the origins and causes of the Asian financial crisis, Japan's interpretation of and response to the crisis, and the lessons that can be applied to the task of rebuilding the international financial architecture. He locates the ultimate causes of the crisis in capital account rather than current account problems, liquidity rather than solvency problems, and the herding behaviour of investors, but notes also how politicians overriding their officials and regulators compounded the problem. Japan's response came initially in the form of a proposal for an Asian monetary fund that was abandoned in the face of US opposition, then with a "New Miyazawa Initiative" of US$30 billion worth of bilateral lending guarantees, proposals to reform the IMF, and new measures to make the yen an international currency. The major lessons of the crisis, Kiuchi concludes, are the need for decisive action at early stages, for enhancing the IMF's authority to deal with capital account problems, and closer regional policy co-ordination, beginning with macroeconomic policy and the development of an Asian bond market to replace short-term borrowing from distant bankers.

Kiuchi's analysis leads him to clear conclusions on many of the key issues in the debate over a new architecture. He rejects dollarisation as a solution for smaller Asian economies, but approves of short terms capital restrictions as a transitional measure, mandatory private sector burden sharing, and state bankruptcy codes. He calls for universal guidelines and processes for accounting, disclosure, bankruptcy, and financial supervision. But he calls for a staged approach to introduce these new measures, tightly tailored to the particular situation of each country, with proper macroeconomic policy reinforcing improved international regulation. Above all, he identifies the role of the G7 in moving toward a *de facto* target zone mechanism, and points to the benefits that further moves in this direction could bring.

In Chapter 4, "The G7, International Finance, and Developing Countries", Duncan Wood analyses the work of the G7 in operating and reforming the international financial system from the perspective of the developing countries, in particular, that of the ten large emerging market economies. The chapter first explores the record of the G7 during the decade from the late

1980s to the late 1990s, identifying how the developing countries have been affected by G7 initiatives in macroeconomic co-ordination, debt renegotiation and reduction, and international financial system reform. It then focusses on the main achievements of the 1999 Cologne Summit that affect developing countries, notably the Cologne debt initiative, broadening the membership of the Financial Stability Forum, and the increased importance accorded to the IMF Interim Committee, now renamed the International Financial and Monetary Committee. Wood also examines why and how the G7 might move toward a more meaningful dialogue with, and inclusion of, the major emerging economies, in the interest of improving the effectiveness and legitimacy of the international financial system being shaped to govern the global economy of the future.

Wood's conclusions are critical yet constructive. He judges that the G7 in the past has inadequately incorporated the views of developing countries as it has dealt with the issues that directly concern them. While the Cologne Summit brought some improvement, its advances remain inadequate to the need to involve the large emerging economies as they rise in relative power, and as their economic performance becomes ever more consequential to that of the G7 countries themselves. The clear need is to devise better processes for regular, formalised G7-emerging economy dialogue and consultation, based in part on the models that other international institutions have recently evolved.

In Chapter 5, "The Dynamics of G7 Leadership in Crisis Response and System Reconstruction", John J. Kirton explores the role of the G7, and of the lesser members within it, in responding to the crisis and constructing a new international financial architecture. He traces the diplomacy of and within the G7 through the three phases of the Asian crisis of 1997-98, the global crisis of 1998 and the reconstruction effort culminating at the Cologne Summit in June 1999. In doing so he highlights how it was the G7 collectively that ultimately prevailed, rather than the US alone, the IMF as a broad multilateral organisation locked in a neo-liberal model, or private sector markets and multinational corporations. Further affirming the leadership of the G7 collectively, rather than as a support group for American leadership, Kirton demonstrates how Canada and Britain, the least powerful members, were able to provide effective intellectual, policy, and structural leadership by advancing distinctive positions, combining with other members, and persisting to see their principles and positions prevail in the end.

Kirton's analysis challenges the traditional theories of why and how effective G7 co-operation has been achieved. In contrast to theories based on the indispensable element of an American willingness and ability to lead, he shows how the G7 came together at the initiative of other members in the face of a reluctant America deterred and immobilised at first by Congressional opposition to authorising the US share of a quota increase for the IMF, and in September 1998 by panicking market players on the verge of freezing its domestic credit system. Nor of great relevance in inducing collective G7 action were common lessons from the distant past, a false new consensus about the impotence of governments in the face of powerful markets and private capital flows, transnational coalitions involving sub-governmental and societal actors, or traditional differences between G7 members. Rather, the autonomous power of international institutions was evident as Canada and Britain were able to use their prerogatives and legacy as G7 hosts, and the G7 norms of consensus decision making to take and sustain a leadership role. Most importantly, it was the particular character of the G7 as a modern international concert, in the face of a systemic crisis, that allowed the smaller members to lead the G7, and the G7 to lead the international community with success.

Part II moves from the crisis, its consequences, and its containment to the particular core issues that dominated the debate over the principles and procedures on which a new international financial system should be based.

In Chapter 6, "Transparentising the Global Money Business: Glasnost or Just Another Wild Card in Play?", George M. von Furstenberg explores the different meanings of the now highly fashionable concept of "transparency". Noting that greater transparency always involves a redistribution of power, he distinguishes between statistical transparency and political transparency, or glasnost, and highlights how both were evident in abundance in the decisions of financial system reform at the Cologne Summit.

Given the many forms of uncertainty that exist in economic analysis, and the capacity of both "offensive" and "defensive" players to benefit from more information, von Furstenberg calls for greater skepticism on the part of policymakers and commentators about the progress to be made by securing greater statistical transparency alone. Indeed, he notes, a denial of data had little to do with the outbreak of recent financial crises in developing economies, and he judges that the greater transparency currently envisaged by the G7 will do very little to reduce the risk of future financial crises. He does, however, judge political transparency to be important, if it is linked to a comprehensive program of reform, while highlighting how it is the rich players in the rich countries who are likely to benefit the most.

In Chapter 7, "Global Capital Flows: Maximising Benefits, Minimising Risks", Joseph P. Daniels examines policy responses of the G7 in light of the perceived benefits and problems of liberalised capital markets. He first explains the economic benefits of liberalised financial markets and high quality intermediaries. Next he considers the problems that pervade financial markets and the constraints that capital mobility places on macroeconomic policy. Additionally the role of foreign speculators in the East Asian crises is considered.

Given the preceding arguments, Daniels considers the proposals put forward in the G7 Finance Ministers' *Strengthening the International Financial Architecture: Report of the G7 Finance Ministers to the Köln Economic Summit*. He finds that many recommendations support the principle of minimal market interference and avoid creating additional risk or diminishing country credibility. Unfortunately, he also finds that the G7 has offered little to the likely candidates of future financial meltdowns, the larger developing nations at an intermediate stage of financial development. Hence, he concurs with the general view of Duncan Wood in Chapter 4. Daniels concludes by suggesting a set of responsibilities for the G7 in the reform process.

In Chapter 8, "The New Financial Architecture for the Global Economy", Norbert Walter takes up the debate over transparency, and over several other central issues, notably the new Financial Stability Forum, equity ratios for financial institutions, supervision, and the broader questions surrounding Russia and the international trade system. Declaring that little has been done to reform the system to cope with another financial crisis that is sure to come, he casts doubt of the adequacy of the G7's emphasis on surveillance and the responsibility of each country to maintain a sound economic policy. Useful advances such as the Financial Stability Forum and improved equity ratios for financial institutions still require further work on the important details. Additionally, calls for greater transparency and surveillance suffer from the fact that in a world of "Snow White and the Seven Dwarfs", the resulting systems will be based on American models that other G7 governments, such as Germany, will resist.

More important, in Walter's view, is the fact that two fundamental issues have yet to be satisfactorily addressed. The first is the need for a mechanism to allow bankruptcy to take place in the financial sector. The second is for G7 governments to stop the recapitalisation or excessive capitalisation of ailing financial institutions.

In Chapter 9, "The Role of the International Monetary Fund as Lender of Last Resort", Curzio Giannini examines how a lender of last resort can deal with financial instability at the national level and whether the concept of an international lender of last resort makes sense in today's globalised economy. At the national level, he notes, the monetary framework and hence the lender of last resort function has now become very different from those specified in the classic model, as independent central banks have arisen to practice "illuminated discretion" in pursuit of a stability-oriented monetary policy. At the international level, while the founders of the Bretton Woods system kept the lender of last resort function at the national level, the question is now what can be done as a lender of last resort in a global environment.

Gianninni's conclusion is that very little can be done, as any grand design to transfer the lender of last resort function to the international level should be regarded with suspicion. Indeed, the IMF is already moving in the other direction, by providing credibility so otherwise financially frozen countries can borrow for private capital markets, by lending into arrears, and by involving private creditors through informal means in the Korean rescue package. Ginannini thus approves of the creation of contingent credit lines, and further moves to make creditors more sensitive to the risks they take, through either improved worldwide regulation and supervision or debt moratoriums with negotiated restructuring. The new Financial Stability Forum, with its emphasis on the former, faces a daunting task. But its very creation and early emphasis suggest that the IMF should refine its role of a provider of credibility, support smoother workout procedures, and avoid thinking of itself as a world central bank.

Part III moves from the debate over core financial questions to the broader issues closely related to them and ones whose treatment could well affect the particular measures selected and the success of their use.

In Chapter 10, "Practising Exchange Rate Flexibility", Olivier Davanne and Pierre Jacquet examine the question, now at the centre of the debate, of the appropriate exchange rate regimes for emerging and developed economies, and of the best international mechanism for ensuring the needed stability in the face of ever-threatening volatility, misalignment, and sometimes brutal shifts from an unduly fixed to a free floating regime. They outline the current consensus regarding the dangers of fixed exchange rates for emerging economies, and the costs of the alternative, forcibly adopted by many in the wake of the 1997-99 financial crisis, of freely floating regimes. They then examine the advantages of a managed floating regime, and the role the G7 and IMF play might play in effectively managing it.

Through their detailed economic and institutional, theoretical and empirical analysis, Jacquet and Davanne make a powerful argument that the current consensus needs to be rethought. Both economic rationality and the record of past decades show that exchange rate flexibility is necessary, and that highly fixed exchange rate regimes should be relied upon only exceptionally. Yet there is a broader array of available options, within which stands out an "adjustable reference parity" regime. In managing such a regime, the G7 and IMF, working in tandem, can do much to strengthen monitoring and surveillance, and thus contribute substantially to exchange rate stability.

In Chapter 11, "Can Small Countries Keep Their Own Money and Floating Exchange Rates?", George M. von Furstenberg looks inward at a central issue of finance - that of exchange rates - and outward from the G7 at the smaller countries in the system. He asks in particular what choice of exchange rate regimes exist for small countries that have fully opened up to international capital markets and free trade in financial services when they are located in the vicinity of a large country or group of countries whose currency is in wide international use. With G7 Finance Ministers in the lead up to Cologne advising that such countries' should generally not defend fixed exchange rates with borrowed money, and with most countries save for China having lifted traditional capital controls, the options for such countries reduce to floating exchange rates, currency boards, and monetary unions.

Von Furstenberg concludes that the first two of these options, for small and medium-sized countries with low credibility currencies, brings major problems of currency substitution and incomplete hedging, to the point where policy makers are driven to look at monetary union as a safe haven. Monetary union can take the form of unilaterally adopting as legal tender the strong international currency of a nearby country, or the multilateral Euroland route of deep financial integration on the basis of equality. The trend is thus toward regional currency consolidation, the disappearance of many lesser currencies, and the separate exchange rates and national monetary policies that accompany them.

Finally, in Chapter 12, "From Globalisation to Regionalism: The Foreign Direct Investment Dimension of International Finance", Alan M. Rugman broadens the focus from the activities of short-term investors in financial capital to the long-term foreign direct investment of multinational corporations (MNCs). He traces the rise and role of MNCs, how they vary widely by sector in their degree of globalisation, and the political power they exert in the face of national governments and intergovernmental organisations. In doing so, he takes issue with those who emphasise the destabilising impact of volatile short-term financial flows in a world of globalised "casino capitalism".

Rather, Rugman argues, the process of international integration is driven by the stable, foreign direct investments of MNCs, which engage overwhelmingly in a regionalism based on the rich triad countries of the US, Europe, and Japan, rather than any comprehensive globalism. For both triad-based MNCs in their production and marketing, and for governments in their efforts to support and regulate the process by creating international trade and investment regimes, it is the home region rather than the wider world that is primary. The collapse of Asian economic growth in 1997 and the contagious worldwide economic slowdown and contagion of 1998-99 was a result in part of the failure of Asian-based firms and governments to develop, through the Asia Pacific Economic Cooperation Forum (APEC) or otherwise, as strong and successful a regional strategy and regime as those of their North American and European counterparts with the North American Free Trade Agreement (NAFTA) and the European Union (EU). Further, the crisis of 1997-99 has driven all to turn even more away from global strategy to the relative safety of their regional bastions.

Agreement on Fundamental Issues

Amidst the wealth of insight and analysis that these chapters contain, there are underlying agreements on many fundamental issues. Above all, the contributors critically assess and challenge many core elements of the emerging consensus in policy and outside intellectual circles about the new system currently being constructed. Avoiding any temptation to celebrate the accomplishments of the G7 guided effort thus far, they offer at best a cautious confidence that much of the crisis response and system construction effort is proceeding with competence and often in the correct direction. They see, however, that there is no ground for complacency or inaction.

In "Challenges and Contributions to the Conventional Wisdom", the final chapter of this text, Kaiser, Kirton, and Daniels summarise the views of the various contributors by issue area. On the five fundamental questions at the heart of the intellectual debate and policy effort, the contributors offer an array of views, but also a large measure of agreement on what was, is being, and should be done. Taken together, these make a substantial contribution to our understanding of the debate over the international financial system the world needs to cope with in the twenty-first century.

Part I
The Crisis and its Legacies

2 The G7 Summit's Contribution: Past, Present, and Prospective

NICHOLAS BAYNE

Introduction

International financial questions occupied the G7 Summit repeatedly during the first 25 years of its life. This chapter reviews the occasions when the summits, up to and including the Cologne Summit of 1999, contributed to the design of the world's financial and monetary system. From this review of past and present performance some lessons can be drawn on what the Summit can do best and where it should concentrate in the near future.[1]

This enquiry is defined narrowly, being limited to Summit activities which were concerned with the international system as such. It therefore excludes all the G7's attempts to improve the coordination of macro-economic policy or exchange rates among themselves, such as the Plaza and Louvre agreements of the 1980s. It concentrates on what the annual Summits themselves did, as distinct from the G7 (and earlier G5) finance ministers and their supporting officials. The chapter speaks of G7 throughout, even though Birmingham 1998 and Cologne 1999 were called G8 Summits because of the addition of Russia.

Under this definition, four important episodes stand out in the Summit record. These are:

- The Legitimisation of Floating Rates: Rambouillet 1975.
- The Commercial Bank Debt Crisis: Versailles 1982 to Paris 1989.
- Debt Relief for the Poorest: Toronto 1988 to Cologne 1999.
- The Speculative Financial Crisis: Halifax 1995 to Cologne 1999.

The first two episodes are from the past and can be considered closed. The second two are still running their course, though Cologne 1999 marked important achievements in both of them. In each of these episodes, the Summit's achievements are judged against a range of criteria, as follows:

- *Leadership.* Did the Summit succeed in resolving differences which could not be overcome at lower levels?
- *Effectiveness.* Did the Summit exercise its talent for reconciling domestic and external pressures?
- *Durability.* Did the agreement reached at the Summit provide a lasting solution to the problem?
- *Acceptability.* Was the agreement reached among the G7 leaders readily accepted by the wider international community?
- *Consistency.* Did the Summit's decisions on international financial issues fit in well with the policies adopted on other subjects?

The judgements form the basis for the overall conclusions, as well as some recommendations for the future. These are summarised in the following paragraph.

First, the leaders must use the Summit as the occasion to resolve disagreements between them which have persisted at lower levels. If this chance is wasted, the Summit's purpose is lost. Second, the issues must have maximum advance preparation, to limit the issues for resolution at the Summit. If the leaders are confronted with too many problems, they will temporise or fudge. That will allow damaging differences among the G7 to persist. Third, experience shows that informal arrangements do not endure. Reforms to the financial architecture must be integrated into formal institutions and given legal force. The Summits must also keep up the pressure to ensure that whatever they agree is properly carried out. Commitments which are not fulfilled or are allowed to drag on undermine the authority of the Summits. Fourth, the G7 Summits must give a lead - that is expected of them - but they must not expect others to follow blindly. They must explain their proposals persuasively, responding to the concerns of others, especially poor and vulnerable countries. They must also justify their policies before the wider public, who are growing suspicious about who gains and who loses from globalisation. Finally, they must correct their neglect of trade policy while they concentrated on the financial system. Their failure to reach a common approach to the next trade round, which would respond to the needs of developing countries, contributed to the collapse of the World Trade Organization (WTO) ministerial at Seattle. This undermines their financial achievements. Restoring the international trading system must therefore be the first priority for Okinawa 2000.

Episode 1. The Legitimisation of Floating Rates: Rambouillet 1975

The first episode dates from the dawn of summitry. It focusses on the struggle to agree a new monetary system, to replace the regime of fixed par values which collapsed in 1971. French President Valéry Giscard d'Estaing was the original creator of the G7 Summit, with German Chancellor Helmut Schmidt as co-founder. Monetary stability was Giscard's highest priority. "What the world calls a crisis of capitalism", he said, "is in fact a monetary crisis".[2] When Giscard invited his five colleagues to Rambouillet in November 1975 (Canada only joined the group in 1976), his first objective was to achieve agreement on the reform of the monetary system, i.e., on new international financial architecture.

In fact, France itself was the main obstacle to agreement. Hitherto France, almost alone, would not agree that the International Monetary Fund should permit floating exchange rates as a legitimate currency regime, as opposed to a temporary expedient in times of crisis. At Rambouillet Giscard compromised: he agreed to legitimise floating, in return for undertakings from the United States and the others to intervene to counter short-term currency fluctuations.[3]

The agreement reached at Rambouillet was based on meticulous advance preparation between the Americans and the French. This took some of the others by surprise, but they had already indicated their readiness to accept whatever France and the United States could agree among themselves. The provisions concerned with legitimising floating were fed into the international community and led to rapid results. Within three months the IMF had agreed amendments to its Articles which embodied the Rambouillet agreement. It laid the foundation for today's financial architecture, with all its merits and its weaknesses.

The understanding on countering short-term fluctuations was more controversial. The Americans were lukewarm from the start and during President Ronald Reagan's first term (1981-84) ignored it altogether. The focus on exchange rates, which the French wanted, became absorbed into the process of multilateral surveillance of macro-economic policy, which was first agreed at Rambouillet 1982. In Reagan's second term, with James Baker at the US Treasury, this became the principal activity of the G7 Finance Ministers, as it remains today. Exchange rates were the focus of the Finance Ministers' meetings at the Plaza in 1985 and the Louvre in 1987. But this interest proved short-lived and the exchange rate regime has never returned to the Summit.[4]

The Rambouillet episode scores highly against the criteria and is instructive in illustrating what the Summit can do:

- The Summit showed *leadership* in resolving the persistent dispute between France and the US, in ways acceptable to the others. Rambouillet is still regarded as among the most productive summits in terms of co-operation achieved.[5]
- The Summit proved *effective,* not from the intellectual brilliance or originality of the participants, but because of the meticulous advance preparation. The Summit endorsed and gave its authority to the detailed provisions worked out beforehand.
- That part of the Rambouillet agreement proved *durable* which was incorporated into a legally binding instrument and applied worldwide. But the part which just relied on informal co-operation between the G7, to intervene in exchange markets, did not endure for long.
- The Rambouillet agreement was *acceptable* to the wider membership of the IMF, though there was some criticism from the IMF staff that it was imprecise and inelegant.
- There was no problem of *consistency* with that part of the Rambouillet agreement that went on to the IMF. But the informal arrangement on countering short-term fluctuations came under strain because G7 countries adopted economic policies which were not compatible with currency stability.

Episode 2. The Commercial Bank Debt Crisis: Versailles 1982 to Paris 1989

The first episode showed the Summit in a generally favourable light. The second episode concerns the crisis over the debts owed by middle-income countries to commercial banks, which occupied most of the 1980s. This time the Summit does not emerge so well.

By the Versailles Summit of 1982, the G7 countries had been pursuing restrictive economic policies for four years, aimed at countering the inflationary effects of the second oil crisis. The policies were successful in that aim, but led to a world-wide recession. The Summit itself was highly contentious. Agreements were reached with great difficulty on East-West trade and on surveillance of the G7 economies - only to crumble a few days later. The leaders were obsessed with these issues and ignored the signs of an imminent debt crisis among developing countries, despite warnings from Helmut Schmidt, attending his last G7 Summit.[6]

During the 1970s, oil-importing countries had been spared the full impact of the two oil crises by the device of "recycling". This worked by the commercial banks lending on to oil-importing countries the accumulated financial surpluses which the oil-exporters deposited with them. But the world recession made it impossible for many middle-income countries to earn enough dollars to service their debts. The crisis broke in August 1982, with Mexico threatening to default, followed by other major debtors like Brazil, Argentina, and Poland. Many international banks were highly exposed to these countries, so that default threatened a systemic crisis - the worst before the Asian upheaval of 1997.

Even after Versailles, however, the Summits gave the debt crisis very little attention. Since many leading debtors were in Latin America and American banks were the most exposed, the United States took the lead in proposing solutions. But the Reagan administration only once brought debt issues to the Summit, when the London Summit of 1984 endorsed the innovation of debt resheduling agreements covering several years, instead of one year at a time.

With President George Bush's arrival all that changed. His Treasury Secretary, Nicholas Brady, developed a new strategy for resolving this persistent problem The Brady Plan introduced the concept of debt reduction, i.e., writing down the debts below their market value. It was a radical idea for banks and their governments to accept that debts would not be paid in full. The IMF meetings in spring 1989 could not agree on it. Bush and Brady decided to raise the issue to Summit level and secured the endorsement of the Paris Arch Summit of July 1989. This was followed by agreement on the Brady Plan at the IMF annual meeting in September and the long-standing crisis was effectively resolved.[7]

The Summit's record in this second episode is more mixed than in the first. In general, the Summits from 1982 to 1988 score badly, while the results of Paris 1989 score well, as follows:

- For a long time, the Summits showed no *leadership*. Their neglect of this subject in the mid-1980s almost certainly prolonged the crisis, which dragged on for seven years. However, in 1989 the authority of the heads of government was successfully used to get acceptance of the radical new concept of debt reduction. (The 1984 agreement on multi-year rescheduling had the same effect, on a smaller scale.)

- Likewise, the Summits were largely *ineffective*, up to 1989, in reconciling the domestic pressures from the creditor banks with the external requirements of the debtor countries. The Americans under Reagan made very little use of the Summits, preferring to work at lower levels.
- A *durable* solution only emerged with the Brady Plan in 1989. Once that was in place, the problem went definitively off the agenda.
- Debt reduction had been rejected by the IMF in early 1989, but it became generally *acceptable* after it had been endorsed by the Summit.
- The *inconsistency* of G7 policies contributed to the outbreak of the debt crisis. The G7 encouraged the recycling of oil-producers' surpluses, leading to mounting debts for oil importers. But this was undermined by the world recession, provoked by the G7's tight economic policies. The leaders at Versailles did not foresee the problems and let themselves be taken by surprise. In general, the Summits have a poor record in anticipating financial crises.

Episode 3. Debt Relief for the Poorest: Toronto 1988 to Cologne 1999

The third episode concerns the Summit initiatives on debt relief for low-income countries, which go back to the Toronto Summit of 1988 but remained active up to Cologne 1999. The record here, despite some weaknesses, is much better than over middle-income debt. Effective arrangements for very poor countries are a neglected part of the international financial system and need to be integrated into any reforms.

Both middle-income and low-income countries accumulated large stocks of debt as a result of the oil crises. The debts owed to commercial banks by middle-income countries were so large that they threatened the system. The debts owed to governments by poor countries were much smaller in total and thus non-threatening; but they were a much heavier burden to the countries concerned. As the crisis eased for middle-income countries, the G7 Summit came to recognise the special problems of the poorest.[8]

The first initiative, agreed on at Toronto in 1988, offered relief on debt owed to governments by poor countries following IMF programmes. Toronto terms were fairly modest. But once the Brady Plan had been accepted, debt reduction could be given to poor countries too. Thus more generous terms were endorsed at London III 1991 and again at Naples 1994. The Lyon

Summit of 1996 expanded these into the Heavily Indebted Poor Countries (HIPC) initiative. This provided further relief not only on debt owed to governments but also on debt to the IMF, the World Bank, and other institutions. A large proportion of low-income countries' debt was owed to these bodies. Hitherto the institutions had refused debt relief for fear of weakening their credit rating. But they now agreed to replace existing debt with new loans on much softer terms.

Though the HIPC initiative looked more generous than what went before, it soon revealed its drawbacks. Poor countries had to endure IMF discipline for a very long time - usually six years - before benefiting from debt relief. The amounts of relief, once received, often proved insignificant. The financing of the scheme was not assured, in part because of dissent over the use of IMF gold.[9]

Despite pressure from articulate public opinion, led by the Jubilee 2000 Campaign, Birmingham 1998 could only agree on modest changes. But Cologne 1999 produced a complete overhaul. The amount of debt relief on offer was doubled and the qualifying period was halved. The financing commitments were less clear at the Summit, but they were tightened up at the annual meeting of the IMF and World Bank in September. This meeting agreed on a scheme to make use of IMF gold and produced the necessary voluntary commitments. While Okinawa 2000 may well wish to review this subject, because it takes place in Jubilee year, further action may not be needed.[10]

The review of the Summit's performance on this issue yields a broadly positive judgement:

- The Summit has consistently shown *leadership* since it took up this issue. It is clear that if the heads of government themselves had not pushed for action on debt relief for the poorest, nothing would have happened at all. The initial proposals were not adequate for the scale of the problem. But the G7 leaders were not content with a single initiative; they remained engaged and kept coming back to improve it.
- The Summit did have problems of *effectiveness* in reconciling domestic and external pressures. These measures to help the poorest were not provoked by any systemic crisis or major threats to the G7's economic interests; they were driven by a clear ethical motivation. For a long time, this was not strong enough to ensure agreement among the G7 on sufficiently generous terms of debt relief or

adequate financing. But by Cologne these problems seemed to be overcome, helped by the change of government in Germany.[11]

- The Summit likewise found it hard to agree on a *durable* debt-relief programme. Every year or so the leaders had to come back and adapt it. But this reflected their determination to come up with a programme which would really achieve its objectives.
- Successive debt-relief programmes emerging from the Summits had no real difficulty in winning *acceptance* internationally. Each of them was endorsed by the full membership of the IMF and World Bank and any problems arose within the G7 itself. More recently, the summit also faced the test of *acceptability* from the charities and other nongovernmental organizations (NGOs) that made up the Jubilee 2000 Campaign. They were deeply disappointed with the results of Birmingham 1998, but gave a cautious welcome to Cologne 1999, provided it was fully implemented.
- The judgement on *consistency* raises wider issues. Debt relief is about the only area where the G7 Summits have directly addressed the problems of the poorest countries. In other fields of direct concern to these countries, notably aid policy and trade access, the Summits have done much less. This question will be treated further in the final recommendations.

Episode 4. The Speculative Financial Crisis: Halifax 1995 to Cologne 1999

The fourth and final episode concerns the current search for new international financial architecture, provoked by the crisis which broke out in three Asian countries just a few days after the Denver Summit of 1997. It took 18 months to bring it under control. While calm has returned in 1999, this may be deceptive.

The crisis did not in fact begin in 1997. It was a revival, in a more acute form, of the troubles which overwhelmed Mexico at the turn of 1994 and 1995. Like the more recent upheavals, the Mexican crisis was marked by the collapse of exchange rates, the haemorrhage of volatile capital and rapid contagion both around the region and further afield. It was checked by an exceptional IMF-led programme, on the record scale of $50 billion, early in 1995. The 1995 Halifax Summit was largely concerned with reforms to IMF and World Bank provoked by the experience of Mexico.

Halifax agreed a four-point plan, which was rapidly adopted by the IMF and the World Bank. The four elements were stronger IMF surveillance for all countries, based on better data; a new emergency financing mechanism, backed by extra funds; better cooperation between regulators of financial institutions; and exploring procedures for countries comparable to insolvency for firms.[12]

At Halifax, French President Jacques Chirac, in a striking image, denounced international speculators as the AIDS virus of the world economy. The Halifax measures were intended to deter further outbreaks of the disease. Instead they only provided a period of remission, before the crisis broke out worse than before. This was because the implementation of the Halifax programme was tardy and incomplete. To take the four elements in reverse order: the G10 declared "insolvency" impractical for countries; G7 Finance Ministers reported only limited progress on regulation to Lyon 1996 and Denver 1997; the funds for the new mechanism were committed far too slowly; and that left stricter surveillance as the only defence. Surveillance on its own was not enough, as countries in difficulty had every incentive to conceal unwelcome data.[13]

As a result, the work on reform - on new financial architecture - had to start again in the light of what happened in Asia. This differed from the Mexican crisis not only in its scale - US$112 billion had to be mobilised for Thailand, Korea, and Indonesia - but also because it was caused by the errors of the private sector, not of government. The IMF's traditional remedies attracted wide criticism.[14] In early 1998, the G7 Finance Ministers assembled a package of reforms, which were endorsed by Birmingham 1998. But they were overtaken by renewed crisis in Russia (only months after the first G8 Summit) and in Brazil. A much more extensive range of measures was prepared for Cologne 1999. The leaders endorsed them once again, and they are now being put into effect by the IMF and the World Bank.

The details of these measures are analysed elsewhere in this book and are not the concern of this chapter. The measures build on the Halifax programme and greatly expand it. Surveillance is strengthened by codes of conduct prescribing greater transparency. Co-operation between regulators is promoted by the new Financial Stability Forum. The Halifax emergency mechanism is now fully funded, while a new IMF Contingent Credit Line should help responsible countries resist financial contagion. There are elaborate provisions for involving the private sector in financial rescue operations. The work of the G7 and IMF is reinforced by a new G20, associating the larger developing countries with the preparation of reforms.

These measures are extensive, but none is really radical, and there seems no great confidence that they can deter future crises and the contagion that goes with them.[15]

The Summits from Halifax to Cologne get a mixed but generally favourable assessment, as follows:

- The Halifax 1995 Summit demonstrated *leadership*. While the rescue of Mexico had been contentious among the G7, the Summit restored harmony to the pursuit of IMF reform. Birmingham 1998 and Cologne 1999 were less clearly decisive. They provided the focus for their Finance Ministers' work, but contributed nothing themselves, in contrast to their personal involvement with debt relief.
- All three Summits were *effective* in reconciling domestic and external pressures. As at Rambouillet 1975, the key was thorough and detailed preparation, carried through by the G7 Finance Ministers and their officials.
- The Halifax reforms were manifestly not *durable*. This was because of slow and incomplete implementation, without sufficient pressure from Lyon 1996 and Denver 1997 to get things done. After the crisis broke out again in Asia, the Summits have been concerned not to make the same mistake again.
- All the reform proposals emerging from the Summits have proved widely *acceptable* in the IMF and World Bank. The G7 did not leave this to chance, but took care to involve other parts of the membership in the reform process. This was chiefly done through the G22, which was launched by the Americans in 1998 and brought in some of the key Asian countries. The new G20, forecast at Cologne 1999 and confirmed at the IMF annual meeting, puts this wider consultation on a permanent footing.
- Once again, the judgement on *consistency* opens up wider issues. The question is whether the Summits, by focussing too much on financial architecture, have neglected other parts of the international economic system, notably the trade regime. This issue will be addressed in the final recommendations.

Lessons from the Past and Present

It is now possible to draw some lessons from the Summit record in handling issues concerned with the international financial system. This section concentrates on their performance under the first four criteria. The fifth criterion - consistency - provides the basis for the main recommendation for the future, which is treated in the final section.

Leadership

The heads of government must use the Summit as the occasion to resolve disagreements between them which have persisted at lower levels. If this chance is wasted, the Summit's purpose is lost. The achievements of Rambouillet 1975, Paris 1989, and Halifax 1995 all demonstrate this, as do the Summits from Toronto 1988 onward which dealt with debt relief for the poorest. In contrast, the world suffered from a lack of leadership from the Summits of the mid-1980s.

Effectiveness

The issues coming to the Summit must have maximum advance preparation, to limit the items requiring resolution at the Summit itself. Effective Summits, from Rambouillet right through to Cologne, clearly demonstrate this. Without proper preparation, the leaders will be confronted with too many problems and they will temporise or fudge. This leads to disagreements persisting among the G7, which can undo any apparent consensus at the summit. This was the main weakness of the G7's work on debt relief for the poorest, so that it required constant reference back to the Summit itself.

Durability

There are two lessons to be drawn from the Summit record on how to make its agreements durable. The first, based on the experience from Rambouillet, is that informal arrangements do not endure. Reforms to the financial architecture, such as those agreed at Birmingham and Cologne, must be integrated into formal institutions and given legal force. The second concerns proper implementation. The Summits must keep up the pressure to ensure that whatever they agree is properly carried out. Commitments which are not fulfilled, or are allowed to drag on, undermine the authority of the Summits.[16] This was the mistake made after Halifax, which left the world vulnerable to the Asian crisis. By far the most important task for the Okinawa Summit of 2000 in the financial field will be to ensure that the decisions of Cologne, on both debt relief and financial architecture, are being thoroughly implemented.

Acceptability

The demands made on the Summit under this criterion have grown over the years. The G7 must give a lead from the Summit - that is expected of them. But they must not expect others to follow blindly. They must set a good example of international behaviour - no one will respect new rules if the G7 themselves do not do so. They must explain their proposals persuasively within the global institutions, such as the IMF, responding to the concerns of others, especially poor and vulnerable countries. They must also respond to a wider public. There is increasing doubt and suspicion about who gains and who loses from globalisation. Charities and other NGOs, loosely grouped under the banner of "civil society", are keen to correct what they see as the dangers of globalisation, for example for the poorest countries. The Summit leaders have to be ready to explain and defend their decisions before this audience, too.

The G7 Summit will not get everything right. Problems only come up to the Summit which have defied settlement lower down. But while mistakes of judgement may be forgiven, the G7's reputation will not survive the refusal to exercise leadership, persistent disagreement among themselves or the failure to implement what they have agreed.

Recommendations for the Future

The analysis suggests that consistency is the hardest criterion for the Summit to satisfy. None of the four episodes examined in this chapter shows a wholly satisfactory record. Part of the Rambouillet understanding failed because G7 members adopted policies incompatible with currency stability. The debt crisis of 1982 broke out because the recycling of oil surpluses could not survive the recession provoked by tight economic policies. The Summits' attention to debt relief, from 1988 onwards, contrasted with how little the G7 had otherwise done to help the poorest countries.

Most serious of all, the last two Summits - Birmingham and Cologne - have given close attention to financial matters but have neglected international trade. Blair did not push trade at Birmingham, in his wish to limit the Summit agenda. Before Cologne, the Germans were preoccupied with Kosovo. Thus the Summit discussions on trade were perfunctory, on both occasions, and the conclusions did not resolve the underlying differences. The discussions also had to accommodate the Russians, who were not even members of the WTO.

The Summit has paid a heavy price for their neglect of the trade dossier. The financial system enters the new millennium in conditions of calm, though no one is sure if this is a settled state or just another period of remission from the virus of contagious speculation. But the trade system, which had looked so strong up until then, enters the millennium in confusion and disorder, after the WTO ministerial at Seattle failed spectacularly to launch a new round of trade negotiations. Many factors combined to cause this failure. But the G7 Summit cannot escape its share of the responsibility.

By the criteria used to judge their achievements on finance, the Summit's recent performance on trade reveals very poor scores. Neither Birmingham nor Cologne showed the necessary *leadership* to resolve the differences in G7 approaches to the trade negotiations. Instead, the European Union persisted with its comprehensive "millennium round", while the US advocated a more limited agenda. The tensions between domestic and external pressures were not *effectively* resolved. Instead, the Americans, with presidential elections in sight, leant towards the protectionist demands of their labour unions, while the Europeans did not stand up to their agricultural lobbies.

The G7 did not only fail to resolve their own differences. They launched proposals which were not *acceptable* to the wider membership of the WTO. While the developing countries were wanting action on textiles, anti-dumping, and the implementation of the Uruguay Round agreements, the G7 members were pressing labour and environmental standards or investment and competition rules. The streets of Seattle also attracted massive anti-globalisation demonstrations, but the G7 members seemed more inclined to humour the protesters than defend the merits of open markets. This further alienated the developing countries. So the G7's approach proved the opposite of *durable*, in that the new round of negotiations did not even get started.[17]

This neglect of trade has undermined what the Summit has done on financial issues, especially on debt relief for the poorest countries. Michel Camdessus, the IMF Managing Director, made that very clear in his speech to the WTO plenary. He said:

> The international community has actively endorsed the enhancement of the Initiative for Heavily Indebted Poor countries (HIPCs).... But these initiatives will be seriously weakened if the developing countries are not given the most fundamental opportunity: to produce and export a growing range of goods and services.... Providing unrestricted market access for all exports from the poorest

countries, including the HIPCs, should receive priority and be brought to an early resolution so that the poorest countries can begin to benefit without delay. They account for such a small proportion of world trade - less than one half of one per cent - that such access would not be costly or unduly disruptive.[18]

The idea of duty-free access for the exports of least-developed countries was launched by Renato Ruggiero, the last Director-General of the WTO, at the Lyon 1996 Summit, nearly four years ago.[19] In the Birmingham 1998 communiqué the G8 leaders said that they "undertake to help least developed countries by... providing additional duty-free access for their goods" and this was explicitly reaffirmed at Cologne 1999.[20] At Seattle the EU, Japan, Canada and the United States all went further and announced commitments on free access for the exports of the least developed. But none was comprehensive, all contained conditions and exceptions, and implementation remains uncertain.

The main recommendation for the immediate future therefore must be that the Summit should reverse this neglect and give high priority to restoring the international trade system. The Summit has devoted much time and effort to financial architecture, widely defined. Now the international trade architecture demands no less attention. The G7 members should show leadership in resolving their internal differences and restoring authority to the WTO. They should work to make both their own policies and the WTO itself more responsive to the requirements of developing countries, especially small and poor ones. This is the only way to make the Summits' work on the new financial architecture consistent with their responsibilities for the world economic system in its entirety.

Trade should be the first priority for the Okinawa 2000 Summit and for the Summit to be held in Italy in 2001 as well.[21] This will help to ensure that a new round of WTO trade negotiations can be properly prepared and successfully launched, with strong momentum, after the disaster of Seattle. The last time the Summit met in Japan, in 1993, it was preceded by a meeting of the trade ministers in the "Quad" (EU, US, Japan and Canada). The trade ministers' meeting and the Tokyo III Summit which followed it provided the necessary impetus to bring the Uruguay Round finally to a successful conclusion by the end of 1993.[22] That provides an example for the Summit to follow in 2000, in order to restore its reputation for leadership and effectiveness, and for producing durable, acceptable, and consistent results.

Notes

1. This chapter draws heavily on Bayne 1999, especially chapters 10 and 11, updated in the light of the outcome of the WTO ministerial meeting at Seattle in November/December 1999.
2. Quotation from Giscard's interview with Hearst press, in *Le Monde* and *Financial Times*, 9 July 1975. For Giscard's ambitions in launching the first Summit, see Putnam and Bayne 1987, pp. 27-34.
3. The monetary agreement from the Rambouillet Summit is analysed in Putnam and Bayne 1987, pp. 38-41.
4. The Plaza agreement of September 1985 was a rare public appearance of the secretive G5. The Louvre meeting of February 1987 was meant to be of the G7, but the Italians refused to attend. For the foundation and early activities of the G7 Finance Ministers, see Putnam and Bayne 1987, pp. 215-222 and 233-234, and Funabashi 1988. For later critiques of the G7, compare Dobson 1991 with Bergsten and Henning 1996.
5. Rambouillet, with a grade of A-, is regarded as the most productive Summit after Bonn I 1978 in the table given in Putnam and Bayne 1987, p. 270, updated in Bayne 1999, p. 195.
6. For Versailles' neglect of the impending debt crisis, see Putnam and Bayne 1987, pp. 174-175.
7. Jacques Attali, President François Mitterrand's sherpa, covers the Paris 1989 Summit in detail in his memoirs (Attali 1995). For the Brady Plan at Paris 1989, see also Bayne 1992 and Bayne 1999, p. 64.
8. Evans 1999 gives an insider's account of how the Summits came to focus on debt relief for the poorest and how agreements were reached.
9. A pre-Birmingham critique of the inadequacy of the HIPC programme was produced by Christian Aid, the leading charity in the Jubilee 2000 campaign (Lockwood *et al.* 1998). Bayne 1998 describes the disappointing outcome of the Birmingham Summit on this issue. Criticism continued right up to the Cologne Summit; see *Financial Times*, 12 June 1999.
10. For an assessment of the Cologne Debt Initiative, see Bayne 1999, pp. 182-185.
11. The German change was signalled in an article by Chancellor Schroeder in *Financial Times*, 21 January 1999.
12. Accounts of the monetary reforms proposed at Halifax are in Bayne 1995 and Bayne 1999, pp. 118-124. See also Cooper 1995 for proposals offered in advance.
13. Initial assessments of the Halifax programme had been generally satisfied with the progress and did not expect a new crisis to break out. See Kenen 1996, which has an introduction by Lawrence Summers, then Deputy Secretary of the US Treasury.
14. Stanley Fischer, Deputy Managing Director of the IMF, replied in *Financial Times*, 17 December 1997, to attacks by Martin Wolf and Jeffrey Sachs, *Financial Times*, 9 and 11 December 1997. See also the exchange of articles in *Foreign Affairs* by Feldstein 1998 and Fischer 1998. Camdessus and Wolfensohn 1998, prepared for the Birmingham Summit, gives a joint defence on behalf of both the IMF and the World Bank.
15. In general, the Summits favoured cautious, piecemeal measures, such as those advocated in Eichengreen 1999, rather than radical changes. An assessment of the work by the Birmingham and Cologne Summits on new financial architecture is in Bayne 1999, pp. 171-178.

16 See Kokotsis and Daniels 1999, and Kokotsis 1999 for assessments of the general Summit record of compliance with commitments.

17 For a judgement on the outcome of Seattle, see *The Economist*, 11 December 1999. The outcome of the meeting and the accompanying demonstrations received wide media coverage.

18 From Camdessus' speech to the WTO ministerial on 30 November 1999. Text on the WTO's website, www.wto.org.

19 Ruggiero's plea at the Lyon summit is recorded in *Financial Times*, 1 July 1996. It received no direct response at Lyon or at Denver 1997. For commentary, see Bayne 1997.

20 The references are to paragraph 5 (last tiret) of the Birmingham communiqué and paragraph 10 of the Cologne communiqué. Both texts available on the website of the University of Toronto's G8 Research Group, www. g7.utoronto.ca.

21 If the new WTO trade round can be re-launched in 2000, the Okinawa Summit can provide the necessary impetus. It is more likely, however, that the round can only begin after the US presidential elections, with a new American administration in place. In that event, the following Summit, to he hosted by Italy, should have a decisive role in getting the new WTO round started in mid-2001.

22 For an account of the final stages of the Uruguay Round and the part played by the Tokyo III Summit, see Croome 1995 and Preeg 1995, Chapter 7.

References

Attali, J. (1995), *Verbatim III*, Fayard, Pads.

Bayne, N. (1999), *Hanging In There: the G7 and G8 Summit in Maturity and Renewal*, Ashgate, Aldershot.

Bayne, N. (1998), "Britain, the G8 and the Commonwealth: Lessons of the Birmingham Summit", *The Round Table*, No. 348, pp. 445-457.

Bayne, N. (1997), "Globalisation and the Commonwealth", *The Round Table*, No. 344, pp.473-484.

Bayne, N. (1995), "The G7 Summit and the Reform of Global Institutions", *Government and Opposition*, 30(4), pp. 492-509.

Bayne, N. (1992), "The Course of Summitry", *The World Today*, 48(2), pp. 27-29.

Bayne, N. and R.D. Putnam (1995), "Introduction: The G7 Summit Comes of Age", in S. Ostry and G.R. Winham (eds.), *The Halifax G7 Summit: Issues on the Table*, Centre for Policy Studies, Dalhousie University, Halifax.

Bergsten, C.F. and C.R. Henning (1996), *Global Economic Leadership and the Group of Seven*, Institute for International Economics, Washington, DC.

Camdessus, M. and J.D. Wolfensohn (1998), "The Bretton Woods Institutions: Responding to the Asian Financial Crisis", in M. Fraser (ed.), *The G8 and the World Economy*, Strategems Publishing Ltd, London, pp. 6-8.

Cooper, R.N. (1995), "Reform of Multilateral Financial Institutions" in S. Ostry and C.R. Winham (eds.), *The Halifax G7 Summit: Issues on the Table*, Centre for Policy Studies, Dalhousie University, Halifax.

Croome, J. (1995), *Reshaping the World Trading System: A History of the Uruguay Round*, World Trade Organization, Geneva.

Dobson, W. (1991), *Economic Policy Coordination: Requiem or Prologue?*, Institute for International Economics, Washington DC.

Eichengreen, B. (1999), *Towards a New International Financial Architecture: A Practical Post-Asia Agenda*, Institute for International Economics, Washington DC.

Evans, H. (1999), "Debt Relief for the Poorest Countries: Why Did It Take So Long?", Development Policy Review, 17(3), pp. 267-279, Overseas Development Institute, London.

Feldstein, M. (1998), "Refocusing the IMF", *Foreign Affairs*, 77(2), pp. 20-33.

Fischer, S. (1998), "In Defense of the IMF", *Foreign Affairs*, 77(4), pp. 103-106.

Funabashi, Y. (1988), *Managing the Dollar: From the Plaza to the Louvre*, Institute for International Economics, Washington DC.

Hajnal, P.I. (1999), *The G7/G8 System: Evolution, Role and Documentation*, Ashgate, Aldershot.

Hodges, M.J., J.J. Kirton and J.P. Daniels (eds.) (1999), *The G8's Role in the New Millennium*, Ashgate, Aldershot.

James, H. (1996), *International Monetary Cooperation Since Bretton Woods*, International Monetary Fund, Washington DC.

Kenen, P.B. (ed.), (1996), *From Halifax to Lyons: What Has Been Done About Crisis Management?*, Essays in International Finance no. 200, Princeton University, Princeton.

Kenen, P.B. (ed.), (1994), *Managing the World Economy: Fifty Years After Bretton Woods*, Institute for International Economics, Washington DC.

Kokotsis, E. (1999), *Keeping International Commitments: Compliance, Credibility and the G7, 1988-1995*, Garland Publishing, Levittown.

Kokotsis, E. and J.P. Daniels (1999), "G8 Summits and Compliance" in M.J. Hodges, J.J. Kirton and J.P. Daniels (eds.), *The G8's Role in the New Millennium*, Ashgate, Aldershot, pp. 75-91.

Lockwood, M., E. Donlan, K. Joyner and A. Simms (1998), *Forever in Your Debt? Eight Poor Nations and the G8*, Christian Aid, London.

Putnam, R.D. and N. Bayne (1987), *Hanging Together: Cooperation and Conflict in the Seven-Power Summits*, SAGE, London.

Preeg, E.H. (1995), *Traders in a Brave New World: The Uruguay Round and the Future of the International Trading System*, University of Chicago Press, Chicago.

3 The Asian Crisis and Its Implications

TAKASHI KIUCHI

Introduction

What have Japan and its Asian neighbours learned from the Asian financial crisis of 1997-99? Amidst such unprecedented calamities as the *de facto* bankruptcy and ensuing nationalisation of the Long Term Credit Bank of Japan and other major financial institutions, for the first time in 50 years many Japanese professionals and workers have faced the harsh reality or agonising uncertainty of unemployment. In this respect as in many others, Japan's new situation, coming on top of close to a decade of stagnant economic growth (Watanabe 1999), resembles the broader crisis faced by Asia as a whole.

To understand the dynamics and impact of the crisis and the ensuing approach to strengthening the international financial system from a Japanese and Asian perspective, it is important to consider in turn three central issues. The first includes the course and the causes of the financial and economic failure flowing from the hitherto highly success model followed in Asia. The second is the way in which Japan, the central economic engine and only G7 member of the region, interpreted and responded to the Asian crisis. The third involves the implications that can be drawn for the future efforts of Asia, Japan, and the G7 to rebuild the international financial architecture to place it on a more stable foundation.

Such an analysis suggests that the ultimate causes of the crisis lie in capital account rather than current account problems, liquidity rather than solvency problems, and the herding behaviour of investors. Yet, it also stems importantly from politicians intervening unwisely to override their officials and professional regulators. Japan's response to the crisis came in the first instance in the form of a proposal for an Asian Monetary Fund (AMF), which was quickly abandoned in the face of US opposition. Japan then followed with the "New Miyazawa Initiative" of US$30 billion worth of bilateral lending guarantees, proposals to reform the International Monetary Fund

(IMF), and new measures to make the yen an international currency. The major lessons of the crisis are the need for decisive action at early stages, for enhancing the IMF's authority to deal with capital account problems, and for closer regional policy co-ordination. The latter should start with macroeconomic policy and the development of an Asian bond market to replace short-term borrowing from distant bankers.

The Asian experience suggests several further conclusions. Dollarisation offers no solution for smaller Asian economies. Short-term capital restrictions as a transitional measure, mandatory private sector burden sharing, and state bankruptcy codes have an important role to play. Universal guidelines and processes for accounting, disclosure, bankruptcy, and financial supervision are also valuable. What is required is a staged approach to introducing these new measures, tightly tailored to the particular situation of each country, with proper macroeconomic policy to reinforce improved international regulation. Above all, the G7 should provide leadership in catalysing and guiding a move toward a *de facto* target zone mechanism, for substantial benefits will flow from further moves in this direction.

The Asian Crisis and Its Causes

A fairly solid consensus already exists among experts regarding what went wrong with the Asian economy, starting with the meltdown in Thailand in the summer of 1997 (Eichengreen 1999, Goldstein 1998). Most of these conclusions are well taken. Unsound economic management bred various forms of bubbles or asset price inflation. Typically, these involved property (typically in Thailand and Malaysia) and other prestige projects (typically in Indonesia and Korea) which did not serve at all to enhance the export competitiveness that had long lain at the heart of the Asian economies' economic miracle. Highly geared financing made the institutions involved particularly vulnerable. Excessive dependence upon short-term bank borrowing without cover from abroad proved fatal. A massive exodus of capital crippled balance sheets beyond repair. Weak institutions and the inadequate oversight of them were then blamed for the reckless business practices which had prevailed in the preceding years.

In essence, as already pointed out, the Asian crisis was a capital account problem rather than a trade account problem, and a liquidity problem rather than an insolvency problem. This was vividly exemplified by that fact that the sharp depreciation of the currencies brought about immediate and substantial improvement in their trade balances but could not arrest further depreciation. In relation to these problems, the herding behaviour of lenders as well as of investors was especially disturbing. It seemed to have intensified inflows as well as outflows of capital. It is very indicative that the region's economic downturn bottomed out when most of the mobile foreign capital moved out and the efforts to hold it by high interest policy were finally abandoned. Suspicion persists that this herding might be a part of the inherent problems in a now globalised financial market.

There are, however, two additional factors that warrant emphasis. The first concerns the importance of sound economic policy. It is unlikely that any new international financial system can eliminate bubbles. Even meticulous regulation still has many loopholes. But prudent economic management can minimise the size of bubbles. It was apparent that in the lead-up to and in the early stages of the Asian financial crisis, politicians overruled official experts frequently in the conduct of macroeconomic policy. Here politicians sought to favour their constituent interest groups at the expense of economic rationality. Moreover, there is even some truth in saying that politicians stole credit for spectacular economic success which was in fact brought about by the technocrats' sound and prudent macroeconomic management in the preceding years.

Secondly, regulations were also distorted for the same purpose. The liberalisation of capital markets, including the creation of offshore banking centres, was pursued single-handedly in order to attract foreign money. A continuing inflow of capital provided a convenient excuse for neglecting the growing insufficiency of the relevant regulations. In retrospect, it would have been wiser to let currencies float and appreciate in earlier years. However, politicians reportedly quickly silenced such a recommendation. It should be pointed out that, in the preceding decade, the region's authorities chose currency devaluation from time to time to correct trade imbalances. It was almost evident that the governments held on too long to the dollar peg, due to a desire not to discourage international investors by any means.

The Japanese Response

Japan's response to the crisis began with an ill-fated proposal for the establishment of an AMF. This proposal is often cited as a leading example of Japan's desire to exhibit a new activism. The proposal was to create a fresh US$100 billion multilateral facility for Asia, to which Japan pledged to contribute half the quota. The proposal was later abandoned in the face of the staunch opposition of the United States. The US argued that the AMF would undermine IMF leadership and lead to the weakening of conditionality. As a result, the Manila Framework was agreed upon to enhance the capability of the IMF to deal with the Asian crisis.

In fact, the AMF proposal was very vague in specifics when it was launched. One interpretation was that it was done intentionally so that specifics could be hammered out in further consultations with the United States and other G7 nations, because its relations with the IMF, World Bank, Asian Development Bank, and other international financial institutions produce obvious complexities. In other words, it is somewhat difficult to make an accurate and fair appraisal of the AMF proposal at this point in time. It was also reported that more than once the Japanese government stated its readiness to the US government to tailor the proposal through further consultation so as to make it compatible with the IMF.

Despite its rapid rejection and withdrawal, there remains considerable merit in the AMF proposal. At the very least, a supplemental fund could be useful if the IMF remains poorly equipped to handle large-scale financial crises. The IMF's enforcement of austere fiscal and monetary policy in the affected Asian economies was a tragic mistake. The combination of a high interest rate policy with cuts in fiscal spending was a serious blow to the region's economies, where balance sheet problems mercilessly deprived the private sector of fresh spending capability. Clever crisis management is different from appropriate structural reform, which can be a perfect recipe for disaster if introduced in the midst of crisis. It is also noteworthy that Japan was quicker to notice the potential danger of contagion than were many others far removed from the region, caught up as they were in the Washington consensus. There seems agreement among Japanese opinion leaders that it is good thing that future discussions on IMF reform must include what was suggested by the AMF proposal.

Currently, the Japanese government is acting on a third proposal, in the form of the New Miyazawa Initiative. This is a bilateral US$30 billion scheme in which, in addition to direct lending, Japan offers guarantee programs to enhance the Asian nations' borrowing capabilities in the market. The scheme has been very well received by the rest of Asia. It is not surprising at all to see that what the rest of Asia needs to get out of their economic turmoil is a fresh inflow of capital, and this was offered by the Japanese government. In this respect, Japan has been making the greatest contribution to the rest of the Asia to date. The Japanese government, however, should not be praised for this response without reservation. An economic recovery is what Japan can do most to help the rest of Asia with. It has not yet been very successful on this front.

Subsequently, the Japanese government announced several recommendations to strengthen the IMF. The first component of its proposal is to expand the facilities, for example, by allowing the IMF to borrow aggressively in the market. The second is to foster a wider participation in the IMF's deliberation process. The third is to enhance monitoring of capital flows on the investor's side. The first component may not be enjoying anonymous endorsement in Japan and can be somewhat controversial. However, the second and third components seem to be generally supported widely in Japan.

It is worthwhile noting in this regard that Japan has made an apparent turn in its policy toward promoting the yen as an international currency. The Japanese government has taken several measures, notably the diversification of Japan Government Bond (JGB) maturity structures, including short-term bills, exemption of withholding taxes for nonresident JGB holders, and improvements on the settlement systems.

In fact, the Japanese financial community in general has long been arguing for yen's internationalisation. This is mainly because of the fear that without a fully functioning international currency, the future of Tokyo as an international financial centre would remain hopelessly crippled when compared with New York and London, and, moreover, with Singapore and Hong Kong. However, the practical obstacle was the necessity of keeping deregulation on this front in line with deregulation on the domestic side, which progressed extremely slowly. It is probably fair to say that the disruption to the financial market in the last couple of years finally crushed any argument in favour of gradual approach. Accordingly, the government has come to side with the notion that yen's internationalisation would have a pivotal role in completing the overdue financial market deregulation on the domestic front.

The idea underlying these reforms regarding yen's internationalisation is to make yen asset markets readily accessible and to make the yen viable as another international currency. The actual replacement of the US dollar by the yen is not the objective. This would be meaningless in light of extensive interdependence among Asia, Japan, and the United States. Any nation in the Asian region has to do a substantial portion of trade not only in dollars, but also in yen. But the opportunity to diversify currency risks through these Japanese government measures will be beneficial. They are more likely to help mitigate the difficulty in economic management arising from violent realignments between the two currencies.

Implications for International Financial System Reform

What lessons can be drawn from the Asian crisis and from the Japanese response for the ongoing effort to rebuild the international financial architecture? One feature of the Asian crisis was the fierceness of the contagion, which the global financial market tended to amplify. Any attempt to contain this contagion requires very prompt decisions and decisive, concerted action at an early stage. This requires restructuring the IMF to deal with capital account problems more effectively. Otherwise some new mechanism should be explored to supplement the IMF. There is wide acknowledgement among Japanese experts that the IMF was not fully prepared for this kind of crisis, which was somewhat clear from the fact that the IMF praised some of Asian nations only several months before the eruption of crisis.

Another aspect of contagion is that, during times of crisis, panicked investors do not distinguish one nation from another in a region. In other words, professional fund managers cannot guide end-investors properly once liberalised financial markets enable far wider participation by amateur investors in speculative emerging markets. Nations within the region have a common stake in preserving investors' confidence. The time is thus ripe for closer regional policy co-ordination, a process that could begin with the task of macroeconomic policy consultation. Global efforts in this direction deserve further exploration, but will take more time to achieve. For example, proposals for a world financial organisation for this purpose look premature and too ambitious. It is evident that the nations in the Asian region have recently demonstrated far keener interest in pursuing any collaborative attempts to preempt repetition of the crisis. One such useful step can be to develop an Asian bond market linking Tokyo, Hong Kong, and Singapore. This would enable businesses to resist the seduction of short-term borrowing. Furthermore, the merits of an AMF should not be lightly cast aside.

In this connection, the birth of the Euro has aroused renewed interest in forming some form of currency union in the future among Asian nations. At present, however, the existing diversity of these nations seems to make this concept impractical. The only viable exchange rate policy thus seems to be the so-called "two corner" solution: a floating rate system or a currency board.

Dollarisation as well does not appear to be a solution for Asia, in view of the strong economic ties with Japan that the countries of the region maintain. Consequently, some kind of currency basket remains attractive as a realistic target of exchange rate management. It is widely agreed in Japan that the internationalisation of the yen would be helpful in this regard. A currency basket regime itself contains many difficult points to be managed, but the discussion is becoming lively in the recent months.

On the other hand, the classic "Trinity dilemma", or "trilemma", seems to prevail. Thus, there are grounds for introducing some form of restriction on short-term capital as a transitional measure employed by small economies which could be overwhelmed by capital flight. This is true, even though capital control in general does not appear to function well in practice. Incidentally, the Japanese government seems to be keen in defending short-term capital controls against some scepticism from the United States.

The Asian nations themselves must do many things on their own to strengthen their financial systems. Yet, the advanced industrial nations, led by the G7, can help them to develop guidelines to meet that goal. Globalisation requires more universal guidelines. A number of suggestions made to meet this objective are valuable. These include improved accounting system with enhanced disclosure, practical bankruptcy procedures, prudent banking practices, and effective supervisory agencies.

Nonetheless, in considering these measures, several points need to be respected. Firstly, all these systems cannot be installed overnight. The fact that the economies that need these measures are called "emerging markets" underscores this fact. Therefore, the next step should be a realistic step-by-step application of the core principles. This application should be highly country specific. In some particular cases, the independence of the country's central bank can claim priority as a needed measure. In other cases, the separation of commercial banks and commerce can be critical.

The enhancement of governance in Asian economies is also of vital importance. This should be achieved by engineering a web of checks and balances among institutions and thereby fostering professionalism. Otherwise, the implementation of sound, high-standard guidelines may fail. To put it differently, overlooking of the importance of institutional infrastructure could lead to confusion as was seen in Russia.

Secondly, elaborate regulations alone may not be able to eliminate bubbles. There is a clear possibility that professional fund managers cannot calm panics among their clients, namely amateur investors. Once that panic grabs the market, rationality ceases to guide it. In this regard, the borrowers' transparency alone may not be a perfect insurance policy. It is thus vitally important to monitor investors intensively. It seems that panic is often very much due to the fear that each investor could be outsmarted by other investors without knowing it or that the market can be manipulated by oligopolistic investors, whether it is true or not. This conviction is natural to all who have had experience as economic forecasters and thus have faced the formidable difficulty of projecting interest rates amidst a lack of information regarding investors' positions in the market.

Here, once again, macroeconomic policy co-ordination, especially in regard to monetary policy, can be very useful. In the late 1980s, the Bank of Japan appears to have been fooled by an apparent price stability, which was brought about by intensified global competition for tradable goods and services. Instead, asset price inflation was growing unnoticed by the monetary authorities. Thus, any sign of stretched financial gearing and abrupt changes of money flow should be taken into proper account in determining monetary policy, both by developing and developed nations. It seems to be a new challenge for any central banks in the globalised financial market. It is hoped that the recent monetary tightening by the Federal Reserve reflects its acute awareness of this complexity of the financial market and its assiduous efforts to aim at achieving a soft landing of the US economy. In the Asian region, most of the nations are recently becoming distinctively positive toward closer communication and consultation with each other on current macroeconomic management.

Debt rescheduling is also required to resolve a financial crisis. It should be said that the Latin American debt crisis was stabilised only when the US administration set out the Brady plan. Indonesia may well need the same kind of arrangement before it could eliminate the troubles caused by the current Asian crisis, as it is only debt rescheduling that can provide an economy with a fresh foundation with which to nourish a renewed growth momentum. There should thus be progress made in permitting the collective representation of private sector creditors when the nations involved agree on the necessity of debt rescheduling. Some mandatory provisions in debt contracts and something close to state bankruptcy codes deserve further consideration.

Finally, the debates on devising a new international financial architecture should not be concluded without revisiting the notion of a target zone mechanism, which aims at stabilising exchange rates, especially among the principal currencies of the dollar, the Euro, and the yen (Williamson and Miller 1987). It appears operable only with participants' strong commitment to making their economic management compatible. Admittedly, the idea remains unrealistic as long as the US is unconvinced of the merits of this mechanism. This is despite the fact that every wild swing of the yen-dollar exchange rate in the past, with all the harm those swings brought to the real economy, was unanimously preceded by a significant shift in US monetary policy. To be more precise, sharp appreciations of the yen against the dollar were frequently preceded by intensifying trade friction between the two nations but corrected only after the Federal Reserve finally tightened its monetary policy to curb growing trade deficits. Apparently, investors' herding behaviour is not guided by sober analyses of the fundamentals but rather by signals sent by Washington.

The more the world moves toward the so-called "mutual surveillance" of each other's economic management (Funabashi 1988), the more G7 coordination comes to resemble a *de facto* target zone mechanism. One day, it will be possible that an outright admission that this is taking place could be just a final stroke of reckoning for what already exists. G7 surveillance and co-ordination should thus be continued. In any event, sovereignty over macro-economic policy has to be compromised considerably in an age of a globalised financial market.

References

Eichengreen, B. (1999), *Toward a New International Financial Architecture: A Practical Post-Asia Agenda*, Institute for International Economics, Washington DC.

Funabashi, Y. (1988), *Managing the Dollar: From the Plaza to the Louvre*, Institute for International Economics, Washington DC.

Goldstein, M., (1998), *The Asian Financial Crisis: Causes, Cures, and Systemic Implications*, Institute for International Economics, Washington DC.

Watanabe, K., (1999), "Japan's Summit Contributions and Economic Challenges", in M. Hodges, J. Kirton and J. Daniels, eds., *The G8's Role in the New Millennium*, Ashgate, Aldershot, pp. 95-106.

Williamson, J. and M. Miller (1987), "Targets and Indicators: A Blueprint for the International Coordination of Economic Policy", *Policy Analyses in International Economics No. 22*, Institute for International Economics, Washington DC.

4 The G7, International Finance, and Developing Countries

DUNCAN WOOD

Introduction

Is the G7 an exclusive organisation and, if so, does it matter? The answer to the first part of this question is obvious. The G7 has been an exclusive institution since its inception in 1975, being the organ representing the interests and policy goals of the seven largest economies in the world. The mere name suggests a country club-like exclusivity to which those left on the outside can only aspire. And indeed the G7 has thrived on such a narrow basis for mutual decision making. The identification of common interests has been relatively simple, given the similarities of economic development and political systems and the high level of interdependence among its members' economies. More importantly, the co-ordination of economic policies that has taken place since 1975 has centred on the most important markets of the world.

The second part of the question, however, is more interesting, and the answer has changed over time. In the 1970s, the exclusive nature of the G7 reflected the dominance of seven states over the global economic system. Not taking into account moral considerations, the exclusion of the developing world was only significant in that the same period witnessed a rise in less-developed country (LDCs) activism with calls for a New International Economic Order (NIEO). By the 1990s, however, this situation had changed. The rise to prominence of several developing country economies, shifts in world trade and competitiveness, and the increasing vulnerability of the global financial system made the separation of the G7 from the developing world, in particular from the large emerging markets, an anachronism.

Beginning with the search for a lasting solution to the debt crisis of the 1980s, the G7 focussed its attention on financial issues, although other issues have also emerged, and for a very good reason. The international financial system since the early 1980s has gone through a period of profound change, with developing countries and, in particular, the large emerging markets, playing a increasingly important role in that system. Along with growing emerging market importance, the fragility of the system also increased. This is largely as a result of problems in the financial and economic systems of the developing world but also due to the liberalisation process taking place across the world's financial markets.

This chapter has three parts. First, it analyses the activities of the G7 from the point of view of emerging markets and offers a critical perspective on the institution, arguing that in the future G7 decision making will have to be more inclusive of the views of certain large emerging markets. In doing so the chapter examines the actions taken by the G7 since the late 1980s with regard to the international financial system, and how these actions have affected the developing world. It explains the issues of macroeconomic co-ordination, debt renegotiation, and debt reduction, and the recent moves towards reform of the international financial architecture. This last issue in particular highlights the weakness of the G7 approach to global governance but offers some hope for a solution to that debility. Though the discussions over the reform of the international financial architecture, though at a minimal level, saw the involvement of an expanded group of countries, it must be added that the inclusion of LDCs in the reform process has thus far been limited. This chapter argues that the G7 should continue to use, and indeed should expand, a collaborative approach to the management of global financial affairs if it is to become a central instrument of global governance at the beginning of the 21st century, as some have predicted (Kirton and Daniels 1999).

Secondly, the chapter examines the achievements of the Cologne Summit, focussing on the report of the Finance Ministers and on what these achievements mean for emerging markets. It argues that the Cologne communiqué does indeed make a significant contribution to strengthening the international financial architecture, but that it does so in a way that continues to exclude the most important emerging market economies from the decision-making process. The Cologne debt initiative, the broadening of the Financial Stability Forum (FSF), and the increased importance of the International Monetary Fund (IMF) Interim Committee, now renamed the International Financial and Monetary Committee (IFMC), are all steps in the right direction. Those efforts made to broaden the decision-making community, however, do not go far enough. Nor do the reforms thus far undertaken solve many of the most important challenges to the system.

The third part of the chapter argues that an adequate response to these challenges can only be found if the policymakers of the G7 consult their counterparts in the most important emerging markets. This argument is made for one very simple reason. The creation of the G7 in the 1970s was essentially a response to a fundamental structural change in the world economy, namely the end of the Bretton Woods regime and the rise of Europe and Japan as economic rivals to the US. The state of the world economy in the late 1990s shows a similarly fundamental change. The rise of new economic powers in the developing world, the increasing mobility of finance, and the growing vulnerability of the international financial system present a new challenge to the world's leading economies. The G7 standing alone would appear to be an inadequate mechanism to address systemic weaknesses and crises in this changed world.

The G7 and Developing Countries

As far back as 1988, at the Toronto Summit, the final communiqué from the group mentioned the growing importance of the newly industrialising economies (NIEs) in the global economy. It noted the fact that dynamic, export-led growth had trebled the NIEs' share of world trade since 1960 and that such countries should match their increased economic importance with "greater international responsibilities and a strong mutual interest in improved constructive dialogue and co-operative efforts in the near terms between the industrialised countries and the Asian NIEs, as well as the other outward-oriented countries in the region" (Hajnal 1989). The emphasis here was clearly on incorporating the most important liberal emerging markets of Asia into the G7 decision-making process, a step "which would facilitate multilateral discussions of issues of mutual concern and foster the necessary co-operation", even if only at the level of "informal processes".

Another significant G7 proposal came from the 1996 Lyon Summit. It forward the idea of "a new global partnership for development". The rhetoric of this announcement focussed on co-operation, burden sharing, and partnership, of "a spirit of common purpose and efficiency" aimed at the goal of sustainable development. The communiqué placed primary and "fundamental responsibility" firmly on the shoulders of the developing countries themselves. The intent, however, seemed to be to build strong foundations for a co-operative future in the world economy in the twenty-first century.

Such co-operation, however, never materialised. The G7, even taking into account its inclusion of Russia, continues to be an exclusive club of the rich which nonetheless is a major determining factor for the economic future of both wealthy and poor states. Instead the G7 has attempted to move into the next millennium without the involvement of the largest developing economies. This threatens to pose a serious problem for the institution in terms of its effectiveness and its legitimacy as an organ of global governance. This section critically examines the work of the G7 from the perspective of LDCs.

Macroeconomic Co-ordination

There can be little doubt that the G7 has achieved considerable success as an organ of macroeconomic stabilisation for the world system during its existence. Wealthy states responded to the turbulence of the post-Bretton Woods world by forming what has been described as a concert system to manage the future of the global economy (Kirton 1999a). They have, in general terms, been highly successful in that endeavour. The G7 has, through the co-ordination of macroeconomic policies and foreign exchange intervention, managed to obtain relative currency stability between them.

An increased level of stability in the global economy has undoubtedly been beneficial for the world's economic development in general, but the benefits have been concentrated in the developed states. For these states have been able to achieve a kind of co-operative competition among them, while LDCs exist in an environment of fierce competition with little, if any, co-operative mechanisms or institutions in place. It could even be argued that higher levels of co-ordination of policies among the G7 states has been detrimental for the developing world in one way: greater stability in the economic cycles and currencies of the wealthy economies have pushed speculators toward the more volatile, higher returns of the developing economies, resulting in higher levels of instability for them. Of course, this kind of counter-factual claim is difficult to prove or refute. It is a fair assumption, however, that the low interest and inflation rates of the industrialised world has made the developing world more attractive to those investors who are more prone to greater risk-taking.

Developing Country Indebtedness

The response of the IMF since the onset of the debt crisis in the early 1980s was dictated by the interests of the industrialised, creditor countries and their private financial institutions. The adoption of a case-by-case approach was fundamental to securing these interests by denying the possibility of a unified response from the debtor states. The IMF and the G7 have consistently argued that this approach was essential for the IMF to assess each country's situation adequately, and for debtor governments and international creditors - both public and private - to negotiate an outcome to the crisis. The G7 was a consistent and constant supporter of the case-by-case approach throughout the late 1980s and early 1990s: G7 communiques stressed that "the case-by-case approach remains the only viable approach" to the resolution of the debt crisis.

This approach to crisis management, however, was widely criticised at the time and since as nothing more than a policy of "divide and conquer". By dealing with each debtor state individually, the IMF, the Paris Club, and private banks were able to extract greater concessions from them than by negotiating *en masse*. Not only was the burden of responsibility for the debt crisis placed firmly in the hands of debtor countries, but the price for IMF assistance was also the establishment of programs of economic liberalisation and structural adjustment (see below).

What of the claim that a case-by-case approach was necessary so that the debt re-scheduling could be fine-tuned to the needs of each individual debtor state? In fact, exactly the opposite can be argued, namely that a standard, orthodox solution was applied to all debtor states, regardless of their specific political and economic circumstances. If anything, this led to a higher level of costs for debtor countries and for their citizens.

Going even further than this, it can be argued that the case-by-case approach prevented a more complete solution to the general problem of international indebtedness. The G7 and IMF's way of dealing with developing countries remained *ad hoc*, an approach which had begun much earlier in the 1950s (Strange 1998). By refusing to seek a structural reform of the international financial system in the 1980s, the G7 and IMF left the system vulnerable to the problem of developing country debt in the future.

Another aspect of the G7's approach to the debt crisis was the group's endorsement of market-based structural adjustment policies and export-oriented recovery strategies for heavily indebted countries. Throughout the late 1980s and early 1990s, the G7 continued to support the orthodox policies of structural adjustment. While this may in the long term bring about economic growth and a sounder basis for national economies, in the short- and medium-term it has meant severe hardships for many groups within the societies of LDCs. It is only at the end of the 1990s that the G7 has explicitly recognised the intimate connection between IMF reform packages and social disruption. Political protests against the hardships imposed by structural adjustment were a cause of political instability in several Latin American countries in the late 1980s, in particular Venezuela.[1]

Market-oriented structural adjustment can also be partly blamed for the crises of the 1990s. In many cases, particularly in Latin America, countries that applied IMF programs rushed headlong towards economic liberalisation. Whilst this brought definite, recognisable benefits in the short- and medium-terms, poorly supervised and regulated capital market liberalisation exposed LDCs to a high degree of risk. Although a step in the right direction, full-blown capital liberalisation proved that it is possible to have "too much of a good thing", especially if it happens too fast.

Reform of the International Financial Architecture

G7 moves toward changing the international financial system began in earnest after the Mexican peso crisis with the Halifax Summit of 1995, a year which also marked the 50th anniversary of the Bretton Woods institutions (Cooper, 1995). The G7 states called on the Basle Committee for Banking Supervision (hereafter Basle Committee) of the Bank for International Settlements (BIS) to assist in this reform by developing minimum standards for banking supervision. The Basle Committee undertook this work and came up with its Core Principles for Effective Banking Supervision, or Basle Core Principles, published in 1997. These principles constitute an attempt to define minimum standards for banking supervision in all countries, developed and otherwise, to increase safety and soundness of banking markets. Though a useful beginning, the Basle Core Principles suffer from a lack of specificity. They are merely guidelines for supervisory behaviour and do not assist national authorities in the day-to-day business of supervision. This was probably unavoidable, given the mandate to design basic principles for all types of banking markets. But neither the Basle Committee nor the G7 has called for these principles to be defined any more clearly, or in a more applied fashion. The only effective way to do so would be to consult more closely with regulatory and supervisory authorities in LDCs. Unfortunately, there appears to be little enthusiasm to build on this foundation and carry it forward.

The BIS itself has moved toward a more inclusive structure since the Mexican peso crisis, accepting new central banks into its membership. In 1996, the BIS recognised the importance of emerging market monetary and financial authorities in the new international financial architecture by inviting Brazil, China, Hong Kong, India, Korea, Mexico, Russia, Saudi Arabia, and Singapore to become new members.[2] Though it is difficult to determine any solid contribution to international financial stability from the new membership of the BIS, continued co-operation and information exchange between these authorities and their counterparts in the developed world will certainly aid crisis prevention and management.

Another major initiative came from the United States. The creation of the G22 in 1998 as an *ad hoc* grouping of developed and developing states constituted an attempt to pull together the highly varied experiences of national policymakers.[3] This demonstrated the importance attached to incorporating LDCs into the process of international financial reform. The G22 formed three working groups that examined the issues of international financial crises, strengthening financial systems, and transparency and accountability. Each working group was co-chaired by officials from one developed country and one developing country. The transparency and accountability committee, for example, was co-chaired by the US and Mexico. Despite this co-operative atmosphere, the G22 did not survive long enough to make a significant contribution to either international financial architecture reform or longer term LDC-G7 co-operation. The group was dissolved after it had published its reports, with the United States deciding that it had served its purpose.

By the middle of 1999, confidence had more or less returned to emerging markets. By the time of the G7 Summit in Cologne, there was less urgency than had been felt a year earlier in Birmingham. The achievements of the Cologne Summit with regard to reform of the international financial architecture will be examined a little later in this chapter. It should be noted, however, that there were several references to working more closely with developing and emerging market country authorities. The question remains as to whether these references will solidify into real commitments.

Evaluating the Cologne Summit 1999

The 1999 meetings of the G7 Finance Ministers took place in Frankfurt rather than Cologne, but the final communiqué was released in the Summit host city. This document, entitled *Strengthening the International Financial Architecture: Report of the G7 Finance Ministers to the Köln Economic Summit*, examined the issues of strengthening international financial institutions (IFIs), enhancing transparency and promoting best practices, strengthening macroeconomic policies and financial regulation and supervision in emerging market economies, improving crisis prevention and management, and promoting social policies. The following section of this chapter analyses each of these issue areas from the perspective of developing countries before turning to the issue of debt relief.

Strengthening and Reforming the International Financial Institutions and Arrangements

Two initiatives in this area are of direct relevance to developing countries. The first was the G7's decision to broaden representation in the recently formed Financial Stability Forum (FSF), with member countries agreeing that such a broadening should be carried out in way "that provides for effective dialogue" between participating countries, both "industrial and emerging". The FSF was originally made up of the finance ministries, central banks, and leading regulators of each of the G7 countries. Also represented were the chairs of the international regulatory organisations and representatives of the IFIs. Of course, this left the FSF as another exclusive organisation that neglected both the input and the interests of developing countries.

The call for a broadening of FSF membership, however, seemed to offer the prospect of a significant step forward in securing international financial stability. It suggested a true dialogue between industrial and emerging market countries in which a better understanding of the particular problems of financial regulation and supervision in LDCs, as well as their interests, could be put on the table and taken into consideration.

The outcome thus far, however, has been very disappointing. The BIS announced the four new members of the FSF but the new expanded membership list does little to give LDCs a strong voice in the institution. The new members are Hong Kong, Singapore, Australia, and the Netherlands, leaving aside the important Latin American nations such as Argentina, Brazil, and Mexico as well as China. The justification for this can be found in the BIS press release. It announced that the four new countries had been invited to join in response to "the statement of the Heads of Government of the G7 countries that the Financial Stability Forum should be broadened to include significant financial centres" (BIS 1999). Clearly, to the G7, Mexico, Brazil, Argentina, and China do not constitute "significant financial centres", and it would be difficult to argue that they do at this point in time. But this misses the point. The interdependence of global financial markets means that authorities cannot merely concentrate on the top 11 financial centres. As the crises in Asia and Brazil threatened to prove, a crisis in a large emerging financial market can rapidly spread to the rest of the system.

The second aspect of immediate significance to developing states in this area was the changes made to the IMF's Interim Committee. In addition to renaming it the International Financial and Monetary Committee, the G7 states committed themselves to the transformation of the committee into a council. The committee is to be given a permanent standing with deputy-level meetings twice a year, just before the Ministerial meetings. The goal of this change is to allow for greater input from the IFMC into the Ministerial meetings, something that had been achieved in April of 1999. This is a welcome initiative from the point of view of developing states. The strength of G7 commitment to making it a *de facto* and *de jure* central part of decision making in the IMF, however, remains to be seen. It must be remembered that the Interim Committee itself was more or less supplanted by the G7 as the main locus of international economic decision making in the 1970s, and there is little evidence to suggest that the wealthy states want to give up this control.

Enhancing Transparency and Promoting Best Practices

Since 1995, one of the central issues for IFIs has been increasing transparency and disclosure of information, in particular from LDC governments. The IMF's Special Data Dissemination Standards (SDDS) form the most obvious manifestation of this concern. Work continues on improving the availability of data. The Cologne communiqué contained many proposals for furthering and strengthening this work, by incorporating transparency evaluation into the IMF's annual Article IV consultations, developing a core set of accounting standards, and ensuring that private sector firms engage in transparent practices.

While increasing transparency is unlikely to be detrimental to the stability of the international financial system, the Finance Ministers report (along with all previous attempts to improve transparency) fails to recognise the many and particular reasons why data gathering and transparency are so difficult to achieve in LDCs. First, many LDC governments have a very real interest (usually political) in preventing the truth about their economies from being known. Second, it is difficult to develop standards that are suitable for such widely varying financial systems as, for example, the US and Mexico. Third, developing standards is one thing, implementing them is yet another. Mexico has been using the internationally recognised Generally Accepted Accounting

Principles (GAAP) for a few years, but their Mexican-style implementation has led to them being called the "Tex-Mex GAAP". Their effectiveness is in doubt.

It is likely that the search for full disclosure of data and practices will continue in years to come. The overwhelming liberal bias amongst G7 countries and in the IMF's management is pushing them towards the realisation of a classical liberal assumption: that a market will work perfectly under conditions of perfect information. Whether or not the assumption can ever be realised, or even if it is a correct assumption, remains to be seen.

Strengthening Macroeconomic Policies and Financial Systems in Emerging Markets

This section of the Finance Ministers report (following on from a section on improving financial regulation in industrialised countries) contained a set of recommendations concerning the activities of LDC governments in the areas of exchange rates, debt management, capital flows, and financial systems. The problem is, of course, that the G7 document was accepted and signed only by G7 states, not by those to whom this section applies. As such, it exists solely as a set of suggestions. The one area where potential exists for a real contribution is in Section 31, where the report states: "It is our objective to help emerging economies adapt their policies and organisations to those required to participate fully in the world economy", and "The IFIs and other international bodies should enhance their co-operation in terms of giving useful advice and assistance to emerging economies". This is where the G7 states could make a strong contribution to international financial stability, by giving technical assistance to developing states to help them design policies and approaches that lead to a reduction in systemic risk. Unfortunately, there seems to be little enthusiasm to develop such assistance at the international level.[4]

Improving Crisis Prevention and Management and Involving the Private Sector

The two main areas of interest from an LDC perspective concerned the IMF's new Contingent Credit Line (CCL) and "bailing in" the private sector in crisis resolution. The CCL was hailed by the G7 Finance Ministers as playing "an important part in crisis prevention". Its goal is to provide a line of credit to countries following sound macroeconomic and structural policies and with reasonable debt structures so that they are protected from contagion during currency and financial crises. While this seems a positive form of assistance, in the view of some it actually threatens financial stability by encouraging moral hazard. The argument is simple: if a country following sound policies knows it has access to the CCL, the danger exists that it will be tempted to adopt more risky practices in the knowledge that a bail-out is already available.

The second element of this area, namely involving the private sector in crisis resolution, focussed mainly on securing private creditor co-operation, and negotiated deals between debtors and creditors during a crisis. Of course, there is a historical example on which to draw: the Latin American debt crisis of the 1980s. Then private sector banks were persuaded by the IMF to provide further financing for debt management. But the same example highlights the priorities of the wealthy states and of the IMF in such situations. The clear focus for the US and other leading IMF shareholders was to protect the interests of their large banks. The adoption of the case-by-case approach reflected this.

Promoting Social Policies to Protect the Poor and Most Vulnerable

In regard to social policies that protect the poor and most vulnerable, the G7 Finance Ministers focussed on the link between crisis resolution and social costs. Of direct relevance to LDCs was the implicit recognition that IMF programs in the past have not adequately taken into account the social and political costs that structural adjustment entails. This led the G7 to call on the IMF and the World Bank to design their programs to allow recipient countries enough latitude to continue with social spending priorities. This promises to be an important departure for the international financial institutions (IFIs) if social policy becomes a key indicator in the implementation of their packages. However, there is room for scepticism. Since the late 1980s, the World Bank and the IMF have claimed to be sensitive to the issue of poverty in their programs, but the IMF's rescue packages continue to follow the traditional Washington consensus of liberalisation and government austerity.

The Cologne Debt-Relief Initiative

In the 1990s, the issue of the indebtedness of the poorest countries has remained on the agenda of the G7. At the Cologne Summit in 1999, the G7 countries announced a far-reaching package of debt reduction for the Highly

Indebted Poor Countries (HIPC). This debt-reduction package allows for debt forgiveness through the IMF and the Paris Club. Hailed as a great achievement by many, the package saw proposals for debt forgiveness totalling anywhere up to US$90 billion. The issue of debt relief for these countries has, however, never been a priority issue for the stability and growth of the world economy as a whole. What really affects global economic growth are the borrowing practices of, and capital flows in and out of, the largest emerging markets, most of which are seen as middle income. One should be careful, therefore, not to over estimate the importance of the HIPC debt-reduction program.

Having said this, the Cologne debt initiative has the potential to provide significant relief to those poor countries trying to maintain both their international and domestic commitments. Thirty-three countries could benefit from a huge reduction in the level of foreign indebtedness to official creditors.[5] The question remains, however, as to the conditionality of the debt relief. Early drafts of the proposal included statements to the effect that recipient states would have to follow procedures of good governance and economic liberalisation, but the final version was silent on this issue. It will no doubt be left to the IMF and individual creditor countries to work out the specifics.

Prospects for a More Inclusive and Effective G7

Studies have shown that by the year 2050 the developing world will be responsible for over 50 percent of world trade with the "Big Ten" emerging market economies accounting for over half of that total.[6] Such projections are always fraught with danger. If the projections are correct, however, then these states will join the most important players in the World Trade Organization (WTO), particularly as their levels of consumption rise and they become important markets in their own right. Effective trade policy must include them, and the WTO will be forced to be flexible if it is to survive. Jeffrey Garten (1998) warned of the impact of the new economic powers on the international system. Although his conclusions were controversial, the new distribution of power will undoubtedly require a reorganisation of the international economy. In the area of finance, the recent years of global financial turbulence have emphasised both the interdependence of the world's financial system and the central place now occupied by emerging markets in that economy.

This chapter has argued that large emerging market countries have traditionally been excluded from the decision-making process in the international economy that is led by the G7. Despite repeated commitments to strengthening the dialogue between the industrialised and developing world, the G7 has repeatedly approached international economic governance through the concerns and interests of its members. Sometimes this has been at the expense of poorer states, but until the late 1990s, this has not been an issue that threatens the stability of the economic system. This is no longer the case as global financial interdependence and the rise of new economic powers in the early twenty-first century will force a revaluation of the role and practices of the G7 and force them to be more inclusive of the perspectives and interests of the most significant developing countries.

Simply attaching a small number of the largest emerging market economies to the G7 policy process would be a popular policy in several ways. First, the effectiveness of the G7 should (in theory) be increased, as the group's policy decisions will more fully account for their impact on developing countries. Second, the legitimacy of the institution will be increased, particularly in the eyes of citizens in emerging market states. Third, those developing countries that are invited to participate will likely respond favourably, particularly if they see benefits in terms of external validation such as those that followed from Mexico's accession to the Organisation for Economic Co-operation and Development (OECD) in the early 1990s.

A further point that should be made concerns the nature of international institutions and international leadership. In the 1970s, British scholar Fred Block noted that international monetary arrangements "both reflect and influence the distribution of political-economic power among the major capitalist states" (1977, p. 1). The same can be said for all important international organisations and institutions. As the structure (understood here as the distribution of power among states) of the international system shifts in the favour of the large emerging market economies (though not necessarily away from the G7 states), successful international institutions and organs of global governance will have to reflect that new structure. If they do not, they will fail to secure the necessary approval and acceptance of the world's most important powers.

Moreover, the work of Duncan Snidal (1985) argued that the relative size of economies is vital in ensuring leadership in the international economy. He used the concept of k-groups to show the costs of leadership would be outweighed by the benefits for a small number of large states. Snidal was looking at the possibility for tripartite leadership of the international economy, shared between the US, West Germany, and Japan. These three states, he argued, represented a sufficiently large proportion of the global economy that for them the benefits of international leadership outweighed the costs. However, the same logic can be used to explain collective action in the G7. In the aftermath of US hegemony, the G7 provided the basis for co-operative action in the world economy. By pulling together the world's seven largest economies, the group generated a form of collaborative leadership in which the benefits outweighed the costs. It is true, of course, that the US has been central to this process. However, the institution would not have achieved the level of success it has without being sensitive to the interests and concerns (both economic and political) of all member states, nor without sharing the costs that leadership and co-operation entails (Kirton 1999b). The share of G7 economies in the global economy will continue to decline in the twenty-first century and if the benefits of economic management are to continue to outweigh the costs, then the k-group must change.

In the next century, the distribution of economic power and thus the structure of the global economy will change, and the G7 must be prepared to be flexible if it is to meet the coming challenges of that age. Incorporating the largest emerging market economies into its decision-making process will ensure that it continues to achieve desirable results and the legitimacy it needs to do so. The steps taken at Cologne to make the IMF International Financial and Monetary Committee a more central part of international economic decision making is a good start. An effective dialogue, however, must be established if systemic risk is to be contained, and global economic growth sustained.

How should this be achieved and what precedents exist for such co-operation between industrialised and developing states? The G7/8 should not be expanded to include the most important emerging market countries and thus become the G15 or G17. Rather, each of the rounds of G7 negotiations and discussions should include the largest emerging market states at a formal level of consultation so as to incorporate at least partially the perspective of the world's most important developing countries.

An important example that has a special relevance for the G7 is clearly the IMF's Interim Committee. This decision-making body of the IMF was created in the 1970s to be a forum for incorporating the interests and perspectives of both developing and industrialised states over the issue of reform of the international monetary system in the aftermath of the US destruction of the Bretton Woods arrangements. However, the creation of the G7 later in that decade shifted the most important locus of monetary power away from the Interim Committee and centred it firmly with the former body. The renamed

International Financial and Monetary Committee has a chance now to represent the views and interests of the developing world.

Other examples include the recent expansion of two international institutions, the OECD and the BIS, during this decade to include LDC states. The OECD's motivation in doing so was as much political as economic. The US government press for Mexico's inclusion as a way to convince dissident Congress representatives that Mexico was truly on its way to developed country status. The BIS invited certain emerging market financial and monetary authorities into its organisation as a way of recognising the changing nature of world finance and as a precautionary measure designed to help prevent and manage future financial crises.

Conclusion: The Future for the G7 and Developing Countries

The challenge for the G7 in the late 1990s and early twenty-first century lies in the fact that the wealthy states have been joined as the "heavyweights" of the international economy by the large emerging markets. Countries such as China and Brazil have grown so rapidly since the late 1980s that they have emerged as rivals to the position of countries such as Canada and Italy in the rankings of the world's largest economies. Effective macroeconomic co-ordination among the largest economic powers will not maintain its effectiveness as a stabilising influence on the global economy if it excludes the most important emerging markets.

This is not, of course, to suggest that the G7 plus the largest emerging market economies should attempt to co-ordinate the macroeconomic policies of countries at such different levels of development. The economic, let alone the political, factors weighing against such co-ordination would render such attempts impossible and most likely counterproductive. However, a system of consultation between the G7 and major emerging market economies would have a beneficial impact on efforts to bring greater stability to the global economy. A process through which the impact of macroeconomic policies in the developed world on the economies of the major LDCs can be fully evaluated would be a great benefit to global stability.

It would be of particular importance in the area of capital flows. Reducing the risk-adjusted differential between interest rates, and co-ordinating capital liberalisation processes in particular would have a beneficial effect. The risk-adjusted interest rate differential between emerging markets and the world's major financial markets has been a significant factor in recent crises, and was of central importance in the Mexican peso crisis. The sequencing of capital liberalisation has also been identified as a contributory factor in financial crises. Co-ordinating the liberalisation of financial markets in developing countries with the work of supervisors in mature financial markets should add to safety and soundness.

The effective management of the international financial system is now impossible without the input of the large emerging markets. It is there that the largest threat to international financial stability exists. A combination of political instability, incompetence and corruption need to be overcome before economic and financial stability becomes a permanent feature of their systems. This will require significantly higher levels of assistance (both financial and technical) from the industrialised states.

Moreover, it is no longer prudent to ignore the interests of the largest emerging market economies. As the size of the largest emerging market economies continues to grow, so will the levels of mutual - but asymmetrical - interdependence between them and the industrialised world. Increasingly, it will be impossible to define G7 interests without reference to those of countries such as Brazil and China.

To steal from the G7's own rhetoric, the growing importance of the institution as a mechanism of global governance should be matched by a "growing international responsibility" to include other major players of the present and future global economic systems. In Cologne, the G7 once again made just such a commitment. This time, however, it is crucial that the rhetoric be followed up with real steps toward a more inclusive organ of global governance. To neglect to do so now threatens both the well being of the developing world, and the stability of the international economy. The years of a "them and us" approach are long gone.

Notes

1 This connection has been noted by Andres Serbin, Andres Stambouli, Jennifer McCoy, and William Smith (1993).

2 These new members were represented by the Banco Central do Brasil, the People's Bank of China, the Hong Kong Monetary Authority, the Reserve Bank of India, the Bank of Korea, the Banco de México, the Central Bank of Russian Federation, the Saudi Arabian Monetary Agency, and the Monetary Authority of Singapore respectively.

3 The G22 consisted of Finance Ministers and Central Bank Governors from Argentina, Australia, Brazil, Canada, China, France, Germany, Hong Kong SAR, India, Indonesia, Italy, Japan, Korea, Malaysia, Mexico, Poland, Russia, Singapore, South

Africa, Thailand, the United Kingdom, and the United States. The heads of the BIS, IMF, OECD, and the World Bank, as well as the Chair of the IMF Interim Committee, attended as observers.

4 One exception is, of course, the Toronto Centre, where the Government of Canada and the World Bank have set up an institute to train financial supervisors from emerging markets.

5 These countries are, Benin, Bolivia, Burkina Faso, Burundi, Cameroon, CAR, Chad, Congo (DR), Congo (Rep), Côte d'Ivoire, Ethiopia, Ghana, Guinea, Guinea-Bissau, Guyana, Honduras, Laos PDR, Madagascar, Malawi, Mauritania, Mozambique, Myanmar (Burma), Nicaragua, Niger, Rwanda, Sao Tome, Senegal, Sierra Leone, Tanzania, Togo, Uganda, and Zambia.

6 The "Big Ten" are China, Mexico, Argentina, Brazil, India, Indonesia, Poland, South Africa, South Korea, and Turkey.

References

Bank for International Settlements (1999), "Broadening Representation in the financial Stability Forum", Press Release 21, June, www.bis.org/press/index.htm.

Block, Fred (1977), *The Origins of International Economic Disorder*, University of California Press, Berkeley.

Cooper, Richard N. (1995), "Reform of Multilateral Financial Institutions", in Silvia Ostry and Gilbert R. Winham, eds., *The Halifax G-7 Summit: Issues on the Table*, Centre for Foreign Policy Studies, Halifax.

Hajnal, Peter (1989), *The Seven Power Summit: Documents from the Summits of Industrialized Countries*, 1975-1989, Kraus, Millwood, NY.

Kirton, John (1999a), "Explaining G8 Effectiveness", in M. Hodges, J. Kirton and J. Daniels, (eds.), *The G8's Role in the New Millennium*, Ashgate, Aldershot, pp. 45-68.

Kirton John J. (1999b), "Canada as a Principal Financial Power: G7 and IMF Diplomacy in the Crisis of 1997-99", *International Journal*, vol. 54, pp. 603-624.

Kirton, John J. and Joseph P. Daniels (1999), "The Role of the G8 in the New Millennium", in Michael R. Hodges, John J. Kirton and Joseph P. Daniels, eds., *The G8's Role in the New Millennium*, Ashgate Publishing Ltd., Aldershot, pp. 3-18.

Serbin, Andres, Andres Stambouli, Jennifer McCoy and William Smith (1993), eds., *Venezuela: La Democracia bajo presion,* Editorial Nueva Sociedad, Caracas.

Snidal, Duncan (1985), "The Limits of Hegemonic Stability Theory", *International Organization*, 39(4), pp. 579-614.

Strange, Susan (1998), *Mad Money: When Markets Outgrow Governments*, University of Michigan Press, Ann Arbor.

5 The Dynamics of G7 Leadership in Crisis Response and System Reconstruction

JOHN J. KIRTON[1]

Introduction

The global financial crisis of 1997 to 1999 represented the most severe threat to the international economic order in the half century since the end of World War Two. Beginning in Asia in the summer of 1997, the crisis had spread a year later to post-Communist Europe, and by the autumn of 1998 to the Americas, both South and North. Amidst its devastating destruction and cascading contagion, it threatened to obliterate the hard-won prosperity of the Asian "tiger" economies and with it the world's confidence in the model of an open, export-oriented, market-based approach to economic development that had finally gained virtually universal acceptance in the 1990s. With the devaluation and default of Russia in August 1998, the crisis further imperilled the most striking achievement of the international community in the 1990s - the peaceful transformation of post-Communist Russia into a democratic polity and market economy to which real measured growth had at long last returned. Most importantly, with the September 1998 collapse of the US hedge fund Long-Term Capital Management (LTCM) and the imminent freezing of the US credit system, the crisis came to the brink of crippling the world's most powerful economy, at the peak of its most sustained prosperous performance ever.

Containing this crisis and constructing a new international financial architecture in its wake were the central challenges the world faced as the twentieth century came to a close. Reconstructing the international financial system for a new era of intensifying globalisation had first been identified as a priority task, well before the 1997-99 crisis erupted, at the conclusion of the 1994 G7 Summit in Naples. Here US President Bill Clinton proposed, with the support of Canadian Prime Minister Jean Chrétien as 1995 host, and of his other G7 colleagues, that the next Summit focus on meeting such challenges of global governance in the twenty-first century. Within a year, the meltdown of the Mexican currency and economy offered an acute example of the costs that open globalised finance combined with poor national policy could bring. It also brought another instance of the United States leading, with the support of North American partner Canada and more distant G7 partners, to mount a successful response.

This portrait of a US uniquely willing and able to lead seemed to provide a successful formula for coping with any financial crises to come. The decade-long rise of the United States, in the wake of the Cold War's end and a globalising world, as the world's only "superpower", also offered a model for reconstruction, inspiring President Clinton, at the 1997 Denver Summit, to recommend to his G7 partners and the world that they adopt the American way (Bayne 1997). Prolonged economic stagnation in Japan and major structural problems in the German and other European economies widened the once steadily narrowing gap in gross domestic product (GDP) between the United States and its leading economic rivals (Kirton 1999a, Fry *et al.* 1998). And at the bottom of the G7's hierarchy of relative capability and status, Canada, afflicted by recurrent national unity challenges, sluggish productivity growth, and a declining currency, also watched with trepidation as the gap with the neighbouring US increased.

The Asian financial crisis, which erupted in Thailand in July 1997 only a few weeks after the Denver Summit, at first appeared ready to unleash the familiar dynamic of American hegemonic leadership. A uniquely powerful and prosperous United States stood able to act as the sole international lender of last resort. A weak and paralysed Japan formed part of the problem. A self-absorbed Europe seemed unconcerned with a distant, merely regional problem. And a relatively small, very open, commodity-intensive and hence vulnerable Canada braced itself for the assault on its markets and currency that the Asian crisis would bring (Kindleberger 1998, Rowlands 1999, IMF 1998).

This portrait proved to have some accuracy as the Asian-turned-global financial crisis unfolded over the following two years. The always formidable capacity of the US for structural leadership was increased as the league-leading growth in the US economy, relative rise in the value of the US dollar propelled by capital inflows into the safe haven of the US economy, and America's leading role as a globally stimulating "spender of last resort" proved to be powerful assets for it in the bargaining to come. Indeed, from 1997 to 1998, the US share of G7 GDP in current US dollars rose from 39.9 percent to 42.4 percent.[2] The similarly valued GDP of the major G7 members that could provide the US as strong second, relative to that of the US, all declined, with Japan falling from 62.1 percent to 51.6 percent of the US total, Germany from 30.2 percent to 26.8 percent, France from 19.8 percent to 18.5 percent, and Italy from 15.0 percent to 14.7 percent. During the following two years, US leadership and success were regularly evident, as the US, at times with the traditional strong seconds, prompted the IMF to lend to the three embattled Asian economies in 1997, to Russia in July 1998, and Brazil in the autumn of 1998. It further appeared in the Americans' leadership in establishing the G22 at the APEC leaders meeting in November 1997, in creating the IMF Supplementary Reserve Facility in December 1997, in the US role in ensuring private banks rescheduled Korean debt during the Christmas holidays in 1997. The US President and Federal Reserve also moved swiftly with a bold vision and interest rate cuts in the dangerous early autumn of 1998, and succeeded in securing a new IMF-based Contingent Credit Line (CCL) in the following months. The American impact was further felt in transforming the G22 into the G20 beginning with the IMF's endorsement of the concept in October 1999, on the new ideas and procedures for transparency, regulation, and crisis management.

Yet, as the crisis compounded, this familiar portrait of unique American leadership proved to be incomplete, inaccurate on several important occasions, and inadequate as an account of describing how and why the G7 successfully led the international community and its major international institutions into producing a substantially successful, if often slow, response. From the outset of the crisis, the United States and the multilateral international organisation it traditionally dominated, the IMF, were at important moments significantly constrained. These constraints on US leadership were due most immediately to the difficulty US policymakers and IMF leaders had in abandoning the deeply held, long-successful neo-liberal model and "Washington consensus" that a contagious globalisation was now rendering less effective. It was due more deeply to a constraint on structural leadership flowing from domestic politics - the reluctance of a suspicious US Congress to authorise the US share of the IMF quota increase that would give the institution the funds needed to combat the burgeoning crisis. Most importantly, as the crisis continued, ultimately to threaten the financial system of the American "Goldilocks" economy itself, the mania of the private markets newly liberated by globalisation revealed an equally vulnerable America, genuinely dependent upon the concerted action of the other major market democracies in the G7 (Kirton 2000).

An apparently ascendant America, now rendered vulnerable alongside the other G7 members by intensifying globalisation, required collective G7 action through mutual adjustment on zero-sum issues and convergent and common contributions in the larger positive-sum domain.[3] It enabled effective influence and leadership, at different times and on different issues, to come from any, even the least powerful, G7 partner. At a time when Japan was emasculated by an unprecedented decade-long stagnation and acute recession, when a slow-growing Germany was absorbed by the prospect and reality of a historic electoral realignment, and when its continental European neighbours were preoccupied with the launch of the new Euro single currency, it was often left to Britain and Canada to play consequential catalytic and influential roles. Their ability and willingness to do so were underscored by their position, however modest, as the only two G7 members to have their relative capability, conceived as GDP in current US dollars, increase from 1997 to 1998, with Britain's rising from 15.9 percent to 16.0 percent and Canada's from 7.6 percent to 7.7 percent. In the case of Tony Blair's Britain, the legacy of its longstanding role as a global hegemon past, the continuing relevance of London as one of the world's leading financial centres, and Britain's transatlantic orientation, offered natural advantages for a Britain able and willing to lead and to stay the course to a successful conclusion (Fraser 1998). In the case of Canada, however, the very lack of league-leading history and issue-specific financial capabilities highlighted how the institutional character of the G7, as a concert of effective equals, allowed even the least capable country to play a consequential leadership role.

Specifically, Canada, along with Britain, the United States, and other G7 members, acted successfully as an effectively equal "principal power" within the institutional confines of the G7.[4] Canada displayed intellectual leadership by offering, along with most other G7 members, comprehensive programmes and initiatives for coping with the crisis and defining a new international financial architecture (Eichengreen 1999). Canada's leadership, first apparent at the Halifax Summit in 1995, continued with its peer supervision plan and "roadmap" concept in the spring of 1998. It culminated with a Six Point Plan of 29 September 1998 and debt-relief plan of March 1999.

Moreover, Canada, along with its partners, mounted policy leadership by identifying in advance, and consistently pursuing to ultimate success, distinctive positions based on specific Canadian interests, values, and experience. In place of the inflation-fighting, fiscal-consolidating, neo-liberal stance that dominated G7 policy in the previous decades, Canada individually or jointly pioneered the push for properly sequenced and controlled capital liberalisation, financial system surveillance and peer supervision; private sector burden sharing, social responsibility in adjustment and debt-relief packages, fiscal stimulus, and enhanced Official Development Assistance (ODA).

Finally, Canada displayed structural leadership by contributing more than its proportionate share, as a member of a G7 concert serving as a collective lender of last resort, to contain the crisis of confidence and contribute to debt relief for the poorest. It contributed multilaterally as a leading member of the IMF, the International Bank for Reconstruction and Development (IBRD), the Asian Development Bank (ADB), the Inter-American Development Bank (IDB), General Arrangements to Borrow (GAB), and New Arrangements to Borrow (NAB). It also acted plurilaterally by providing national funds to South Korea in December 1997, to Thailand in April 1997, and to Brazil in November 1998. Moreover, it joined in cutting interest rates in the autumn of 1998, when the resources of a financially and congressionally paralysed United States were insufficient to stave off the burgeoning global crisis. And Canada stood ready to provide new ODA to ensure a successful debt-relief initiative at the 1999 Cologne G7 Summit.

Throughout the two years of the crisis, Canada pursued its preferences by combining, not only with traditional, geographically proximate, far more powerful partners, but also with a shifting array of G7 allies on different issues and at different times. Moreover, it often opposed the initiatives of both the United States and Britain. Ultimately, through persistence, skilled concert diplomacy within the G7 club, and changes in international context as the crisis compounded and its effects became clear, Canada had a discernible impact in shaping outcomes in the direction of a more humane, socially responsible form of globalisation.

While Canada's contribution most clearly shows the G7 to be a forum for collective management, in which even the weakest member can influentially lead, Britain's diplomacy during the crisis further sustains this case. Britain, with its global financial centre in London and prerogatives as host of the 1998 Summit, took the lead in several areas, notably in capital account liberalisation and in the push for transparency and comprehensive international codes of conduct for national financial systems. It pioneered the quest for debt relief for the poorest, which, when joined by the new German government of Chancellor Gerhart Schroeder, proved to be a major achievement of the 1999 Cologne Summit. While Britain often worked in tandem with the US, it was often Britain that moved most rapidly, and often joined with other G7 members against the preferences of the US, as on installing principles of good practice in social policy in the World Bank. And its impact was felt at the end on these issues, and on the architecture of the new Financial Stability Forum (FSF).

The ability and willingness of the United States to lead remained important in shaping the G7's agenda, action, agreement, and its ultimately successful impact on the global financial crisis and resulting new international financial architecture. Overall structural and specialised capability still counted, and here the Americans enjoyed an impressive and increasingly lead. Yet, in the rapidly globalising world of the 1990s, capability was joined by an ever more acute vulnerability that afflicted all G7 members more equally, as a factor that was felt and that forced a much more genuine form of collective leadership from the G7. The impact of intervulnerability[5] was reinforced by a crisis that was new in its content, contagion, and severity, and by the distinctive norms and institutional procedures of the G7 in response. The new intervulnerability and crisis bred by globalisation, and the new concert-based approach to global governance embedded in the G7, had come to reinforce and in important respects replace America's unique hegemonic leadership in guiding the international financial system as the twentieth century came to a close.

Phase 1: The Asian Crisis of 1997-98

The substantial role that the G7, and Canada and Britain within it, played in countering the 1997 Asian crisis began soon after the 1997 Denver Summit.[6] At Denver itself, amidst its aura of American triumphalism, the G7 leaders followed President Clinton's preoccupation with welcoming Russia as a virtually equal member to the newly christened "Denver Summit of the Eight", as a tradeoff for Russian acquiescence in the US-led project to expand NATO to include three Eastern European countries. With only a very short, semi-secret session among themselves "at seven" to discuss serious economic matters, they devoted no time to considering the early signs of the crisis brewing in Asia (Hajnal 1999). Even their G7 Finance Ministers, who debated financial regulation at some length, did so with no sense of urgency, on the assumption that the measures identified at Halifax and those invented in response to the Mexican crisis would suffice.

When Thailand precipitated the crisis by devaluing its currency in early July, there was little sense of a common or systemic threat. European G7 members saw the issue as a regional Asian responsibility. The United States was equally prepared to leave the problem to the Asians. By August 1997, when a US$17 billion package for Thailand had been assembled, Japan, which was regionally affected, was the only G7 member to contribute national funds.

By September 1997, however, when G7 Finance Ministers met in Hong Kong at the time of the semi-annual IMF meeting, they moved decisively to authorise an ambitious array of innovative measures to strengthen the international financial system in the face of such crises. They agreed to a 45 percent increase in IMF core resources, to amend the Articles of Agreement within the year to make the IMF formally responsible for sweeping capital account liberalisation, to strengthen IMF involvement in financial sector reform, to improve national governance by reducing corruption, and to expand the allocation of Special Drawing Rights (SDRs).

In the diplomacy behind the Hong Kong reform package, Canada and Britain acted as equal members of the G7 concert. Here different members, including the least capable, led on specific issues, and all ultimately adjusted to create a new and effective consensus. On the IMF quota share increase, all G7 members combined to persuade a resistant and internally divided US, which feared congressional opposition, to accept at the last minute the 45 percent addition. On capital account liberalisation, it was the British who led, with an initiative adopted by IMF Managing Director Michel Camdessus and supported by the US.[7] Yet, this initiative met with strong opposition from Canada, which succeeded in blunting initial enthusiasm for a blanket grant of authority to the IMF for unrestricted liberalisation. Canada, working with the United States and Japan, made progress on its push, begun at the 1996 Lyon Summit, for banking and financial sector reform. The United States, with Canada in strong support, secured an IMF agreement to discuss governance issues. Canada encouraged the IMF to double the SDR equity allocation and to devote the proceeds to the new members of the IMF. With the US in the lead and Canada in support, the G7 also made it clear that the IMF, rather than any regional support fund proposed by Japan, would remain at the centre of the Asian rescue effort.

Britain's approach at Hong Kong, most evident in its leadership on capital account liberalisation, flowed naturally from its current position as one of the world's leading financial centres, and its past success over two centuries in periodically creating and flourishing within an open global financial system. Canada's approach, particularly its strong opposition to capital account liberalisation, also derived directly from its distinct interests, values, and experience. Canada's position had been recently developed in its programme for international financial institution (IFI) reform as host of the 1995 G7

Halifax Summit, and its experience with the financial crisis that erupted in fellow NAFTA member Mexico on 20 December 1994 (Kirton 1995a, Martin 1997). Both cases reinforced in the minds of Prime Minister Jean Chrétien and Minister of Finance Paul Martin, a strong scepticism toward unrestricted capital flows, as allegedly rational markets proved prone to panic in ways that could have enormously destructive consequences for individual citizens and the public good. Martin's scepticism was further manifested in 1996, when he led Canada to allow Chile to preserve its system of limiting the outflow of short-term capital during the first year after its investment in the provisions of the bilateral Canada-Chile free trade agreement forged that year. Spurred by the collapse of Barings Bank in 1995, Martin had also developed a proposal for Halifax for improved supervision of national financial institutions. The concept was extended after Martin participated in a meeting of western hemisphere Finance Ministers in Santiago, Chile, in December 1996, where the core of a proposal for peer supervision through a new international supervisory authority was born.

Behind the specific lessons of Halifax and Mexico lay domestic imperatives and international experiences. The first was a continuing concern with national unity and an acute awareness that separatist forces in Quebec could use a fall in the Canadian dollar or denationalisation of the federal government's capacity for financial management to further their cause. The second was the domestic value that Canada placed on equalisation, through automatic federal fiscal transfers, to guarantee all Canadians a similar, high-standard social safety net. And the third was a long history of international successes, ranging from Canada's pioneering role with flexible exchange rates as an adjustment device, through its position as a *de facto* permanent member of the IMF executive board and the G7 Finance Ministers forum, to its attachment to the world's poorest states through the Commonwealth and la Francophonie.

These factors continued to exert an impact as G7 decisiveness and Canada's role expanded in response to the spreading crisis during the autumn of 1997. When a support package for a beleaguered Indonesia was assembled, the United States joined Japan as a contributor to a "second line of defence" of national funds, to be deployed if those of the IMF and other IFIs proved insufficient. In November, Canada and its G7 colleagues formalised the second line of defence and moved to ensure that all had the legislative authority to contribute to it.

In early December, the G7 agreed to a support package for South Korea of US$35 billion from the IFIs, to be reinforced, if necessary, by a second line of defence. To this second line, Japan pledged US$10 billion, the United States US$5 billion, each of the European G7 members US$1.25 billion, and Canada US$1 billion. Shortly after, when the South Korean won plummeted, G7 members agreed to activate the second line in return for an agreement from their private banks, pushed by the US and others, to roll over and reschedule their South Korean loans. This private sector burden sharing agreement was particularly valuable in light of the difficulty the United States government was having in securing congressional authorisation for its share of the IMF quota increase. The United States Secretary of the Treasury, Robert Rubin, who had hoped that the mere existence of a large package with a second line would reassure markets, now agreed with his other G7 partners that American dollars would be forthcoming. The 24 December announcement that national funds would indeed flow proved sufficient to stem the market's assault on the won. No national funds actually had to be expended in exchange markets. G7 governments acting together had beaten panicking markets in this new globalised game of financial deterrence.

These actions lessened the pressure on the surrounding Asian economies, although Suharto's Indonesia, which was resisting IMF prescriptions, suffered further attacks. As its situation deteriorated, the United States, reinforced by Germany and supported by the other G7 members, intervened. On 15 January 1998, the IMF and Indonesia negotiated a letter of intent under which Indonesia accepted revised economic targets and more far-reaching structural reform.

The next threat to Asian economies arose in April 1998, when it became evident that both South Korea and Indonesia would be unable to meet their pledges, made in the summer of 1997, to the support package for a still struggling Thailand. Here, Canada (1998c) displayed structural leadership, by assuming the Indonesian share of $500 million. Canada did so on the grounds that Thailand was honouring its programme with the IMF and thus deserved the funds promised in return. Canada was the only country from outside Asia to make a contribution to Indonesia. The American administration, concerned about congressional criticism of a "bail-out" and any use of the Exchange Stabilization Fund (as in the Mexican rescue package of 1994-95), refused to contribute. In giving when the United States could not, Canada became part of a "first line" programme. Its disbursements, which started to flow in June, ultimately totalled US$300 million.

The Asian phase of the crisis was thus contained through concerted, if just in time, G7 action. In a clear display of their power over markets, G7 governments often prevailed, and did so at times without actually expending national funds. Instead, they induced the IFIs, banks, and other private sector actors to provide the required liquidity. Moreover, in mobilising these additional moneys, a congressionally constrained US was led to follow the policy leadership of its G7 colleagues, and often rely on the structural leadership which these partners, from second-ranked Asian Japan through sixth-ranked European Britain to seventh-ranked North American Canada, made available in the form of new national funds. In such a situation, intellectual leadership also flowed freely and effectively from the G7's lesser members. Britain and Canada, on opposite sides, drove the debate over capital account liberalisation, and Canada, with relatively few Asian investors of its own to protect, pushed with some success for significant private sector participation.

With the acute phase of the Asian crisis over, G7 leaders and Finance Ministers turned their attention from crisis response to system reform for the Birmingham Summit in May 1998. At Birmingham, British Prime Minister Tony Blair, taking full advantage of the institutional advantages of serving as Summit host, introduced some historic reforms to ensure that the G7 would avoid the distractions of Denver and focus on the central challenge of finance (Kirton and Kokotsis 1997-98, Hodges *et al.* 1999, Bayne 2000).[8] He chose a highly concentrated rather than comprehensive agenda, with finance and the related issues of employment and crime as the central items. He forced the leaders themselves to focus on them, by having their ministers prepare a thorough set of recommendations immediately prior to the Summit and leaving the leaders alone without attending ministers, for the first time in Summit history, to shape them as they saw fit. To enhance this process and diminish the preoccupation with media messaging, he introduced an informal leaders retreat. Finally, he gave G7 leaders a full half-day immediately prior to the opening of the G8 to focus on finance and economic issues, rather than forcing them, as at Denver, to find a few minutes between G8 sessions to deal with the subjects that had historically been at the G7's core.

Here they stressed the need for improved transparency, early warning, and private sector burden sharing. Canada secured an endorsement for the concept behind its major initiative of establishing a mechanism for peer review of national banking and financial system supervisory authorities. Its proposal, first unveiled at the April 1998 Washington meetings of the IMF's Interim and Development Committees, included a call for a new international supervisory authority, with a small new secretariat for assembling multinational teams of supervisory experts. Because France preferred to invest the supervisory function in the IMF under its Article 4 consultations, and

Britain wanted to use a joint IMF-World Bank mechanism, the decision on how to implement the concept was left to the G7, IMF, and World Bank meetings in the autumn.

Phase 2: The Global Crisis of 1998

The second phase of the crisis came in the summer and autumn of 1998, when the financial crisis went global. Following further disquieting events in Asia, on August 17 Russia unilaterally devalued its currency and rescheduled its debt only three weeks after receiving yet another large IMF support package that mobilised the funds of the GAB for the first time in two decades. Although no one within the G7 had been enthusiastic about the prospects for the July package, the speed of Russia's collapse and the shock of a default and devaluation brought home the message that no country, even a member of the G8, was too big to fail. It was soon apparent that the IMF, which still lacked the agreed-upon quota share increase as a result of American political stalemate, might not have sufficient funds to cope with crises on this scale.

The contagion, driven by plummeting commodity prices, soon spread to the emerging economies of the Americas, as interest rate spreads ballooned in all emerging markets. Brazil, which had a large fiscal deficit financed at floating interest rates, was particularly hard hit. As its interest rates soared, capital started to flee the country at the rate of up to US$1 billion a day. In early September, Colombia devalued its currency. Moody's downgraded Brazil's foreign currency bonds. Stock markets in the United States, Canada, Mexico, and the rest of the Americas continued the sharp fall begun in mid-summer.

By late August, the most powerful and prosperous US itself came under attack. As even healthy companies in the United States found it difficult to borrow money at reasonable rates, fears of an international credit crunch emerged. The crisis peaked in mid-September with the *de facto* collapse of LTCM, an American hedge fund, and its rescue by major American financial institutions under the guidance of the Federal Reserve. While the rescue was reassuring, the fear that similar hedge funds might be on the verge of collapse compounded the move toward a freezing of credit markets in the United States. Along with continuing congressional refusal to authorise the United States share of the IMF quota increase, this meant that the world was deprived of its traditional reliable lender of last resort. Indeed, the hitherto vibrant American economy was itself on the verge in the minds of many of being engulfed by the cascading crisis.

Throughout, Canada, along with the United States, Britain, France, and others, provided intellectual and policy leadership in the IMF and other fora, by producing and pressing for detailed proposals on many items on an expanding crisis response and system reform agenda. The US offered intellectual leadership on 17 September, when President Clinton publicly outlined a package that emphasised the desirability of interest rate cuts, a new IMF precautionary lending facility, and support for Brazil. Canada's Paul Martin, dissatisfied with the central thrust of the American plan and judging that markets needed a stronger signal that governments were in control, prepared his own package. This he unveiled at the Commonwealth Finance Ministers Meeting in Ottawa on 29 September, just before the 3 October meeting in Washington of G7 Finance Ministers (Canada 1998a).

The Canadian plan began, in congruence with the Americans, with a call for stimulus - a carefully worded admonition to focus on "the risks of an extended global slowdown" through, implicitly, an immediate lowering of interest rates by G7 central banks. But the remainder of its Six Point Plan marked a sharp departure in intellectual conception and policy emphasis from the core of the plan President Clinton had proposed. The second element in the Canadian plan was social targeting - a call to tailor IMF programmes to local conditions, particularly through a less restrictive fiscal policy in some Asian countries than IMF orthodoxy prescribed. The third element, reinforced by the recent experience in Asia and Russia, was to extend international supervision to domestic banking and financial systems. The fourth element was capital control - a plea to adjust the move to capital account liberalisation by allowing weak economies to impose transitional, nondistortionary controls on capital, particularly short-term capital inflows. The fifth was the introduction of the Emergency Standstill Clause, negotiated in advance and covering all private sector instruments, including bank deposits. The clause could be invoked by countries suffering a crisis of confidence to preserve capital until payments could be restructured in an orderly fashion. In Canada's view, the failure of markets to differentiate between good and bad risk in the wake of the Russian devaluation underscored the need for an international bank holiday. Finally, the development and debt needs of the world's poorest countries were addressed.

The most urgent Canadian concern - a shift in focus from the threat of inflation to that of recession - was a form of policy leadership with immediate origins and an immediate impact. By September, the Canadian economy had suffered four months of no growth. On 27 August, after the Canadian dollar plummeted to an historic low of just over 63 cents to the United States dollar in the aftermath of the Russian devaluation, the Bank of Canada raised interest rates by a full percentage point. The day of Martin's speech, the United States Federal Reserve and the Bank of Canada immediately lowered interest rates by 25 basis points. In mid-October, the Federal Reserve instituted a further unexpected cut, which Canada again matched. By the end of the month, Britain, Italy, and Japan had followed. By November, the continental European countries did the same. From 1 October to the end of 1998, a total of 34 central banks lowered interest rates on 66 occasions.

Canada's early call was by no means the major cause of the emergency action or of the historic shift in the G7's decade-long macroeconomic focus on fighting inflation. Yet the United States-Canadian-British initiative provided the policy leadership which met the short-term needs of the Canadian economy and proved critical in combating a potentially paralysing liquidity crisis in the United States that would have brought global collapse.

The second Canadian priority was to tailor IMF programmes to the particular situation in each country, with an emphasis on fiscal stimulus within them when necessary. In IMF and G7 discussions over the programme for Indonesia during the autumn, Canada repeatedly pressed for greater fiscal flexibility in the IMF adjustment programme. This, the Canadians argued, would allow the Indonesian authorities to increase their spending, especially on targeted social programmes, development programmes, and public infrastructure. Canada also favoured a relaxation in the pace of privatisation of Indonesian state enterprises.

Canada's other priorities made progress at the 3 October G7 Finance Ministers meeting in Washington. Held amidst what President Clinton called the worst financial crisis in 50 years, the meeting produced a communiqué which reflected several major Canadian concerns (G7 1998b). Notably, it signalled an easing of monetary policy to provide needed liquidity. At the end of the meeting, Canada, the United States, and Britain promised to maintain conditions for sustainable growth.

The communiqué also supported IMF programmes and a proactive role for the G7, through the IMF, G22, and elsewhere on the issues of architectural reform and a consensus on the core principles to guide it. Canada, along with Britain and the United States, pushed successfully for an emphasis on transparency. Although the American and British approach to banking and financial system supervision largely prevailed, Canada made some progress in principle. An emphasis on private sector involvement as a way of avoiding moral hazard reflected one of Martin's concerns, although here a German conviction dominated and no particular mechanism for private sector "bail-in" was endorsed. Canada's greatest gain was in the crisis-bred diminished enthusiasm for rapid capital account liberalisation, as the process for amending the IMF articles of agreement, initially slated for completion at the meeting, was extended another one to two years.

Despite this momentum, the G7 failed to provide the badly needed immediate, co-ordinated macroeconomic management required to stem a still burgeoning crisis in Brazil and in credit and equity markets in the United States and the rest of the developed world. In early October, the IMF (1998) cut its earlier estimate of world growth to a modest 2 percent. Some relief came when Congress passed the American IMF quota share increase on 14 October, and Japan's Diet passed its banking bill shortly thereafter. But the situation remained unstable.

For Canada, continued deterioration during October posed a particular threat. Its primary fear was that the assault on Brazil would spread to Argentina and other Latin American countries, especially Mexico. With its credit market still gripped by uncertainty, it was unclear whether the United States would have the will or the ability to contain any threat in Mexico as swiftly and surely as it had in the wake of the 20 December 1994 crisis. Mindful of how the Mexican crisis had threatened the Canadian dollar - of how that dollar, perceived as a commodity currency, was already at an all-time low - and with a looming provincial election in Quebec to reawaken fears of disunity within Canada, the Canadian government concluded that further action was necessary.

With markets clearly not absorbing the G7 message from the 3 October meeting, the British led a campaign to send a stronger collective signal, and to do so at the leaders' level. British Prime Minister Tony Blair, still in the chair of the G7 for 1998, called for a special G7 Summit. He received enthusiastic support only from the French, who also demanded that such a special Summit involve a broader group of countries. The British Chancellor of the Exchequer, Gordon Brown, returned from the Washington G7 meeting of 3 October convinced of the need for a new G7 statement and one which reflected a deeper degree of consensus than had previously been revealed. Canada, along with the United States and Japan, was initially sceptical about the value of either a statement or a special summit, in the absence of anything new to announce. But when Congress finally approved the IMF quota share increase contribution, Japan passed its banking legislation, Brazil approached the IMF for assistance, and the G7 came to an agreement through conference calls on Clinton's proposed precautionary facility (through CCLs that the

United States conceived and secured), Canada concluded that a statement that cast these new developments in a positive light would be useful.

Britain, as G7 host, took the initiative in catalysing the process and drafting the statements, along two tracks. The first was among G7 sherpas, with Blair dealing through Britain's sherpa John Holmes, who was in touch with his counterparts, who were in turn in touch with their leaders. Leaders were also in direct contact with one another by fax and phone. This process included calls from Clinton to Canada's Chrétien, Britain's Blair, and, on several occasions, Germany's new Chancellor and incoming summit host Gerhart Schroeder, whose government was strongly opposed to Clinton's call for a new IMF precautionary facility. The second track was among the G7 Finance Ministers, with Brown working through the finance deputies. At the last minute, the two statements composed on separate tracks were rendered compatible. Despite the rushed nature of the process, with conference calls until the last minute, the substance of the final statement was genuinely a G7 product, and one which reflected most of Canada's and Britain's core concerns.

On 30 October, the G7 released two statements, the first from the leaders and the second from Finance Ministers and central bankers (G7 1998b). In them, Canada succeeded in its goal of securing collective, proactive G7 leadership in a way that reassured global financial markets, redirected policy from a preoccupation with combating inflation, and directed a far-reaching reform of the IFIs in keeping with its Halifax initiative.

On the issue of capital controls, Martin's call for restrictions on short-term capital outflows, in the form of the Emergency Standstill Clause, received some support from other G7 countries. The United States, however, whose own private sector investors would be most harmed by such a proposal, remained adamantly opposed. The 30 October statement included carefully crafted language that amounted to a tacit acceptance of the concept of capital controls. The leaders' statement spoke of the need to minimize the "risk of disruption" for "an orderly and progressive approach to capital account liberalisation" and for "measures to ensure the orderly and co-operative resolution of future crises, in particular mechanisms to involve the private sector". G7 officials were directed to work out the mechanisms to give this principle effect over the next year. The G7 finance deputies and central bank governors took up the issue at a meeting in Paris in mid-November.

A second area of substantial Canadian gain followed from Martin's initiative for stronger banking and financial sector supervision. The Finance Ministers' statement directly endorsed enhanced supervision through "a process of peer review". The IMF, France's preferred forum, also agreed to devote more attention to the quality and capability of such supervision in its annual Article 4 review of members' economies (Canada 1998b).

Canada's influence could also be seen in the emphasis in the leaders' statement on dealing directly with the social dimensions of the financial crisis. The statement began by highlighting the "impact on the poor and the most vulnerable". It endorsed an emergency facility in the World Bank to offset the social damage caused by financial failure and called for principles of good practice in social policy to protect the most vulnerable social groups.

The final element of the G7 response was its support package for Brazil, still being negotiated as the 30 October statement was released. When it was unveiled on 13 November, it contained several novel components. Brazil had voluntarily adopted a restraint package prior to the extension of G7 assistance. In addition to IMF and other IFI funds, it would use bilateral national contributions from all G7 members and other countries as part of a first, rather than a second, line of defence. Of the US$41.5 billion total, the IMF provided US$18 billion, the IBRD US$4.5 billion, the IDB US$4.5 billion, and bilateral contributions, funnelled through the BIS, US$14.5 billion. For the first time, newly available NAB funds were used to support a non-NAB member. These funds were authorised by phone calls to the G7 Finance Ministers, who provided over 90 percent of the total. At US$41.1 billion, the package was well in excess of the US$25 billion initially envisaged or the market-rumoured US$30 billion. A full US$37 billion of the total would be made available during the first year. The size and early availability of the package, and the willingness of all G7 members to put their national funds on the front line to make it this large, was sufficient to demonstrate resolve and to deter markets from continued attack.

Canada's contribution to the bilateral first line of the Brazilian package, determined at a late stage in the process, was a relatively modest US$500 million, or a deliberate one-tenth the United States contribution. The contribution was driven by several considerations. The United States had not contributed to the Thai package in the spring, when Canada bore the burden from beyond the region. As a major contributor to the IMF, IBRD, and IBD, Canada was already contributing in excess of US$500 million to the Brazilian package. Canada was unenthusiastic about Brazil's approach to the IMF and the creation of a new precautionary facility for which it was the first test case. Nor was Canada eager to use NAB funds, which became available on 17 November, rather than the United States quota share, which became available only later, for the IMF's multilateral portion of the Brazilian package.

Canada's concern about the prudent use of IMF resources was again evident in a subsequent G7 debate about the speed of repaying the NAB. Because the United States wanted to show a still sceptical congress that the IMF could function as a profit centre, it preferred to rely as long as possible on the NAB, so as to reap its very high interest rates and delay a use of the IMF's regular quota increase. The French agreed. Canada, along with Britain, Germany, and Japan, wanted to pay off the IMF and revert to the lower cost regular IMF quota as soon as possible. Canada's position was driven in part by a desire to free the resources otherwise constrained by their commitment through the NAB to deter and defend against any currency crises to come.

The United States delay in making its IMF quota share increase available in time for Brazil to use it stemmed in part from a provision of the congressional authorising legislation. It allowed funds to flow only 15 days after the Secretary of the Treasury and the Chair of the Federal Reserve received assurances from the "major shareholders" of the IMF that they were pressing for several conditions as part of IMF programmes. So that Rubin could act, the G7 agreed that their executive directors at the IMF would collectively ask the Managing Director to meet such conditions. This unprecedented collective G7 action, which publicly directed the Managing Director of the IMF to take action, proved effective and indicated that the G7 collectively, and not the United States unilaterally, was the source of effective leadership for the IMF.

Phase 3: System Reconstruction, 1999

The third stage of Canada and Britain's international financial leadership came during the first half of 1999 as the G7 moved through the final instalment of the crisis, in Brazil in early 1999, to the construction of a strengthened system at the Cologne G7 Summit in June. Here, Canada was able to work in close partnership with the new G7 host, German Chancellor Schroeder, and his "red-green" coalition government, to advance its longstanding positions.

Canada's response to the onset of crisis in Brazil was largely channelled through the IMF, using the instruments put in place in the autumn. Canada drew several lessons from the crisis and the particular response of the international community to it. The first was a reinforcement of its belief, based on a close analysis of the Asian crisis, that there were no innocent victims - that Brazil's heavy external debt held in very short-term instruments and the threat of nonpayment by one of its state governments had rendered the country vulnerable and precipitated the crisis. It could not be blamed on any irrational "contagion" at work in a newly globalised economy. The second view, based on the failure of private sector investors to participate in the response to the second Brazilian crisis, was that much stronger measures for private sector burden sharing were required. The third judgement, shared by Schroeder, was that Clinton's preferred precautionary mechanism, the CCL, was a relatively ineffective instrument for dealing with the crises likely to emerge.

Canada took these lessons into the G7 Finance Ministers Meeting in Berlin on 20 February, in Washington on 26 April, and in Frankfurt on 11-12 June, and to the G7 Summit in Cologne on 18-20 June. Canada made some advances in the early meetings. Most notably, the new Financial Stability Forum (FSF), a German initiative, contained a mechanism for peer supervision of national financial systems that gave life to an early Canadian proposal - if in a different institutionalised forum. Moreover, the architecture of the FSF reflected Britain's own proposals for financial regulation supervision even more than the Canadian ones, and the British national who headed the BIS, Andrew Crockett, was appointed the FSF's first chair. Yet, as Cologne approached, significant differences remained on the core architectural issues: private sector involvement, moral hazard and the Emergency Standstill Mechanism, crisis prevention and resolution, international institutions and the role of the IMF, membership in the FSF, debt relief for the poorest, and the overall approach to globalisation.

On private sector involvement, Canada took its lead from the Prime Minister, who retained a strong aversion, evident from Halifax onward, to privatising profits and nationalising losses. Canada thus remained wedded to its Standstill proposal, the option that would force the greatest degree of private sector involvement. The proposal initially evoked strong opposition from the government and leading intellectuals in the United States, whose lenders would be the primary private sector actors called upon to contribute.[9] Yet in the lead-up to Cologne, Canada continued to set private sector participation and the related issues of transparency and disclosure as its three priorities among the six architectural items on which the G7 would focus.

On Standstill, the leading element of Canada's thrust for private sector participation, Canada received support from Britain. However, the continental Europeans remained unconvinced and the Japanese provided no reaction. Rubin continued to see problems with Standstill but did begin to refer to the concept in speeches. On the broader principle of private sector participation,

Canada took real pleasure from an agreement at Cologne to send a clear message to private sector lenders in emerging markets that they could no longer assume that the G7 or IMF would bail them out of all difficulties.

The views of the Prime Minister were also evident in crisis prevention and resolution. Here again, Canada had a strong aversion to relying on public funds to compensate private sector actors for imprudent lending. It thus worked, along with others and with considerable success, to narrow dramatically the conditions under which the US-inspired CCL - with its antithetical approach of lending public money first - could be activated.

On international institutional reform, Canada faced strong demands from France and from the IMF's Camdessus, who wanted primacy for the IMF. Canada had reservations about transforming the Interim Committee of the IMF into what it saw as a *de facto directoire*. On the FSF, the earlier agreement of the G7 Finance Ministers had left to the leaders the issues of how broad participation in the Forum should be and whether more emerging economies should be included. Canada, in notable contrast to the United States, was in the vanguard of those pressing for broader participation.

It was on debt relief for the poorest that Canada's intellectual, policy, and structural leadership was most fully expressed. Since the Canadian-hosted Toronto Summit of 1998, this had been a leading Canadian and British initiative at the G7 (Bayne 1998, 2000). During the spring, the new German government, despite the reluctance of its Central Bank, reversed Germany's longstanding position and agreed that a "Cologne debt initiative", including the sale of IMF gold, would be the centrepiece "deliverable" of its Cologne G7 summit. As spring proceeded, a G7 agreement on the sale of five million ounces of IMF gold led rapidly to a demand for the sale of ten million ounces, to raise the substantial funds required to make the initiative credible. As Cologne drew near, Canada, Britain, and, now, the German Chancellor and Foreign Ministry encountered strong resistance from France and Japan on a second component of the initiative. Both countries had continued their programmes of large ODA loans rather than grants and would thus be faced with large costs to their national budgets in a proposed G7 programme to write off loans.

Here Prime Minister Chrétien also had strong views. Canada had led the G7 long ago in giving ODA in the form of grants rather than loans. It also led the way in writing off its loans from an earlier era. Moreover, Chrétien, having moved Canada from a $42 billion annual fiscal deficit into sustained surplus, was willing to provide a substantial new amount of ODA as part of a balanced package of debt relief from Cologne, as his 1993 campaign Red

Book had promised. The new contribution, in addition to the full credit that Canada's Finance Ministry demanded for its past action, was contingent upon Japan and France writing off their substantial loans so that a credible Cologne package could be achieved.

A final area of emphasis, and another propelled in part by Chrétien's views, was the social side of globalisation. For the Cologne debt initiative, Canada wanted debt relief to lead to sustainable growth rather than recidivist tendencies. Thus, new financial resources would be tightly targeted to social, educational, and human capital spending. Relief would be denied to countries that persisted in violating norms of good governance and that incurred excessive military and other unproductive expenditures. Canada had an interest in not surrendering the levers for promoting these values. In particular, it did not want to use funds for the Highly Indebted Poor Countries (HIPC) to reward Myanmar, a country that continued to violate basic human rights. Canada pressed to include Bangladesh, a very poor Commonwealth partner.

By the end of the Cologne Summit, Canada had made major advances on all of its priorities. On private sector burden sharing, the communiqué bluntly declared that the G7 (1999) would shape expectations "so that private sector creditors know they will bear the consequences of the risks they take". On crisis prevention and resolution, it limited the use of the CCL to countries pursuing (by then strictly defined) "sound and sustainable policies" and emphasised a host of private sector solutions that were at times intrusive. On international institutional reform, a compromise gave the IMF's Interim Committee permanent standing as a new "International Financial and Monetary Committee", but also affirmed other measures, including "an informal mechanism for dialogue among systemically important countries". A clear Canadian victory came on the Financial Stability Forum when the leaders at Cologne agreed to broaden its membership to include emerging economies.

Canada, along with Britain, also enjoyed considerable success on the Cologne debt initiative. G7 leaders affirmed that relief would be "faster, deeper, and broader" through measures to reduce the stock of debt by more than half. The target was for rulings on three-quarters of eligible countries by 2000. To finance the package, the IMF would sell up to 10 million ounces of its gold, creditor countries would forgive most commercial and all ODA debt, and additional contributions would be made on the basis of a burden-sharing formula that took into account Canada's earlier leadership and contributions. Relief was to be directed towards the Canadian priorities of poverty reduction, health education and other social needs, sustainable development, and good governance.

Perhaps Canada's most striking success was in securing an emphasis on a social safety net to offset the negative effects of globalisation. The G7 communiqué heralded the principle that "social policies are the cornerstone of a viable international architecture" and instructed the IMF and other IFIs to invest in education, health, and social needs as an essential part of their policies. The subsequent communiqué of the G8 (now that Russia was included) spoke even more broadly and ambitiously of the need to "strengthen the institutional and social infrastructure that can give globalisation a "human face" (G8 1999). Taken together, the Cologne consensus marked a repudiation of, and replacement for, the neo-liberal approach that had dominated G7/8 thinking at Denver, and during most of the 1980s and 1990s. Notably absent from the Cologne communiqués were any references to capital account liberalisation as a valuable international constitutional principle, let alone one worthy of entrenchment in the IMF Articles of Agreement (Blinder 1999).[10] Emerging economies were now invited to carry out a "careful and well-sequenced approach to capital account liberalisation" and to do so only after they had stronger, better regulated, national financial systems in place.

Conclusion

The 1997-99 Asian-turned-global financial crisis was ultimately stemmed when the US Treasury Secretary, Central Bank governor, and Congress acted at the last hour to lower interest rates and authorize an IMF contribution, thereby preventing the clear and present danger of a financial meltdown that threatened to engulf even a secure United States. However, in acting in this way the United States, constrained by congressional stalemate as an unprecedentedly dangerous moment, and by the advent of frozen domestic credit markets in the wake of the LTCM collapse, was by no means behaving as the classic, self-confident, capable hegemon of old. Rather, in an era in which globalisation rendered the most powerful, relatively closed, and vibrantly growing United States vulnerable along with its lesser partners, the US needed the support of its G7 colleagues to mount an effective response to cope with panicking markets simultaneously on three regional fronts. Moreover, with Japan financially fragile and in recession and Germany initially distracted by a government in transition, the least powerful G7 members - Britain, the 1998 host, and Canada, guardian of the Halifax programme of IFI reform - used their institutional assets to play substantial, multilevelled, leadership roles.

For Britain, the greatest achievement came from the ultimate fulfilment of its October 1998 quest to mobilise the G7 into taking additional collective action to reassure panicking markets in the wake of a congressionally constrained US. It further succeeded, without the additional impulse of crisis, in realising its decade-long quest to obtain large-scale debt relief for the poorest.

Canada's successful leadership was driven by a recognition of its broad economic interests and domestic values, and a systemic sense of responsibility as a member of the governing global concert institutionalised in the G7. During the three phases of the crisis, Canada recurrently displayed intellectual, policy, and structural leadership. Intellectually, it did so in its Halifax programme, peer supervision, and "roadmap" proposals; its six-point programme; its Standstill concept; and its proposal for debt relief for the poorest. In the policy realm, it acted with early interest rate cuts and calls for fiscal stimulus, peer supervision, social responsibility, controlled capital liberalisation, private sector burden sharing, and debt relief for the poorest. Structurally, it often made more than proportional contributions as a G7 member to the supplementary support packages for South Korea, Thailand, and Brazil, and provided its share of the GAB/NAB, IMF, IBRD, IDB, and ADB packages. It was also prepared to finance debt relief for the poorest (along with prospective financial packages for Mexico and other endangered economies) and a Balkan stability package for the reconstruction of Kosovo and its neighbours.

Canada often acted against American preferences, notably on capital account liberalisation, social responsibility, the precautionary CCL facility, and delayed NAB repayment. It assembled issue-specific coalitions from an ever changing array of G7 partners, and its distinctive positions were substantially reflected in collective outcomes. Above all, its diplomacy was effective, as the action of the G7 and a G7-led IMF ultimately contained the looming Asian and then global financial crisis (Dobson 1999).

The successful leadership offered by Canada and Britain during the 1997-99 global financial crisis calls for important adjustment of and extensions to the traditional dominant interpretations of the causes of effective G7 co-operation, in order to take account of the changed circumstances of the rapidly globalising, crisis-ridden world of the 1990s.[11] These theories had argued that such co-operation depended upon the unique and necessary role of a United States able and willing to lead (if, in the leading variant) with support from one of the G7's strongest other members (Putnam and Bayne 1984, 1987; Bergsten and Henning 1996).[12] The G7's response to the 1997-99 global financial crisis and reconstruction of the international financial system was not only or even primarily a case of collective action flowing from a United States alone able and willing to lead, and doing so with the support a second leading G7 power. The US was at key moments a hesitant leader, constrained by congressional stalemate, carried by collective peer pressure from its G7 partners, in the face of compounding crisis, into following a consensus started by others, sharing the intellectual and policy leadership with others, depending on the financial contributions from others, and adjusting to others to produce the "just in time" leadership that the G7 brought. In short, effective co-operation came from a G7 in which even the weakest members, Canada and Britain, along with the US and others regularly led, and the US, along with Canada, Britain and the others, regularly followed, at many levels.

Nor did G7 co-operation during the crisis flow importantly from a shared memory of distant disasters which provided a divergent or common interpretative frame and impulse for leaders as they approached the unknown events of the present and near future. The memories of the stock market crash of 1929 and ensuing depression were far less important to leaders, in a now globalised world, than the more recent and sufficiently successful responses they had mounted to the 1987 stock market plunge and the Mexican meltdown of 1994. At the same time, these recent experiences also inhibited swift and sensitive collective action, as the Mexican model induced European members at the outset to first adopt a regionalised view of the world, rather than one in which all members of the transregional G7 coalition had to be involved. However, ultimately, all G7 members were able to learn that a genuinely global response was required. More broadly, the crisis similarly led G7 leaders, at first constrained by a Washington consensus with neo-liberal values at its core, to change significantly to a quite different policy model. In short, neither the distant memories of the past nor false consensus of the present when the crisis broke did much to determine the G7's effective collective response (Bergsten and Henning 1996).

Domestic-level factors, whether as domestic cleavages permitting mutually supportive transnational alliances or as traditional differences based on overall national or state-defined interests, were important but ultimately not decisive. Congressional resistance did constrain and delay the American administration's preferred actions, and lead Clinton and Rubin to play a variant of a two-level game (Putnam 1989). Yet, it was more the contagion of a crisis that had finally infected the American homeland, rather than a transnational coalition forged with a newly elected German government with a very different orientation than its predecessor that prompted the United States and the G7 to produce the effective consensus by the end of October 1998. And traditional differences were readily overcome, as the United States set aside the quest for rapid IMF-entrenched capital account liberalisation, and the new German government adopted a debt-relief initiative with IMF gold sales as the centrepiece deliverable of its Cologne Summit.

Of some relevance were those factors highlighted by the model of democratic institutionalism (Kokotsis 1999, Ikenberry 1993).[13] At the national level, Finance Ministers, who were most focussed on their country's G7 responsibilities, were largely in the lead, allowing for swift crisis response and continuing system construction efforts in the inter-peak crisis interludes when their heads were personally not engaged. At the international level, the whole process - The G7 Finance Ministers interactions, the international institutions controlled by the G7, beginning with the IMF, GAB, and NAB, and the newer bodies they dominated and created, such as the G22 and FSF, allowed for wider legitimacy for G7 leadership, broader burden sharing, and swifter implementation.[14] In addition, the commitment and popular support enjoyed by key leaders, notably Canada's Chrétien, Britain's Blair and even America's Clinton, enabled them to persist in their efforts to keep the Summit focussed on crisis response and system reconstruction until an adequate solution was found.

More specifically, in accordance with the core tenets of liberal-institutionalist theory, the particular procedures, rules, norms, and principles of the G7 empowered the weaker members and thus enabled them to constrain and collectively change the opening perspectives and positions of the most powerful. Britain and Canada, and Germany subsequently, skilfully used the prerogatives and legacy of the G7's rotating annual hosting arrangements to advance their issues and interests. The norms of consensus and peer pressure allowed each member, including the smallest, to delay action, and induced even the largest United States, from Hong Kong onward, to adjust to the consensus of the others. Moreover the growing Summit-inculcated sense of systemic vision and responsibility, and the accumulated legacy of transregional burden sharing, induced members who were initially instinctive regionalists to contribute to the collective cause.[15]

Above all effective G7 action to contain the crisis and construct a new financial architecture from 1997-99 was driven primarily by variants of those factors at the core of the G7's essential character as a modern international concert, now operating in the face of the acute intervulnerability and new forms of crisis and contagion that a rapidly globalising system brought. These particular international processes and international institutional provisions critically empowered the other, including least powerful members of the G7 to assist the US administration in overcoming domestic constraints on US leadership and adjusting America into the consensus that generated a collective and effective G7 response. G7 capabilities remained collectively dominant in the full system, even as the legitimacy and funds brought by outsiders, and by the G7-led Bretton Woods institutions played important roles.[16] The equalisation of capabilities bred by the new rise of Canada and Britain at the bottom, helped offset the small rise in the US share in the G7 as a whole and the sharp drop in second-ranked Japan and third-ranked Germany. But far more importantly, it was the rapid equalisation of vulnerability brought by the contagion and virulence of the crisis that prompted all G7 members to join together, enabled each to lead, and induced all to adjust to arrive at a consensus, commonly search to construct a solution, and contribute to the collective good. Constricted participation within the IMF and elsewhere, especially in October 1998 among the US, current G7 host Britain and incoming G7 host Germany, proved critical, even though the G7 also reached out from the start to mobilise the resources and legitimacy of the GAB, NAB, new G22, and, later, FSF and G20.[17] Common principles of major power responsibility, market democracy and rule of law, induced all G7 members to support democratising and marketising countries in distant regions, to do so in ways that sustained the move toward genuine market democracy, and the openness and transparency that flow from it. A common core of domestic values ultimately helped all G7 countries, with Canada and Britain in the lead, to recognise that the adjusting countries needed the social safety expenditure that was taken for granted within all G7 countries at home. Political control by democratic and popularity elected leaders through the G7 Summit and ministerial was important in helping allow President Clinton's position to prevail *vis à vis* his Congress, Chancellor Schroeder's *vis à vis* his central bank, and the Canadian Prime Minister and Finance Minister against the economic orthodoxy of their trade and finance officials.

Above all, it was the intervulnerability created and rendered visible by crisis, the recent "first shock" of the 1994 Mexican crisis, and the learning that had begun at Halifax and was reinforced at each stage of the contagion that led to co-operation, and co-operation on a very different set of premises that those that had reigned, amidst the aura of American triumphalism, at the Denver Summit of 1997.

Notes

1 This article is based on papers prepared for conferences on Canadian and Taiwanese public policy at National Chengchi University, Taipei, Taiwan, 18 December 1998, and on The Challenges of Globalization, Bishop's University, 6-8 June 1999. It draws substantially on Kirton (1999). I gratefully acknowledge the comments of colleagues at these conferences, the research assistance of Gina Stephens, Natalie Armstrong, Ivan Savic, Diana Juricevic, Paul Jacobelli and other members of the G8 Research Group, and the co-operation of many interviewees in G7 governments and international financial institutions. I am particularly grateful for the trenchant and detailed comments of Sir Nicholas Bayne on an earlier draft. The responsibility for this chapter remains mine alone.

2 These calculations are made employed the formula and data sources used in Kirton (1999b).

3 On the G7 as a genuine forum of collective management, in which different countries lead on different issues and all contribute, see Bayne (2000).

4 See Dewitt and Kirton (1983), Hawes (1984), Black (1997-98) and Bayne (1999a). For a competing view, see Cooper (1997) and Nossal (1997), and, in the finance field, Webb (1992, 1999).

5 On the concept of "intervulnerability", see Doran (1984).

6 See Kirton (1997) and Kokotsis and Kirton (1997-98), on which this section is based in part.

7 Alan Blinder (1999) notes that "the US government was a primary pusher of this bad advice".

8 For background on the traditional British and Canadian approach to reforming the Summit process and their differences with that of the US, see Hodges (1994), Kirton (1994), and Putnam (1994).

9 For a representative expression of US opposition, see Eichengreen (1999).

10 Blinder's analysis also shows the content and emergence of a new consensus in US intellectual circles more broadly.

11 For an analytical outline, see Kirton and Daniels (1999).

12 See also Kirton (1999b).

13 See also Bayne (1999a) on the importance of persistence.

14 While the creation of the G22 can be attributed to unilateral US (and presidential) leadership, new bodies such as the FSF were clearly a collective G7 product, with Germany's Hans Tietmeyer playing the leading role in initially bringing the body to life. In contrast to those who emphasise the US historic control of the IMF (Hale 1998), the case clearly shows that the crisis rendered the G7 collectively the effective centre of control within the G7.

15 On the dynamics of transregional burden sharing in the G7, see Kirton (1997b). More broadly, see Mansfield and Milner (1999).

16 The one partial exception was China. In accordance with this argument, it was less important for its deployed capabilities than the vulnerabilities it could have created for the G7 had it deployed it major weapons of an exchange rate devaluation, as the G8 acknowledged at the Birmingham Summit of 1998. See Kirton (1999d).

17 For a brief account of the latter bodies, see Kirton (1999d).

References

Bayne, Nicholas (2000), *Hanging in There: The G7 and G8 Summit in Maturity and Renewal*, Ashgate, Aldershot.

Bayne, Nicholas (1999a), "Continuity and leadership in an Age of Globalization", in Michael Hodges *et al.*, *The G8's Role in the New Millennium*, Ashgate, Aldershot.

Bayne, Nicholas (1999b), "Review of Andrew Cooper's Canadian Foreign Policy: Old Habits and New Directions", *The Round Table*, July.

Bayne, Nicholas (1998), "Britain, the G8 and the Commonwealth: Lessons of the Birmingham Summit", *The Round Table*, 348.

Bayne, Nicholas (1997), "Impressions of the Denver summit", at www.G7.utoronto.ca.

Black, Conrad, (1997-98), "Taking Canada Seriously", *International Journal* 53 (Winter): 1-16.

Blinder, Alan (1999), "Eight Steps to a New Financial Order", *Foreign Affairs* 78, September/October, pp. 50-63.

Bergsten, Fred and Randall Henning (1996), *Global Economic Leadership and the Group of Seven*, Institute for International Economics, Washington DC.

Canada (1998a), Finance Canada, "Remarks by the Honourable Paul Martin, Minister of Finance, to the Commonwealth Business Forum", 29 September, Ottawa.

Canada (1998b), Finance Canada, "Minister Welcomes Declaration of G-7 Finance Ministers and Central Bank Governors", 30 October, Ottawa.

Canada (1998c), Finance Canada, "Canada to Join Thailand Assistance Package", 15 April, Washington DC.

Canada (1998d), Finance Canada, "International supervisory and surveillance initiative proposed", 15 April, Washington DC.

Cooper, Andrew (1997), *Canadian Foreign Policy: Old Habits and New Directions*, Prentice Hall, Scarborough.

Dewitt, David, and John Kirton (1983), *Canada as a Principal Power*, John Wiley, Toronto.

Dobson, Wendy (1999), "Fallout From the Global Financial Crisis: Should Capitalism be Curbed?", *International Journal*, vol. 54 (Summer), pp. 375-386.

Doran, C. (1984), *Forgotten Partnership: U.S.-Canada Relations Today*, John Hopkins University Press, Baltimore.

Eichengreen, Barry (1999), *Toward A New International Financial Architecture: A Practical Post-Asia Agenda*, Institute for International Economics, Washington DC, pp. 9, 92, 125.

Fry, Michael, John Kirton, and Mitsuru Kurosawa, eds., (1998), *The North Pacific Triangle: The United States, Japan and Canada at Century's End*, University of Toronto Press, Toronto.

Fraser, M (1998), ed., *The G8 and the World Economy*, Strategems Publishing Limited, London.

G8 (1999), G8 *Communiqué*, Koln 1999, 20 June, www.g7.utoronto.ca.

G7 (1999), *G-7 Statement*, 18 June, www.g7.utoronto.ca.

G7 (1998a), *Statement by the G-7 Finance Ministers and Central Bank Governors*, Washington DC, 3 October, www.g7.utoronto.ca.

G7 (1998b), *Leaders Statement on the World Economy*, 30 October, and *Statement by the G-7 Finance Ministers and Central Bank Governors* (30 October), www.g7.utoronto.ca.

Hajnal, Peter (1999), *The G7/G8 System: Evolution, Role and Documentation*, Ashgate, Aldershot.

Hale, David (1998), "The IMF after Russia's Default", *Foreign Affairs*, Vol. 77, September/October.

Hawes, Michael (1984), *Principal Power, Middle Power or Satellite? Competing Perspectives in the Study of Canadian Foreign Policy*, York Research Program in Strategic Studies, Toronto.

Hodges, Michael (1994), "More Efficiency, Less Dignity: British Perspectives on the Future Role and Working of the G7", *The International Spectator*, 29(2).

Hodges, Michael, John Kirton and Joseph Daniels, eds, *The G8's Role in the New Millennium*, Ashgate, Aldershot.

Ikenberry, John (1993), "Salvaging the G7", *Foreign Affairs*, vol. 72 (Spring), pp. 132-139.

International Monetary Fund (1998), *World Economic Outlook, October 1998*, International Monetary Fund, Washington DC.

Kindleberger, Charles (1988), *The International Economic Order: Essays on Financial Crisis and International Public Goods*, MIT Press, Cambridge MA.

Kirton, John (2000), "Deepening Integration and Global Governance: America as a Globalized Partner", in Tom Brewer and Gavin Boyd, eds., *Globalizing America: The USA in World Integration*, Edward Elgar, Cheltenham.

Kirton, John (1999a), "Canada as a Principal Financial Power: G-7 and IMF Diplomacy in the Crisis of 1997-99", *International Journal*, vol. 54, Autumn 1999, pp. 603-624.

Kirton, John (1999b), "Explaining G8 Effectiveness", in Michael Hodges, *et al.*, *The G8's Role in the New Millennium*, Ashgate, Aldershot, pp. 45-68.

Kirton, John (1999c), "Canada and the Global Financial Crisis: G7 and APEC Diplomacy", *The Canadian Studies Journal*, vol. 3 (forthcoming).

Kirton, John (1999d), "The G7, China and the International Financial System." Paper presented at an International Think Tank Forum on "China in the Twenty-First Century", China Development Institute, 10-12 November, Shenzen, China.

Kirton, John (1997), "Canada, the G-7 and the Denver Summit of the Eight: Implications for Asia and Taiwan", *Canadian Studies*, vol. 2, pp. 339-66.

Kirton, John (1997), "Le rôle du G-7 dans le couple intégration régionale-sécurité globale", *Etudes Internationales*, 28 Juin 1997, pp. 255-270.

Kirton, John (1995a), "The Diplomacy of Concert: Canada, the G-7 and the Halifax Summit", *Canadian Foreign Policy*, vol. 3 (Spring), pp. 63-80.

Kirton, John (1995b), "The G-7, the Halifax Summit and International Financial System Reform", *North American Outlook*, vol. 5 (June), pp. 43-66.

Kirton, John (1994), "Exercising Concerted Leadership: Canada's Approach to Summit Reform," *International Spectator* vol. 29 (April-June).

Kirton, John and Joseph Daniels (1999), "The Role of the G8 in the New Millennium", in Michael Hodges, *et al.*, *The G8's Role in the New Millennium*, Ashgate, Aldershot.

Kirton, John and Ella Kokotsis (1997-98), "Revitalizing the G-7: Prospects for the 1998 Birmingham Summit of the Eight", *International Journal*, vol. 53 (Winter), pp. 38-56.

Kokotsis, Eleonore (1999), *Keeping International Commitments: Compliance, Credibility and the G7, 1988-1995*, Garland Press, New York.

Mansfield, Edward and Helen Milner (1999), "The New Wave of Regionalism", *International Organization*, vol. 53 (Summer 1999), pp. 589-628.

Martin, Paul (1997), "Canada and the G-7", notes for remarks by the Honorable Paul Martin, Minister of Finance, to the University of Toronto G-7 Research Group, (November), at www.G-7.utoronto.ca.

Nossal, Kim Richard (1997), *The Politics of Canadian Foreign Policy*, 3rd ed., Prentice Hall, Scarborough.

Putnam, R. (1989), "Diplomacy and Domestic Politics: The Logic of Two Level Games", *International Organization*, vol. 42.

Putnam, Robert and Nicholas Bayne (1987), *Hanging Together: Cooperation and Conflict in The Seven Power Summits,* Revised Edition, Harvard University Press, Cambridge MA.

Putnam, Robert and Nicholas Bayne (1984), *Hanging Together: The Seven Power Summits*, Harvard University Press, Cambridge MA.

Putnam, Robert (1994), "Western Summitry in the 1990's: American Perspectives", *International Spectator*, vol. 29 (April-June 1994), pp. 81-94.

Rowlands, Dane (1999), "High finance and low politics: Canada and the Asian Financial Crisis", in Fen Hampson, Michael Hart and Martin Rudner, eds. *A Big League Player: Canada Among Nations*, Oxford University Press, Toronto, pp. 113-36.

Webb, Michael (1999), "The Group of Seven and Political Management of the Global Economy", University of Victoria (10 June).

Webb, Michael (1992), "Canada and the International Monetary Regime", in Claire Cutler and Mark Zacher, eds., *Canadian Foreign Policy and International Economic Regimes*, UBC Press, Vancouver, pp. 153-185.

PART II
CONSTRUCTING THE NEW SYSTEM

6 Transparentising the Global Money Business: Glasnost or Just Another Wild Card in Play?

GEORGE M. VON FURSTENBERG

> *More Light to Glasnost!* We want more openness about public affairs in every sphere of life.... Truth is the main thing. Lenin said: More light! Let the Party know everything!... People are becoming increasingly convinced that glasnost is an effective form of public control over the activities of all government bodies, without exception, and a powerful lever in correcting short-comings.... Naturally, it is not enough to know and to tell the truth. Acting on the knowledge of the truth and of understanding it is the main thing.
> - Mikhail Gorbatchev, *Perestroika,* 1987, 75-76.

Introduction

In social, rather than physical science, transparency is not a self-contained static property but a condition facilitating purposeful social acts. The term thus appears with different connotations on a variety of reform agendas. These include initiatives conveyed to the G7 primarily by the International Monetary Fund (IMF) and the Bank for International Settlements (BIS) with active support from the world's major financial centres in London and New York. The agendas listed in Section B of the Report of the G7 Finance Ministers to the Köln Economic Summit on *Strengthening the International Financial Architecture* freely mix narrow prescriptions for achieving greater *statistical* transparency with calls for *political* transparency. The latter is to help furnish both fulcrum and lever for far-reaching reforms and not just the oil that keeps the international financial system from choking up again and again for the emerging economies.

Because *transparency* evokes a diffuse set of strictly positive connotations in the literature on political economy and better governance, it is over-prescribed as if, taking a look-through twice a day would be effective prophylactic against a broad spectrum of social ills. This chapter's goal is to characterise the complex political applications of the term and to dampen claims about the good to be achieved by greater statistical transparency alone.

Perspective

The optimal amount of knowledge about another person's or organization's conditions, motives, plans, strategies, actions, and results is not unbounded in the sense of "the more the better". Not only is the marginal-benefit-to-cost ratio likely to fall as more intense and comprehensive surveillance becomes more resented and less instructive, but there are privacy, property rights, and empowerment issues as well. Indeed, with exceptions defined by law, the government is prevented from opening our mail or from making or requiring disclosures about us, just as it is entitled to use access qualifications and the Secret Service legally to protect its own sensitive information in privileged areas. When legislation was introduced in the United States in the spring of 1999 that would require banks to "know your customer", by profiling and monitoring their clients' sources of income and money flows so as to be able to report any scent, say, of money laundering, to the authorities, there was a public outcry. Making "me" more transparent gives "you" more power to abuse, intimidate and exploit me, and to force disclosure of ever more of my information.

Indeed, transparency in society or social transparency, as distinct from the kinds of transparency implied by being a straight arrow (honesty and predictability, except in certain games) and never lying to one's mother (deference and respect), is not normally of intrinsic value or even necessarily desirable per se. For instance, publicly held corporations are required to issue releases as soon as they become aware of actual or impending adverse material change in their business condition. However, this disclosure rule is imposed to be fair to all stockholders by keeping insiders from benefiting from exclusive knowledge, and not for the sake of transparency *per se*. Privately held companies normally would be ill-advised to disclose such information and may withhold it though not necessarily from their bankers. Countries have their Official Secrets Acts, or the like, because they know the high cost of their own transparency in adversarial situations such as high-stakes poker or war, where feints may be needed.

Calling for greater transparency involves a certain redistribution of power. It amounts to taking sides in a game in which one set of actors attempt to defend their information advantage against the information extraction and revelation strategies pursued by the opposite parties to a deal. The review called for in Section 19 of the G7 Finance Ministers' report of "ways to improve market disclosure, including a model template for public disclosure of their exposures and risk profile by institutions engaged in trading, investment, and lending activity, both regulated and unregulated" clearly needs to take account of this partiality. More information usually benefits one side more than the other. For instance, it may be used for more sophisticated derivative constructs to further exponentiate and leverage financial structures. The construction of derivatives on higher moments of the return distributions, such as on volatility and outlier segments of index distributions, with moments above the second covering deviations from normality, has only just begun. More data allow more risks to be appraised and taken. It would be naive to assume that having more statistics *must* be risk-reducing and conducive to improving the welfare of all parties (hence *Pareto-preferred*). In addition, candour can not just kill bad programs but also good ones in a partisan, posturing world like that of some US Congressional committees.

It is often useful to reflect on the literary usage of a term to get its full range of connotations. What is meant if the plot of a novel is described as transparent? Probably that it holds little interest and does not merit careful analysis. What if someone's motives are described as obvious? Probably that the person is a boor. The literary idea then is that transparency can imply artlessness, insensitivity, and a lack of subtlety and appreciation of complexity: *Cine verité*?

Political Transparency

If we grant that the emerging economies principally addressed by the G7 err on the side of too little rather than too much transparency by any standard, we still need to decide where and how more transparency is to be achieved and for what purpose. As Gorbachev's meandering rhetoric makes clear, the call for glasnost, or levelling with the people, amounts to an admonition not to muddy the waters or to hide true intentions in public life. But there are many reasons for powerful political and economic actors to prefer to fish in the dark. Transparency by degrees of light thus has come to be cast as an inverse measure of regulatory opacity or of outright corruption. Conversely, a lack of transparency has come simplistically to be viewed as a cloak for evil deeds which big brother must watch from some privileged institutional superstructure to which the rules of transparency and a lack of ulterior motives, of course, need not apply.

Linking transparency to social progress, and lack of transparency to corruption, a Transparency International (1998) Initiative on Corruption currently is being debated in international fora. Similarly, the IMF (1997, p. 2), like other international organizations, for some time has prided itself on promoting transparency in financial transactions in the government budget, central bank, and the public sector more generally, and on providing assistance to improve accounting, auditing, and statistical systems: "In all these ways, the IMF has helped countries to improve governance, to limit the opportunity for corruption, and to increase the likelihood of exposing instances of poor governance". In the light of subsequent crises, however, the IMF in the judgment of its Managing Director (Camdessus, 1999, p. 179), must not have done enough. For "a lack of transparency has been found at the origin of each recurring crisis in the emerging markets, and it has been a pernicious feature of the 'crony capitalism' that has plagued most of the crisis countries and many more besides".

This conception of both the problem and its remedy echoes a positivism in late nineteenth-century philosophy that equated greater scientific knowledge, though not just more and better data, with assured social progress: growing civic virtue and wisdom, prosperity, representative government, absence of contagion and of herd behaviour, and other good things. In fact, however, things often are transparently wrong and stay wrong. Indeed, knowing what is wrong and not being willing or able to do anything effective about it has become something of a specialty, not just in much of Africa but also in continental Europe, Russia, Japan, and Colombia in the last one to three decades, and the list goes on.

Transparency as Oversight and Quid Pro Quo

In many parts of the world and areas of public life glasnost therefore clearly is not a powerful agent of political and economic reform; it is clearly insufficient, and not always necessary, for such reforms. Nevertheless, as a general rule, transparency of institutions and procedures can be a driver of thoroughgoing political transformation. It is a precondition for building reliably functioning institutions and regulatory bodies, as well as providing legal security and democratic accountability. In the context of political economy, transparency has also been linked to reliable incentives or explicit constraints making the fiscal and monetary authorities, in particular, behave in a manner that is sustainable intertemporally. Fostering such time consistency is the intention behind the IMF's "Code of Good Practices on Fiscal Transparency" and a draft code of *Good Practices on Transparency in Monetary and Financial Policies* noted approvingly in Sections 17.b and 17.c of the G7 Finance Ministers' report.

Transparency of the condition and policies of members also is required by the IMF to reduce program risk. Thus the IMF may require additional reporting, accounting and monitoring to offset the moral hazard implied by its assistance in times of crisis. It may demand greater transparency in order to be able to impose and monitor conditionality under programs with members. Conversely, lack of consistency over time and by case is also an issue for the international financial institutions (IFIs) themselves. The reason is not just that the IFIs set various debt traps for themselves and others under which existing debts of deadbeat members are serviced by issuing ever more debt to defer the inevitable write-off. This is a process familiar most recently from dead-upon-disbursement loans to Russia, and from the HIPC (Heavily Indebted Poor Countries) debt relief initiative announced with much fanfare at the G7 Summit. A deeper reason is that the IFIs have a personality that is split between a self-image of being stewards of the common good and the reality of also being agents for the political will of principal members or groups of member countries. Eichengreen (1999, p. 9) notes, for instance, "the disproportionate influence enjoyed by the US Treasury as a result of its physical and intellectual proximity to the Fund". Friedman (1999, p. 5) finds it "no surprise that today the IMF is widely regarded as the international enforcement arm of the U.S. Treasury". With transparency a political tool rather than an ethical value to all parties, the IMF may be able to use the greater transparency urged on it by member governments, including the United States, to reduce the disproportionate influence of the latter.

Members of the IMF are both its clients and source of funds. Their political control soon may be tightened through the elevation of the Interim Committee to a standing Policy Council, a process started at the Köln G7 summit. Perhaps to counteract this continuing politicisation of the IFIs, calls for increasing their accountability and transparency have been included in Section 11 of the G7 Finance Ministers' report. For a long time the IMF held that confidentiality had to rule in its dealings with member countries in difficulties or it would not be able to obtain the best available information from them at all. The quality of the members' data on one side, and their publication status at the IMF and hence the transparency of IMF operations to outsiders on the other, thus were deemed inversely related. Recently the IMF has taken steps to enhance this transparency with unknown consequences for the quality of what transpires. Simultaneously strengthening the roles of "steward" and "agent" will do little to advance time consistency but is quite capable of promoting institutional self-interest.

This instance may show that the political context in which calls for greater transparency are issued is quite complex: Moves toward greater transparency and professionalism may be linked to other steps which undercut it.

Statistical Transparency: Miracle Drug for Crisis Prevention or Much Less?

Although of the term *transparency* has become *de rigueur* for a wide variety of statistical improvements only in the last few years, the IMF has been in the business of helping countries improve their data collection and reporting for a long time. Reacting to the Mexican crisis that broke into the open in December 1994 and generated a "tequila effect" in much of the region to the south, the IMF has taken significant new steps to require improvements in documentation, quality, coverage, timeliness, and accessibility of the macroeconomic data released by member countries. Its Special Data Dissemination Standards (SDDS), established in early 1996, went beyond the corresponding "General" Standards (GDDS) in imposing special requirements on countries participating in international financial markets or desiring to do so. The IMF does not actually audit or control any aspect of the data reported by countries except for those data recording financial operations with the IMF. Nevertheless its prodding has enhanced the usefulness and international comparability of the information available to the public.

The G7 Finance Ministers, in Sections 20 and 21 of their 1999 report, have called for further improvements in data availability and communication. They called for more timely and complete release of macroeconomic indicators and data on external finance positions. They also urged general adoption of improved internationally accepted accounting and other "transparency" standards and of regulations and codes of good practices that conform to certain core principles everywhere. Britain's chancellor of the Exchequer, Gordon Brown, in April 1999 called for "[equipping] international financial institutions to monitor and enforce the new rules of the game", although these fighting words were muted by the G7 who appeared content with the disciplining effects of publicity and exposure in financial markets.

The Institute of International Finance (1999, p. 16) wants the IMF to do more and "[to] strictly enforce compliance with the SDDS" on all countries "with significant market access". The Institute has also urged the IMF to adopt "more demanding SDDS requirements for [foreign exchange] reserves and potential drains on them" (p. 15), so that the large multinational banks, which are the Institute's members, may be duly warned.

The Köln G7 Statement once again headlines *enhancing transparency and promoting best practices* in Section II.B.: almost every section of the much longer report of the G7 Finance Ministers calls for greater statistical transparency in some respects. Commendable though this is, the cry for ever more, and more transparent, data - a cry that is raised after every major crisis - can easily leave the impression that having enough information may be sufficient to prevent future crises. Indeed complaining about inadequate or misleading data provides a convenient alibi for those who might otherwise be charged with poor judgement and malfeasance. For it leaves the unwarranted impression that if the developing countries that had large net international capital inflows - equal to 5 to 10 percent of their GDP - for several years in a row had only let the statistical truth be known, surely there never would have been the flood of international lending that subsequently was found unsound.

The reason why "more complete information" is too often viewed as a cure-all by economists is closely related to the articles of faith which many of us have (been) taught to uphold. A standard (New Palgrave, 1987, p. 281) rendition of one such key tenet is:

> Rational expectations theory holds that prices are formed within the limits of available information by market participants using standard economic models appropriate to the circumstances. As such ... market prices can not diverge from fundamental values unless the information proves to have been widely wrong.

The corollary of this claim is that, with accurate public information, we can trust market data to reveal the appropriate (equilibrium) price relationships which are in line with (the true economic model's) fundamentals. And indeed, economists always strain to prove that "the price" of financial assets, no matter how levitated or depressed, must somehow be "right". Thus around the time the Japanese stock market bubble burst "for good" a decade ago, it was sporting good fun (e.g., French and Poterba, 1990) to try to demonstrate that Japanese stock prices may not have been far out of line with fundamental equilibrium, misconceptions about outlandishly high valuations notwithstanding. Similarly, a good many analysts now assert that the latest and biggest stock market bubble of the United States that lasted at least through the first half of 1999 surely is no bubble at all, but that the US economy has earned every Dow Jones and Nasdaq record it gets on account of its extraordinarily strong fundamentals.

Of course there are dissenters, such as the dissent appearing in the report, dated June 11, 1999, quoted below, but if there is such uncertainty about the future course of financial markets even in the United States, lack of transparency surely has nothing to do with it.

> With fiscal restraint set to reach its limits and little sign that the private-sector deficit will stop growing, the current account deficit is likely to remain on an upward trend. However, the necessary simultaneous rise in capital inflows is becoming more difficult to achieve. This is because the underlying trend in relative returns on capital – which favored the United States ... – seems to be turning. The resulting strains in the balance of payments raise the specter of a financing crisis, which would hurt the dollar and could reduce U.S. asset prices.
> - *U.S. Economics Analyst,* 1999, p. 1.

This may be a perfectly fine example of analysis based on fundamentals. It weighs the intrinsic uncertainty of public and private sector budget balances and savings behaviour as they relate to such fundamentals. Nevertheless it is clear that if the Goldman Sachs organisation and those whom it manages or advises, as one, would really see this spectre, asset prices, not just in the United States, would have taken a large tumble by June 11, 1999, when the analysis was issued.

Sunspot Activity and Transparency: It's No Use to Look Into the Sun

Perhaps the actual onset of crises has more to do with market uncertainty that is not transmitted through fundamentals, so-called extrinsic uncertainty. Such uncertainty is involved in generating what are known as "sunspots", where there may be large effects from an activity, such as the stampede of a herd, that has some small and fairly accidental trigger event but no known fundamental cause.

Where does this strange term come from? It is certainly not meant to connote "too much light", to spite Lenin or Gorbachev. Rather it refers to something which over a century ago was thought to be fundamental to business cycles: The theory was that predictable cycles in sunspot activity would influence the weather so as to have a predictable effect on agricultural yield rates and hence on output and real income. It later turned out that any grain of truth somewhere in this deduction could not, by itself, have made a detectable mark on the actual course of business cycles. However, if people continued to believe in the validity of the sunspot theory of business cycles and took its predictions seriously in their planning and positioning for the future, the theory could be self-fulfilling. Propelled by common beliefs alone it could hold, even if it had no appreciable basis in fundamentals but was little more than a superstition or fad. Bullard (1990, pp. 337-338) thus aptly describes sunspot equilibria as containing an ultimately "frivolous" variable and explains the origin of the term "sunspots" in economics. These fads themselves could change abruptly for no known fundamental reason, perhaps just because herd leadership had changed, thereby producing a multiplicity of sunspot equilibria. Only under highly restrictive assumptions will learning about the economy arrive at its true structure and settle on a nonsunspot (classical Walrasian) equilibrium.

Sunspot equilibria therefore are not the result of regime-switching or of a mere lottery over fundamentals-based equilibria which derive from an information, learning, and economic structure that allows markets to clear in different states of the world. Rather they expand the set of equilibria in a major, though undesirable (not Pareto-optimal) way:

> (Prevalence) of proper sunspot outcomes came as a big surprise to many rational-expectations theorists. Game theorists, on the other hand, long ago accepted the naturalness of stochastic solutions to nonstochastic games. Mixed strategy equilibria and ... correlated equilibria are examples in which extrinsic uncertainty matters to the outcomes and payoffs of games.
> - *Shell, 1987, pp. 550.*

Thus, blind trust in the market's "correctly" valuing financial assets through the processing of accurate information is misplaced. It is predicated on the unwarranted, frequently implicit, assumption that surely we all know how to enter the right information into the "true" model so as to obtain results consistent with the actual functioning of the economy and of financial markets. Hayek would have called this a pretense of knowledge. Worse yet, if sunspot activity is as prominent in financial markets as in the models of economists, the model with the "true" fundamental relationships may not be of much value, even if it could be nailed down and kept from "switching". If temporary equilibria form a sequence interspersed with sunspots, there cannot even be a definable tendency toward equilibrium in the way Walrasian equilibria pull market activity toward them.

Financial Crises Always Hit Markets Unexpectedly: It's the Nature of the Beast

What we know is that recent international financial crises have been sudden and frequent and that denial of data which anyone in a position to act on them really wanted, and wanted to pay attention to, had little to do with them. Nor were all of these crises precipitated by a dramatic prior change in economic circumstances. Consider this honest appraisal of three major emerging-economy crises in the December 1998 issue of *Finance and Development*:

> All three crises took investors by surprise. Bank lending increased in 1981 to every country later obligated to restructure its debt, and bond and loan interest rate spreads were stable in the first half of 1982. Similarly, Mexico's decision in December 1994 to float the peso was unexpected, despite periods of turbulence for domestic interest rates, stock prices, and the peso-dollar exchange rate in the preceding 11 months. Most investors were also surprised by the scope and intensity of the Asian crisis, in part because of the affected countries' strong record of growth and stability and their cautious fiscal policies. Yield spreads on bonds and syndicated loans declined for most Asian economies between 1995 and 1997, and no sovereign credit rating was downgraded in 1996 or the first half of 1997. In the months leading up to the outbreak of the crisis, Eurobond spreads for Indonesia, Malaysia, the Philippines, and Thailand fluctuated in relatively narrow ranges. Spreads did not spike until the depth of the Korean predicament became known and speculators attacked the Hong Kong dollar in October.
> - *Mathieson, Richards, and Sharma,* 1998, pp. 29-30.

Of course it is fair to note that financial crises must always be unexpected by the mass of market opinion for, if that opinion were to shift, the crisis already would have begun. Hence the proper, though hopelessly counterfactual, question might be to ask which crises did *not* occur, rather than why the crises that did occur came as such a surprise. Even Brazil's recent problems, which were quite conventional and not hidden statistically to any great degree, that failed to be telling to analysts for reasons no amount of data, or statistical warning signs may be able to overcome.

> The obvious question, in light of these easily observable problems, is why crises come as such a surprise. In the case of Brazil, for instance, [a noted analyst at] Westham International concluded in early 1998 that the country's record at economic restructuring "makes it clear that Brazil will not suffer the same fate as Southeast Asia". Merrill Lynch maintained an "overweight" to "neutral" recommendation even in their report dated January 5, 1999 [just days before the

crisis set in]. [Earlier], as the Mexican peso approached collapse in December 1994, a compilation of views by UCLA economist, Sebastian Edwards, revealed that most observers remained optimistic about the country's economic prospects. Indeed, Mexico's *Euromoney* country risk rankings actually improved between March and September 1994! Similarly, Asian mutual funds remained overweighted in Thailand until May of 1997.
- *Rajan,* 1999, p. 3.

The field of finance theory has been famous for generating both directional, magnitude, and excess sensitivity "puzzles" (see von Furstenberg, 1998; and Lewis, 1999, for references). Judged from the pulpit of deeply grounded axiomatic finance theory, it seems that the real world of finance is always unaccountably misbehaving: Correspondence between predictions of theory and empirical outcomes is a rarity. In addition, using up the few degrees of freedom available in the calibration of theoretical models to resolve one puzzle, say the equity premium puzzle, usually just raises other puzzles, such as the puzzle about the minuscule level of the risk-free real interest rate, and the real bond rate puzzle. For those who remember popular renditions of the Heisenberg principle, this may sound familiar.

Given this record, it is not frivolous to suggest that greater transparency will have little net effect on the risk of widespread financial crisis. Rather, more and better data, if in fact used for better analysis and supervision, help both the crisis offence and the defence in international financial markets. Greater transparency may also do little to raise the state of preparedness. The reason is that measures of financial fragility, even when tested successfully out of sample to predict crises that have already occurred, do not appear to have much capacity to predict future crises. Financial markets are extremely good at exploiting the information provided by any emerging pattern. As soon as the profit opportunities it offers have been recognized, they will be seized until that pattern no longer appears. Hence what is seen now will not be seen tomorrow, and the indicators and alarms installed today will not reliably warn of future crises. As Eichengreen, Rose, and Wyplosz (1995) have candidly admitted, even when all else is known about a crisis well past, we may still be left wondering why it happened. Bhagwati (1997; cited in Buria, 1999, p. 10) too is convinced that "markets may do something when you have done nothing wrong and you may have to do something wrong in order to convince the markets that you are doing something right!"

Conclusion

Greater transparency with respect to international finance and the policies, positions, and technical factors that move it - and make it risky - may not achieve its designated goals, but it can have important side effects. Statistical transparency alone comes closest to being both uncontroversial and relatively inconsequential: More complete information will not cure instability when we are still struggling to find the switch for the right models to process that information, knowing deep down that the switch always gets disconnected once one is found. More and more finely measured bodies of data without a reliable model to process them do not even amount to information relevant for prevention because little can be learned from them about how to avoid financial crises. There are many other things that will be learned from such data, for instance how to stretch the construction of financial derivatives even further or how to unhinge this or that borrowing and exchange arrangement. With both the offence and the defence drawing strength from greater calculability and sharper distributions and functions, it is not at all clear which side will win out.

Political transparency ranges from elements of statistical transparency, such as a quick and clean vote count, to procedures for establishing political legitimacy. It frequently involves mixed agendas in which increased transparency may either be the means or the price for achieving something else that is of substantial value in itself to those who seek to impose it.

Glasnost was a program of making government operations and decisions transparent and to give them legitimacy through democratic forms of participation. The transparency called for by the IFIs and the G7, by contrast, is likely to enhance analytical power and say-so at the top of the financial pyramid. This is where finance ministries, central banks, IFIs, regulatory standard setters, leading financial multinationals, and investment gurus who pass for statesmen meet. I doubt that, at the end of the day, it is the individual taxpayers, private pensioners, or small investors who stand to reap benefits from greater transparency. These are the usual address of those who claim to bring "social goods".

At the very least the transparency campaign, on account of its known redistributive effects, aims far beyond innocuous statistical improvements which nobody would oppose. A basic asymmetry arises from the fact that imposing new rules of transparency is a nonevent with regard to the G7 countries' internal business and domestic asset valuations but not for the emerging economies that may be greatly affected.

To hide this asymmetry, the IMF and countries that are host to the world's most sophisticated financial service industry, such as the United Kingdom, have made a display of also applying greater transparency to their own operations and to meet the transparency codes laid down for others. They do so at no cost to themselves since they have a natural antidote to transparency, discretionary power, while gaining leverage over others. They have even promised to consider requiring greater disclosure from their heavily leveraged financial institutions, particularly hedge funds, that rightly view transparency as jeopardizing some of their contrarian strategies. But basically they are demanding much more from others for themselves than from themselves. Already in 1998, the IMF started publishing Press/Public Information Notices (PINs) under the title *IMF Economic Reviews* and more such PIN notices, covering a wider range of the IMF's activities are published, on paper and electronically, ever more promptly. The IMF (1999) has followed up with further steps to enhance public access to its own operations and decision documents without needing to reveal who and what really spur its actions. In April, Britain's chancellor of the Exchequer loudly took credit for the IMF publishing one of its first transparency reports on the British economy: "It demonstrated Britain's commitment to this type of surveillance" (Brown, 1999). Obviously Britain was trembling in its boots.

All told, the greater transparency envisaged by the G7 can do very little to reduce the risk of financial crises. Global finance is developing rapidly in a way that generates new risks and requires ever greater knowledge inputs for highly conditioned analyses. For this reason, the mere ability to improve upon past estimates of probability density functions, correlations, and outliers does not guarantee that future financial crises will cause less damage, or come as less of a surprise, than the crises just past.

What is certain is that under the seemingly technical requirement of greater transparency, other agendas are being served. These relate to the exercise and distribution of power within and between countries and among players, rich or poor, in credit or debt, now inextricably linked with each other in open financial markets. These financial markets themselves, or, more precisely, the content of the news and views, or "belief shocks" (Salyer and Sheffrin, 1998) that move them, are not transparent or easily reduced to fundamentals. Furthermore the deserved and undeserved "disciplines" to which they may subject countries and their policymakers do not necessarily strengthen representative government. Rather, they make national economic policymakers disproportionately accountable, on the surface at least, to "foreign investors, country-fund managers in London and New York, and a relatively small group of domestic exporters" (Rodrik, 1999, p. 151). These are the embodiments of efficiency in financial markets to those of blind faith. The sway of global finance also creates exposure to powerful external trend-setters and opinion-makers, including the international financial press and institutions, who are the opaque guardians of transparency in others.

Transparency, it turns out, is not a simple global public good. It is not even simply good since "the effects of increased transparency on price volatility or the volatility of the economy are ambiguous" (Furman and Stiglitz, 1998, p. 70) not only in theory when risk markets are imperfect, but most likely in actual crisis management well.

References

Bhagwati, J. (1997), "Interview", *Times of India*, December 31.

Brown, G. (1999), "Toward a Strong World Financial System", *The Wall Street Journal*, April 30, p. A14.

Bullard, J. (1990), "Rethinking Rational Expectations", pp. 325-354 in G.M. von Furstenberg (ed.), *Acting Under Uncertainty: Multidisciplinary Conceptions*, Kluwer Academic Publishers, Boston.

Buria, A. (1999), "An Alternative Approach to Financial Crises", *Essays in International Finance*, No. 212, Princeton University.

Camdessus, M. (1999), "Transparency and Improved Standards Are Key to Stable and Efficient Financial System", *IMF Survey*, 28(11), June 7, pp. 177-180.

Eichengreen, B. (1999), *Toward a New International Financial Architecture: A Practical Post-Asia Agenda*, Institute for International Economics, Washington DC.

Eichengreen, B., A.K. Rose and C. Wyplosz (1995), "Exchange Market Mayhem: The Antecedents and Aftermath of Speculative Attacks", *Economic Policy*, vol. 21, October, pp. 251-312.

French, K.R. and J.M. Poterba (1990), "Are Japanese Stock Prices Too High?", National Bureau of Economic Research Working Paper No. 3290, March.

Friedman, B.M. (1999), "The Power of the Electronic Herd", *The New York Review of Books*, 46(12), July 15, pp. 1-8.

Furman, J. and J.E. Stiglitz (1998), "Economic Crises: Evidence and Insights from East Asia", *Brookings Papers on Economic Activity*, No. 2, pp. 1-114.

G7 (1999), *G7 Statement*, Cologne, 18-20 June.

G7 Finance Ministers (1999), *Strengthening the International Financial Architecture: Report of G7 Finance Ministers to the Köln Economic Summit*, Cologne, 18-20 June.

Gorbachev, M. (1987), *Perestroika: New Thinking for Our Country and the World*, Harper & Row, New York.

Institute of International Finance (1999), *Report of the Working Group on Transparency in Emerging Markets Finance*, Washington DC, March.

International Monetary Fund (1997), *Good Governance: The IMF's Role*, IMF, Washington DC.

International Monetary Fund (1999), "IMF Takes Additional Steps to Enhance Transparency",

Public Information Notice No. 99/36, April, pp. 1-3.

IMF (current URL). http://www.imf.org/external/standards/index.htm. source for data dissemination (http://dsbb.imf.org) and fiscal and monetary transparency standards and reports on country transparency practices.

Lewis, K.K. (1999), "Trying to Explain Home Bias in Equities and Consumption", *Journal of Economic Literature*, 37(2), June, pp. 571-608.

Mathieson, D.J., A. Richards and S. Sharma (1998), "Financial Crises in Emerging Markets", *Finance and Development*, 35(4), December, pp. 28-31.

Rajan, R.S. (1999), "The Brazilian and Other Currency Crises of the 1990s", *Claremont Policy Briefs* (99-02), May, pp. 1-4.

Rodrik, D. (1999), *The New Global Economy and Developing Countries: Making Openness Work*, Overseas Development Council, Washington DC.

Salyer, K.D. and S.M. Sheffrin (1998), "Spotting Sunspots: Some Evidence in Support of Models with Self-Fulfilling Prophecies", *Journal of Monetary Economics*, 42(3), December, pp.511-523.

Shell, K. (1987), "Sunspot Equilibrium", pp. 549-551 in J. Eatwell, M. Milgate, and P. Newman (eds.), *The New Palgrave Dictionary of Economics, Vol. 4, Q to Z*, The Macmillan Press, London.

Transparency International (TI) (1998), 1998 Corruption Perceptions Index: A Joint Initiative Undertaken by TI and Göttingen University, Germany, http://www.gwdg.de/~uwvw/CPI1998.html.

U.S. Economics Analyst (1999), Goldman, Sachs & Co. Global Research, (99/23).

von Furstenberg, G.M. (1998), "From Worldwide Capital Mobility to International Financial Integration", *Open Economies Review*, 9(1), January, pp. 53-84.

7 Global Capital Flows: Maximising Benefits, Minimising Risks

JOSEPH P. DANIELS

> Recent events in the world economy have demonstrated that a strengthening of the system is needed to maximize the benefits of, and reduce the risks posed by, global economic and financial integration.
> - *Report of the Finance Ministers to the Köln Economic Summit*

Introduction

Much has been made of the role of capital flows and financial speculators in the context of global integration. Yet in much of the literature on reforms to the international financial system, it is taken for granted that the economic benefits of broader and deeper liberalised financial markets and the economic role that speculators play in these markets is well understood. In the early 1990s, the industrialised countries, particularly the United States and Europe, have unabashedly promoted financial liberalisation as the obvious and inevitable policy choice for developing and emerging economies.

Following the financial crises of 1994 and 1997, however, criticism of globalised financial markets for their shortcomings has been unremitting. Various policy-making fora have also followed this path, concentrating on risks and considering ways in which to contain the level or constrain the pace of financial liberalisation and global activities of financial speculators, as opposed to promoting the benefits of continued liberalisation as they once had. Because of advances in telecommunications and financial engineering, continuing integration of financial markets appears inevitable.

If history has anything to offer us, as James (1999) argues, liberalisation can be reversed. The lack of clear and consistent leadership in international economics may explain, in part, the recent surge in isolationism and protectionism. Leadership in this complicated issue area requires close attention to the normative and positive aspects of financial liberalisation in order to gain credibility to co-ordinate at the international level and advocate at the national level.

Capital market liberalisation has become an appealing goal to many nations because of the perceived allocative benefits and efficiency gains. The risks inherent in this process, however, have been made painfully obvious and, as a result, policymakers have elected to "reform" the financial system - meaning measures designed to prevent possible crises and better manage those that do occur - so as to maximise said benefits while minimising the risks. The overall purpose of this chapter is to offer an understanding of the basis for a strengthening or reform of the international financial system and, therefore, the rationale behind the *preventative* reforms advanced by the G7 Finance Ministers. It seeks to add to the existing literature by identifying and discussing, in an accessible manner, the root benefits of capital market liberalisation, the risks and imperfections inherent in capital markets, and the constraints that liberalised capital markets place on the conduct of microeconomic and macroeconomic policies. The role of financial speculators in the recent financial crises in East Asian is also considered. Instead of offering yet another list of reform proposals, this chapter focusses on those proposals most likely to be acted upon, that is, those drafted by the G7 Finance Ministers in *Strengthening the International Financial Architecture, Report of the G7 Finance Ministers to the Köln Economic Summit*. Finally, as the members of the G7 are the architects of the current international financial system, they have key responsibilities in its reform and management. We outline these responsibilities in the final section.

The conclusion drawn here is that the G7 has put forward worthy proposals for reducing variability and for responding to and containing future crises. These proposals should be acted on with haste. The G7 has fallen short, however, in providing the likely victims of future crises, the larger emerging and developing economies, with solid working proposals and examples appropriate to the conditions of these economies and broader participation in the reform process. The G7 Ministers' report implies that market participants will continue to be the principal agents pressing the integration of the financial systems of the major developed economies with those of the emerging and developing economies. Likewise the market will continue to be the primary supervisor of macroeconomic and exchange rate policies, rewarding nations with sound and credible policy and punishing those without. Nonetheless, the G7 has key responsibilities in the reform process and in managing these markets.

Benefits of International Capital Flows

Advocates of capital market liberalisation argue that unhindered capital movements allow savings to flow to their most productive use and, therefore, financial speculators play an important and beneficial role as they are the agents that provide liquidity, regardless of host location, to projects with potentially high marginal products. Those projects that do eventuate in high returns reward speculators for the risk they have assumed. In this way, resources are directed in the most efficient pattern, resulting in real sector development and productivity increases. Financial speculators, therefore, take the risky side of a financial transaction and provide essential liquidity to the economy.

With access to foreign capital, domestic households and businesses may expand their lending and borrowing activities abroad, allowing agents to continue to spend and invest during domestic economic downturns and repay during periods of economic growth, thereby mitigating typical business cycles. Hence, domestic agents can diversify savings internationally and reduce their exposure to domestic economic shocks. These positive aspects reinforce capital flows as domestic residents enjoy higher risk-adjusted rates of return, spurring yet higher levels of saving and investment activity. In turn, increased saving and investment induce additional economic growth.

For developing nations in particular, access to global capital reduces the cost of financing investment projects considerably. More investment projects are undertaken, leading to real sector development. In the long run, this translates into higher standards of living as higher rates of growth are enjoyed. Private speculative capital, therefore, may substitute for uncertain development aid that often comes with inefficiency costs associated with bureaucratic red tape and constraints.

The Role of Financial Intermediaries

For speculative capital flows to deliver promised real sector development and growth, a well-developed system of financial intermediaries is required. Pagano (1993) identifies three key functions of financial intermediation that lead to economic growth. The first is funnelling savings to firms with minimum x-inefficiencies. The process of intermediation absorbs a fraction of each dollar of savings so that less than one dollar is invested. An efficient system of intermediaries faces low reserve requirements, transaction taxes and unnecessary regulation, reducing these inefficiencies.

Secondly, financial intermediaries make it possible for many people to pool their funds together, thereby increasing the size, or *scale*, of the amount of total amount of savings managed by a central authority. This centralisation of management can reduce average fund-management costs below the levels that savers would incur if they were to manage their savings alone, thereby enjoying financial economies of scale. In this way, intermediaries may increase the amount of savings ultimately invested by reducing unnecessary costs.

Another outcome of an efficient system of intermediaries is the reduction of information asymmetries and an improvement of capital allocation and market stability. An information asymmetry exists when one party to a transaction, say a borrower, has more or better information than does the other party, the lender. For financial markets in particular, information asymmetries can lead to a number of potential problems including inefficient allocation of savings, herding behaviour, and even financial crisis. Intermediaries who specialise in the assessment of the quality of debt instruments and continuously monitor the performance of firms that issue these instruments are able to reduce the degree of information imperfections.

Intermediaries also provide a means for savers to pool risk. If savers are unable to pool risk, they will invest in the most liquid projects. More productive but less liquid projects are not financed, resulting in lower potential economic growth. Hence, intermediaries play a key three-part role: relying on their informational capabilities, they evaluate investment projects and determine those with the highest marginal product and then induce savers to invest in higher risk but more profitable projects through risk sharing at reduced average costs.

Financial Sector Development and Economic Growth

Reduced costs, higher quality information, and the pooling of risk are only some of the ways in which intermediaries may affect the rate of saving in an economy. Economic theory shows, however, that financial sector development may either increase or decrease saving and the effect on economic growth is unclear *a priori*. Improvements in hedging instruments may reduce precautionary saving and improvements in household credit markets may allow agents to dissave in favour of current consumption or low-marginal-benefit projects. Hence, if financial development induces lower saving, economic growth may suffer.

One view on the contribution of the financial sector is that long-run trend performance is determined solely by real sector development. An alternative view is that the development of the financial sector alters economic fundamentals and, therefore, alters long-run performance. Why financial development evolves differently across economies and the casual relationship between financial development and real sector growth is still unclear. Recent empirical literature, however, supports the view that financial development does indeed affect economic growth. Eatwell and Taylor (1998) argue, therefore, that the ultimate measure of a system of intermediaries is the effect on the real sector of the economy.

Misallocation of Capital

The fact that "reform" of the international financial system is being widely discussed is an admittance that unhindered financial markets do not achieve the utopian view of efficient capital allocation expressed above. Such an outcome is the quintessence that one would like to see reached, but there are a number of market imperfections and policy-created distortions that cause the system to fall short. In the presence of a deep and well-regulated system of intermediaries, financial development and capital market liberalisation may positively affect the path of potential long-run growth. Yet, under lesser conditions, intermediaries may channel capital flows in ways that undermine domestic policies, increase shocks and contagion, and trigger financial crises (Crockett, 1997, p. 7). The benefits of efficient capital allocation described above may be offset and economic growth actually suffer.

The potential costs of financial crises is well documented in the literature. For example, it is believed that the costs of the 1980s banking crisis in Argentina equalled one-half of the nation's GDP, while the United States' bailout of banks during the early 1990s totalled at least US$200 billion. The 1995 real estate collapse in Japan resulted in the nonperformance of more than US$250 billion in bank loans. In South Korea more than 10 percent of all bank loans are nonperforming, and for India and China nonperforming loans are estimated to be nearly 20 percent of outstanding loans. Since 1980, the International Monetary Fund (IMF) estimates that 133 of 181 IMF member nations have suffered banking problems it considers to be "significant" (Lindgren, *et al.* 1996).

The conclusion is that there are potential allocative and efficiency gains to be enjoyed from liberalising capital markets. A well-developed and regulated system of intermediaries is necessary for these gains to be realized.

This is not a sufficient condition, however, as there are policy-created distortions and financial markets imperfections that must be dealt with. With the potential benefits of financial speculation and the importance of a well-developed financial market in channelling global funds outlined, the risks and policy constraints inherent in liberalised financial markets are considered next.

Financial Markets and Economic Policy

There are a number of potential imperfections and risks inherent in financial markets. It is useful to focus on those that are central to the stability of global capital markets. For liberalised capital markets to function at the level of practical expectations, microeconomic and macroeconomic policies must be consistent with an environment of free-flowing capital. To promote stability of the system, these policy constraints must be realised and respected, policy-created distortions minimised, and imperfections addressed.

Risks, Distortions, and Microeconomic Policy

One type of market imperfection, that of asymmetric information, is believed by some economists to pervade financial markets in particular (Eichengreen, *et al.* 1999). As discussed above, asymmetric information can induce an inefficient distribution of capital and increased market volatility. Two key problems associated with information asymmetries are adverse selection and herding behaviour. In financial transactions, lenders are often not privy to all of the information - particularly information about risk - regarding a capital investment project. The existence of an information gap between savers and borrowers can result in adverse selection, or the potential for those who desire funds for unworthy projects to be the most likely to want to borrow or to issue debt instruments. A result of adverse selection is that the issuance of poor-quality instruments can make savers less willing to lend to or hold debt instruments issued by those seeking to finance high-quality projects (Daniels and VanHoose 1999). Additionally, poor information may result in herding behaviour. That is, in the presence of information gaps, savers follow the behaviour of someone else they feel is better informed. In a global context, herding behaviour can be a catalyst for contagion and spreading financial instability to regional levels. Herding behaviour can also lead to a reduction of asset prices or currency values that greatly exceeds what is warranted.

In global capital markets, the problem of information asymmetries can be extensive as multinational enterprises engage in transactions spanning the globe. High-quality intermediaries are able to reduce the degree of asymmetric information by having offices around the world, creating economies of scale in information processing. By continuously monitoring and evaluating the performance and activities of multinational enterprises, they are able to reduce, albeit not eliminate, information asymmetries and thereby encourage savings and reduce herding behaviour.

Another potential problem is that of moral hazard, that is the borrower engages in behaviour that increases risk after the debt instrument has been purchased. Again intermediaries are able to reduce moral hazard by continuously monitoring the performance of the borrower. In the context of global capital markets and in light of recent financial crises, moral hazard may arises when a domestic government implicitly guarantees that a firm or bank will not be allowed to fail. International organisations, such as the IMF, have also been accused of creating moral hazard when standing by ready to bail out sovereign nations facing a liquidity crisis.

Finally, capital flows may respond to policy-created distortions, leading to an inefficient and capricious allocation of capital. Cooper (1999) points out that differential national taxation, trade restrictions, and macroeconomic policies are but a few policy-created distortions that may lead to a misallocation of capital. In addition, differential national regulation on financial transactions may generate regulatory arbitrage, when domestic institutions either locate abroad or conduct certain types of operations abroad in order to avoid domestic regulation and supervision. This mitigates the regulatory abilities of governments and exposes domestic intermediaries to the very types of risk regulators seek to minimise. These distortions result from domestic microeconomic policies yet need to be judged in an international context as well. Without proper international co-operation and co-ordination, there exists a potential "race to the bottom" or a move to the regulatory and tax environment of the least stringent nation.

Financial Market Liberalisation and Macroeconomic Policy

Financial market liberalisation also constrains macroeconomic policy in ways determined by the exchange rate regime, one of the most important macroeconomic institutional choices a nation faces. For developing nations, the exchange rate is an extremely important nominal price that affects export performance, the cost of important commodities and inputs, and directing business planning and investment. Pegging the exchange rate, therefore, is an attractive option. The well-known "impossible trinity" of fixed exchange rates, capital mobility, and discretionary monetary policy prescribes that these three conditions cannot exist simultaneously and policymakers must be willing to forgo one aspect.[1] For developing, transitional, and emerging nations seeking to gain exchange rate stability and domestic price credibility through pegged-exchange rates while liberalising financial markets to take advantage of cheaper foreign financing, the lesson is that monetary authorities must be independent and conduct policy in a manner consistent with the first two objectives. This means that discretionary monetary policy via sterilised foreign exchange interventions is not sustainable in the long run. The typical outcome of countries trying to practice all three is an overvalued currency and inevitable devaluation. In turn, the devaluation focusses attention on the improper past conduct of monetary policy and the loss of credibility is dramatic. As a result, the devaluation often leads to a complete collapse of the exchange rate regime and eventual floating of the currency until a new trading floor is found and the currency stabilises.

Developing nations, therefore, face a dilemma; should they choose fixed or flexible exchange rates? Cooper (1999), an advocate of a common world currency, see the only practical choices as being flexible exchange rates and some type of capital controls or capital market liberalisation and strongly fixed exchange rates with the complete loss of discretionary policy. With capital market liberalisation, a developing nation with a flexible exchange rate regime will experience a highly volatile exchange rate that responds primarily to the flow of foreign capital and, as a result, will be driven to capital controls. Otherwise, full capital mobility requires these nations to adopt a true fixed exchange rate regime with the loss of monetary policy, such as in Hong Kong or Argentina.

A pegged exchange rate regime, such as that employed in Thailand, Indonesia, and Malaysia prior to the fall of 1997 is problematic in combination with capital market liberalisation.[2] A key consideration is that under a pegged-exchange-rate regime, currency risk is shifted, to a given degree, from private market participants to the government. To private agents, the marginal benefit of employing hedging instruments appears less than the marginal cost. Many foreign exchange exposures, therefore, go unhedged and the foreign currency denominated debt of firms and businesses will balloon with a devaluation. According to Cooper, at the point when authorities realise that the exchange rate needs to be devalued so do private market participants and currency speculators, who are able to profit at the expense of national reserves. Further, as foreign currency indebted businesses scramble to buy up reserves so as to hedge their exposure, they exert significant downward pressure on the value of the domestic currency. The outcome is a free-falling exchange value. This is combined with the fact that the G7 nations lack an exchange rate policy that provides for long-term stability among their currencies. What this means for developing countries that choose to peg to one or more of these currencies is that, eventually, a revaluation or devaluation is inevitable. If the conduct of macroeconomic policy or microeconomic reform was wanting in the interim, or if the adjustment to parity was postponed too long, markets are likely to make these nations pay harshly for their shortcomings.

Another concern regarding financial liberalisation, somewhat separate from the choice of exchange rate regime, is the potential loss of monetary control. As pointed out by Williamson and Mahar (1998), nations that practised monetary policy through capital controls typically do not have any, or least not well-developed, money and bond markets. Removing these controls leaves authorities with no means to control monetary growth through open-market operations. Eventually liberalisation leads to the development of government securities markets and monetary control is restored. The transition period, however, may prove to be quite unstable, providing one explanation of why many nations experience a financial crisis following liberalisation.

The Role of Foreign Capital in Recent Crises

Before moving on to consider the appropriateness of reforms, it is important to first consider the role of foreign speculators. At the time of the East Asian crisis, Malaysian Prime Minister Mahathir Mohamad blamed foreign speculators for the financial crisis that engulfed the region, sparking a bitter debate with the likes of George Soros. Did foreign speculators truly cause the financial crisis in their blind pursuit of profit, as some claimed? Or, as argued by other, was it the result of improper macroeconomic and microeconomic policies?

Now that some time has passed since the start of the East Asian crisis, empirical assessments of the crisis are beginning to materialise. Though the evidence so far is rather scant, it supports the notion that foreign speculators *were not* the cause of the crisis. One of the most recent studies, by Choe, Kho, and Stulz (1999), considers the role of foreign investors in the collapse of the Korean stock market in 1997. The authors show that the market adjusted quickly to sales by foreign investors and that negative abnormal returns were not persistent following foreign sales. The authors provide evidence of herding behaviour by foreign investors but convincingly argue that such behaviour need not be destabilising. Their results show that domestic buying activity dominated foreign selling activity in the last three months of 1997. Hence, there is no evidence that foreign speculators were a destabilising force. Regarding Thailand, Lauridsen (1999) concludes that private sector intermediaries mishandled short-term capitals flows leading to a misallocation of capital. Though, in the author's opinion, this is the main cause of the crises, it was accompanied by political instability and mismanagement. Jomo (1999) concludes that the reliance on short-term financing, speculation against the currency-basket peg, and injudicious policy responses led to the collapse of the Malaysian ringgit. The "Tequila Crises" of 1994-1995 is examined in a special volume of the *Journal of Banking and Finance*, edited by Calomiris (1999). Though the review of the literature on this episode shows some disagreement on the role of speculators, what is apparent is that is was problems in macroeconomic and microeconomic fundamentals that made Mexico "vulnerable to the whims of speculators" (p. 1458).

Finally, in a theoretical context, Aghion, Bacchetta, and Banerjee (1999) show that economies at an intermediate level of financial development are more unstable than economies with either fully developed or underdeveloped financial markets. As a result, intermediate economies that undergo financial liberalisation may destabilise their economies. Foreign direct investment, however, is not destabilising. The authors suggest, therefore, that economies with financial markets at an intermediate stage of development should carefully plan and pace financial liberalisation, allowing FDI but restricting portfolio flows. The importance of creating incentives for FDI is addressed by Alan Rugman in a later chapter of this text.

Hence, the literature suggests that the sources of these financial crises lies in the mix of inappropriate macroeconomic policy and inadequate microeconomic reform coupled with capital market liberalisation, as opposed to foreign speculation. Whether one blames speculators, the conduct of microeconomic and macroeconomic policies, or the level of financial development for the financial crises of the 1990s, the previous sections of this chapter demonstrate the overarching importance of a well-developed, high-quality system of financial intermediaries. Financial intermediaries exist to save potential holders of financial instruments from incurring the risks and allowing them to enjoy reduced costs, thereby encouraging financial speculation in the most efficient sectors of the economy. In turn, speculators provide the most promising sectors of the economy with the liquidity needed to develop and expand. While these institutions cannot eliminate adverse selection and moral hazard problems, they can collect information about the underlying riskiness of financial instruments and monitor the continuing performance of those who issue such instruments, thereby reducing the extent of these problems in financial markets.

Preventative Policy: G7 Recommendations

With the benefits and risks of unhindered capital flows considered, what type and to what extent should reform efforts take? Should there be a new international financial architecture, or should reforms be modest? Eichengreen (1999, p. 9) makes a compelling, though blunt, argument against proposals that are too grandiose, claiming that they are impractical and have "not a snowball's chance in hell of being implemented". Given the complex and dynamic nature of the system, one must realise that there is no definitive answer to the questions proposed here. Thus, there will be considerable disagreement on reforms that are complex and broad sweeping. As such, grand proposals are non-starters in the current political environment.

As stated at the outset of this chapter, the objective of policy and reform should be to maximise the benefits while minimising the risks associated with capital market liberalisation. The literature has shown that liberalisation needs to be paced according to the level of financial development the nation finds itself at. Microeconomic policy actions should free trade flows, encourage flexibility and competition, and improve regulation and supervision of the nation's system of intermediaries. The deepening of the market for government debt is essential for controlling the money supply and allowing for direct financing. The ability to finance directly reduces the impact of banking crises on the real sector of the economy and provides for long-run stability.

In evaluating the G7's proposals designed to prevent possible future crises, this section reviews those put forward in the Report of the Finance Ministers to the Köln Economic Summit (see the appendix for the full text of the Report). Beginning in Halifax and continuing in Lyon, the Finance Ministers were requested by the leaders to identify key areas of reform in the international financial system and to report on initiatives prior to the summits.

The Köln Report, therefore, is a document that has been in construction for four years and has evolved along the way. It allows for a comprehensive view of the Finance Ministers' assessment of the state of the international financial system, reforms that have taken place, and proposals to date.[3] The report, however, is not necessarily a set of policy commitments. Rather it is a proposal prepared for the G7 leaders' consideration. Nonetheless, it provides a useful means for evaluating the types and likelihood of reforms to the system.

After reviewing the report, the role of the G7 as a body of global governance in the context of the international financial system is considered. In light of the centrality of the G7, the dominance of the G7 economies in global trade and capital flows, and the fact that the G7 nations were the architects of the current system, a set of responsibilities is put forward. Fulfilment of these responsibilities is critical to the success a well-functioning global financial system.

General Overview of Assessment and Proposals

The report of the Finance Ministers reflects well the work that has taken place since Halifax. The document addresses the key areas of strengthening and reforming international financial institutions (IFIs): enhancing transparency and promoting best practices, strengthening financial regulation in industrial countries, strengthening macroeconomic policies and financial systems in emerging markets, improving crisis prevention and involving the private sector, and promoting social policies. At 28 pages in length it is indeed comprehensive in its assessment and long in recommendations. The report reads as a text on various reforms implemented, recommended, and proposed for further study. It does an excellent job of framing the current situation in the most general sense. The overall quality of the document reflects the efficient workings of the G7 Finance Ministers' meetings and the competence of the current ministers and their staffs.

The report makes it clear that no new international organisations are needed (a point which is emphasised again below). The theme of the report is that for international financial markets to work properly, enhanced transparency and disclosure as well as improved regulation and supervision are necessary. Involvement of the private sector in crisis management and prevention, as well as requiring the private sector to bear responsibility for risk assumed, is also emphasised.

Some of the key recommendations are that the IMF and World Bank need not only co-operate, but need also to forge a clear division of responsibilities between the two. Improved and increased transparency and accountability of these institutions and other IFIs is pressed. Involvement of developing and emerging nations is limited to the New Arrangements to Borrow (NAB), the Interim Committee of the IMF, and the new Financial Stability Forum.[4] A number of other proposals are made for reforming and improving the existing IFIs. We leave these to the experts in policy architecture to gauge their merit.

The Ministers' report opens by stating that a "well-functioning international financial system is essential to allow an efficient allocation of global savings and investment, and provide the conditions needed to improve world-wide growth and living standards in all countries". In the process, it is made clear that policy responsibility still rests with national authorities and what is envisioned is international co-operation rather than international regulation. International institutions, particularly the IMF and the World Bank, are asked to improve performance in core responsibilities, increase transparency, clearly delineate responsibilities, and co-operate rather than increase their scope of regulatory and supervisory activities.

Risk Management

Much attention is given to risk assessment, a challenging task in today's environment of sophisticated financial engineering. Banks and other financial intermediaries are the focus of reform, given the important role they play in filling information gaps and allocating capital. The reforms of the Basel Committee are held as the standard that all countries should consider for domestic implementation. Unfortunately, the revisions have come under fire for not doing enough and not being particularly useful to developing country systems. Developing nations have argued that they would be at the mercy of rating agencies, and though the new standards might tighten controls over banks in developed nations, may very well hurt banks in their nations (Diaz, 2000). Clearly the emphasis is minimising market imperfections and improving supervision of financial institution activity rather than regulating it.

Capital controls are suggested for developing nations only as a transitory tool while the financial sector develops and supervisory abilities improve. The purpose is to limit unhedged short-term borrowing of developing country banks. Though not a first-choice policy instrument, the views of the finance ministers are consistent with the literature suggesting that financial development is a necessary condition for stability and foreign direct investment (FDI) is preferred to short-term capital flows, as FDI is not destabilising. Eichengreen (1999) argues that such taxes are indeed warranted in certain cases, but that they are a third-choice, where improvements in risk management and regulatory abilities are the first and second choices. The problem with capital controls is that they reduce the pressures on policy makers to implement the first and second choices. Further, as the report states, they have not been a very effective instrument in most cases.

Private Sector Bail-In and Involvement

Private sector bail-in, that is having private sector investors assume responsibility for risk undertaken, is not only a critical component of crisis management but also crisis prevention, as clear terms for bail-in would reduce moral hazard. By forcing private sector participants to bear the financial consequences of their investment decisions through changes in debt financing and the reduction of domestic and international safety nets, *ex ante* expectations are changed and, it is assumed, a more conservative approach to risk will be adopted.

The report outlines a framework that recommends linking official support to the country's programme of meeting its debt obligations, balancing classes of debt holders if the debt is to be restructured, establishing a reserve floor for private sector contributions in relation to official contributions and allowing lending into arrears and the use of payment suspensions and capital controls in "exceptional" cases. The report further states that no category of private creditors (bondholders) should be viewed as senior to any other group (banks). It concludes, however, with an acknowledgement that the general approach will remain to be applied on a case-by-case basis. This reflects the disagreement that exists between, primarily, the Americans and other G7 members on how to bail in private bondholders. Because bonds do not typically contain collective action clauses, rescheduling of this type of debt is difficult, if possible at all. This has led to a mistaken belief that bondholder rights are held higher than those of other debt holders (*The Economist*, 1999). The problem with these types of provisions, as well as standstill arrangements and exchange controls, is that they may reduce the quality of the debt instrument. Because of this, some have argued that they may actually create an unstable environment that is conducive to a financial crisis.

Co-ordination of Reform

Private sector involvement in crises prevention is also called for. Little detail is forthcoming on how to accomplish this, however. Eichengreen (1999, p. 7) points out the obstacles to IMF-led standard setting and the need to rely on private sector expertise as the "only practical way of promulgating effective standards in the relevant areas". The number and variety of agencies involved in financial architecture reform is quite expansive. In an attempt to categorise the various bodies, the agencies and organisations mentioned *explicitly* in the report are grouped according to their affiliation with international organisations, private sector organisations, and the G7.

Those directly affiliated with the G7, or created by the G7, are the; Financial Action Task Force, created by the G7 at the 1989 Paris Summit and includes 26 member countries; G7 Financial Experts Group on Supervision and Regulation in the Financial Sector; and the G7 Working Group on Financial Crime. International organisations and affiliate bodies are; the World Bank; the IMF; the New Arrangements to Borrow (NAB); the Interim Committee or International Financial Monetary Committee; the IMF / World Bank Development Committee; the Financial Sector Liaison Committee (FSLC); the IMF-World Bank Financial Sector Assessment Programme (FSAP); the United Nations (UN), and the Organisation for Economic Co-operation and Development (OECD). Private sector-based bodies and affiliates are; the BIS; the Paris Club; the BIS Committee on the Global Financial System (CGFS); the Financial Stability Forum chaired by Andrew Crockett, General Manager of the BIS and supported by a small secretariat at the BIS; the Counter-party Risk Management Group; the International Organisation of Securities Commissions (IOSCO); the International Accounting Standards Committee (IASC); the International Association of Insurance Supervisors (IAIS); the Joint Forum on Financial Conglomerates (Basel Committee, IOSCO, and IAIS); and the Core Principles Methodology Working Group (Basel Committee, IOSCO, and IAIS).

Far from being an exhaustive list, the above is merely a subset of the bodies involved in reforming the financial architecture. It does illustrate, however, the Finance Ministers' point that no new international body is needed. Rather what is essential for success is overall management of the process that is already in motion.

Exchange Rate Management: A Special Problem

As discussed earlier, the appropriate approach to exchange rate management is a perplexing problem and continues to be an area of practical disagreement. Many emerging nations choose to peg the value of their currency relative to a vehicle currency because of their dependence on dollar-priced basic commodities, to gain credibility and convertibility, to reduce transaction costs, thereby promoting trade and investment, and as a means of fighting inflation. There are, however, two practical problems with rigid exchange rate regimes.[5] The first is that they require adopting nations to subjugate monetary policy to exchange rate management rather than domestic objectives. Many nations resist this by sterilising exchange rate interventions, a practice that cannot be sustained. Hence, in the long run the conduct of macroeconomic policy is often inconsistent with the exchange rate regime. The second is that it encourages unhedged borrowing, as discussed earlier.

The finance ministers' position is that the exchange rate regime must be backed by consistent macroeconomic polices. Further, they judge that the international community should not provide official financing to countries that peg their exchange rate unless the exchange value is sustainable and "certain conditions" are met. The report is not firm on this issue and no alternative regimes are offered developing countries. Experience shows that basket-pegs and single-currency-pegs will continue to be a popular choice among developing country policymakers. They are, however, difficult to sustain when the G7 nations do not co-ordinate on their own exchange values. What this means for developing countries that choose to peg to one or more of these currencies is that, eventually, a revaluation or devaluation must be made. If macroeconomic policy or microeconomic reform were wanting in the interim, or if the adjustment to parity were postponed too long, markets are likely to make these nations pay harshly for their shortcomings. This was the case for East Asian countries such as Thailand, Malaysia, and Indonesia, which pegged or managed their currencies against a basket that attached a large weight to the US dollar.

Emerging G7 Responsibilities

Fischer (1999) points out that the reform of the international financial architecture really means microeconomic and macroeconomic corrections undertaken by the developing nations - the recipients of capital flows - the developed nations - the originators of capital flows - and IFIs. Clearly the points of emphasis in the G7 report, banking reform and increased transparency for example, are required by all participants of the system, but are primarily directed at the recipient nations. What is the role of the G7 as an institution with global leadership responsibilities?

The G7 nations are in a unique position in regard to the new financial architecture. They are the architects of the current system, as detailed by Nicholas Bayne in Chapter 2. They also dominate global markets in terms of trade and capital flows, and are the issuers of the world's vehicle currencies. They have, therefore, special responsibilities for its reform. Based on the points put forward in this chapter, the following 7 roles for the G7 are suggested.

1. Actively Serve as the New Financial Architecture's General Contractor

The G7 should co-ordinate and set agendas, establish time lines for results, and make recommendations for research. As an institution, the G7 does not have any "turf" issues with other organisations, it is not an agent of any organisation (other than the leaders themselves), and can exercise considerable control over many institutions such as the IMF. Being at the centre of the process, the G7 Ministers must take responsibility for co-ordinating the process, serve as the driving force for implementation, and act as the leading advocates of the benefits of capital market liberalisation.

2. Co-ordinate and/or Co-operate among Themselves

The G7 must actively co-operate, and when practically feasible, co-ordinate microeconomic and macroeconomic polices. Co-operation is needed on microeconomic policies, such as financial market regulations and taxes so as not to create distortions that lead to an inefficient flow of capital. Co-ordination on debt-holder clauses is needed since no country will unilaterally adopt such clauses and run the risk of lowering the quality of their debt. Macroeconomic co-operation is need to maintain a environment conducive to stable capital flows, including exchange rate stability and the avoidance of unsustainable external deficits.

3. Encourage Competition

The G7 must encourage competition, particularly multilateral trade liberalisation and the Multilateral Agreement on Investment (MAI). As discussed earlier, trade liberalisation is a precursor to financial liberalisation. Without it, distortions exist that result in the inefficient distribution of capital with bubbles resulting in particular sectors of the economy. Competition is also required in the banking sectors of both developed and developing nations to ensure a healthy system of intermediaries.

4. *Encourage and Allow for Broader Participation*

The G7 should, and will, remain an exclusive club. It should allow, however and whenever appropriate, broader participation. Inclusion of the developing and emerging nations will enhance the credibility of reforms that are forthcoming from the process and give these nations some "ownership" of the process. These two aspects are certainly needed to summon the political will for change, given the current backlash that exists against integration, and the political will to endure in the midst of a crisis.

5. *Continue Work on Standards*

Because of the dynamic nature of financial markets, financial engineering, and the activities of multinational enterprises, appropriate standards and best practices are not static. The G7 is the body that must see that work on transparency, corporate governance, and risk management standards continues, even though stability may temporarily return.

6. *Provide Incentives*

Many of the reform measures mentioned above require major change and unilateral adoption by developing nations. The G7 must encourage their adoption by providing incentives and rewards for those countries that conform and maintain compliance. The Council on Foreign Relations (1999, p. 172) refers to this as "Rewards for joining the Good Housekeeping Club". These incentives would include conditioning lending terms with performance and reducing regulatory capital requirements for banks. The G7 must also avoid generating market distortions through its own regulatory actions, such as the standards for capital requirements are alleged to have done.

7. Do Not Over-Advertise

The G7 must avoid overstating, or allowing to be overstated, the benefits of modest reform measures such as improved transparency and surveillance. Financial crises will occasionally occur; that is the nature of the beast. Overstating the effects reduces the credibility of reform efforts in the eyes of the most shrewd market participants whilst understating the existing market risk to those participants less savvy.

The international financial architecture is a public good and, therefore, its reform affects many nations outside of the G7. Given the centrality of the G7 in global governance, however, the G7 finds itself in a unique position of responsibility. The seven responsibilities outlined above constitute an important role for the G7 Ministers. Meeting these obligations is critical for a credible and balanced approach to strengthening the international financial architecture.

Conclusion

Capital market liberalisation offers developing nations the capital necessary for growth and increased standards of living. Increasing capital mobility is the means for more efficient capital allocation and world-wide economic gains that result. These benefits, however, are accompanied by risks that pervade financial markets. The appropriate approach to reform of the international financial architecture is one that seeks to maximise the benefits while minimising the risks.

The Report of the Finance Ministers to the Köln Economic Summit is a living document that reflects the efforts of the G7 and various international and domestic organisations reform efforts since the Halifax Summit in 1995. The recommendations contained in the report are conservative in nature and, in cases where differences in opinion remain, maintain a market-oriented approach. As such, few details are given, making implementation in many areas more difficult. Further, as reflected in the report, a vast number of organisations, agencies, and committees are involved in the process and overall co-ordination presents a daunting task. Nonetheless, appropriate private sector expertise is included in forming accounting and auditing standards, and standards for supervision, regulation, transparency, private sector involvement, and risk management are the core elements needed for effective reform. The most important challenge that the G7 now faces is to co-ordinate the process and, as stated in the report, "to encourage implementation". The endurance of the G7 in this regard will ultimately determine the success or failure of reform.

Notes

1 See Jeffrey A. Frankel (1999) for an excellent and intuitive discussion on this issue.
2 See Daniels, Toumanoff, and von der Ruhr (1999) for a discussion of the currency-basket-peg arrangements and estimates of their currency weights for these nations.
3 The reliability of communiques as a public record of policy intentions is now well established in the literature, e.g., von Furstenberg and Daniels, 1992.
4 Hence, we concur with Duncan Wood's position in Chapter 4 that much more needs to be done to include the likely candidates of the next significant crisis, the large developing nations experiencing financial liberalisation and financial development.
5 In addition to the two papers on this subject that appear in this text, see Eichengreen *et al.* (1999) for an analysis of the problem of transition from one regime to another.

References

Aghion, Philippe, Philippe Bacchetta and Abhijit Banerjee (March 1999), "Capital Markets and the Instability of Open Economies", *Centre for Economic Policy Research, Discussion Paper No. 2083.*

Calomiris, Charles (1999), special issue editor, "Lessons from the Tequila Crisis for Successful Financial Liberalization", *Journal of Banking and Finance*, vol. 23, pp. 1457-1461.

Choe, Hyuk, Bong-Chan Kho, and René Stulz (1999), "Do Foreign Investors Destabilize Stock Markets? The Korean Experience in **1997"**, *Journal of Financial Economics*, vol. 54, pp. 227-264.

Cooper, Richard (1999), "A Tour of International Financial Reform: Interview with Richard Cooper", *Challenge*, pp. 5-28.

Council on Foreign Relations Task Force (1999), "The Future of the International Financial Architecture", *Foreign Affairs*, 78(6), pp. 169-184.

Crockett, Andrew (1997), "Why is Financial Stability a Goal of Public Policy?", in *Maintaining Financial Stability in a Global Economy: A Symposium Sponsored by the Federal Reserve Bank of Kansas City*, Jackson Hole, WY: Federal Reserve Bank of Kansas City, pp. 7-36.

Daniels, Joseph, Peter Toumanoff and Marc von der Ruhr (1999), "Optimal Basket Pegs for Developing and Emerging Economies", Working Paper, Marquette University.

Daniels, Joseph and David VanHoose (1999), *International Monetary and Financial Economics*, SouthWestern Publishing, Cincinnati.

Diaz, Miguel (2000), "Bringing Up Basel", *Latin Finance*, No. 113, pp. 44-46.

Eatwell, John and Lance Taylor (1998), "International Capital Markets and the Future of Economic Policy", CEPA Working Paper No. 9, Center for Economic Policy Analysis at www.newschool.edu/cepa.

The Economist (October 2, 1999), "Bail in, Bail Out", p. 19.

The Economist (October 17, 1998), "Turmoil in Financial Markets: The Risk Business", p. 21.

Eichengreen, Barry, Michael Mussa, Giovanni Dell' Ariccia, enrica Detragiache, Gian Maria Milesi-Ferretti and Andrew Tweedie (1999). "Liberalizing Capital Movements: Some Analytical Issues", *International Monetary Fund Economic Issues, 17.*

Eichengreen, Barry (1999). *Toward a New International Financial Architecture: A Practical Post-Asian Agenda*, Institute for International Economics, Washington DC.

Eichengreen, Barry, Paul Masson, Miguel Savastano and Sunil Sharma (1999), "Transition Strategies and Nominal Anchors on the Road to Greater Exchange-Rate Flexibility", *Princeton Essays in International Finance, No. 213.*

Fischer, Stanley (1999), "Reforming the International Financial System", *The Economic Journal,* 109(459), pp. F557-F576.

Frankel, Jeffrey A. (1999), "No Single Currency is Right for All Countries or At All Times", *Essays in International Finance*, No. 215.

James, Harold (1999). "Is Liberalization Reversible?", International Monetary Fund, *Finance and Development*, 36(4), pp. 11-14.

Jomo, K.S. (1999), "Financial Liberalization, Crises, and Malaysian Policy Responses", *World Development*, 26(8), pp.1563-1574.

Lauridsen, Laurids (1999), "The Financial Crisis in Thailand: Causes, Conduct and Consequences?", *World Development*, 26(8), pp. 1575-1591.

Lindgren, C., Gillian, G., and Saal, M. (1996), *Bank Soundness and Macroeconomic Policy*, International Monetary Fund, Washington DC.

Obstfeld, M. (1998), "The Global Capital Market: Benefactor or Menace?" *Journal of Economic Perspectives,* 12(4), pp. 9-30.

Pagano, Marco (1993), "Financial Markets and Growth: An Overview", *European Economic Review,* vol. 37, pp. 613-622.

von Furstenberg, George M. and Joseph P. Daniels (1992), "Economic Summit Declarations, 1975-1989: Examining the Written Record of International Cooperation", *Princeton Studies in International Finance, No. 72.*

Williamson, John and Molly Mahar (1998), "A Survey of Financial Liberalization", *Essays in International Finance, No. 211.*

8 The New Financial Architecture for the Global Economy

NORBERT WALTER

Introduction

The current debate about the new international financial architecture arose as a consequence of the most recent global crisis. This event, running from 1997 to 1999, included both the initial Asian crisis and the emerging market crisis that followed. By the second half of 1999, as the financial markets in those parts of the world calmed, the debate about the new financial architecture subsided as well. Yet this calm can be deceptive. It implies that there will be another financial crisis. Moreover, in addressing it, the international community will be as unprepared as ever.

At present, all consequential policymakers and informed observers agree that the international community should not only improve crisis resolution, but also much more importantly, act in the area of crisis prevention. Here the most important call, repeated time and time again, is for "surveillance". The world is indeed improving its performance at surveillance. But little of substance has genuinely changed. All repeat the old slogans, such as: "It is always necessary to start with the responsibility of each country for maintaining a stable economic policy". At the same time, many of these fashionable phrases do not as yet offer real solutions to the challenges the international financial community faces.

More importantly, the most fundamental issues about the improvement of the international financial architecture are not being discussed with any seriousness. The first and most important factor to improve the international financial architecture is to allow bankruptcy to take place in the financial sector. The second factor, in order to create prudent banking, is to prevent governments from supporting more capitalisation and from providing subsidies to poorly operated banks.

Transparency

All currently agree that greater transparency is required in the world's financial system. Yet, when one asks for more concrete suggestions on what greater degree and form of transparency is required, a much more difficult situation arises.

The only standards that all know internationally and that are thus completely transparent are those of the United States. But the continental Europeans do not prefer them. At the same time, the world outside the US has no alternative but to agree with what the US Federal Reserve or regulatory authorities in the United States and the institutions in the US private sector are doing. This is obviously not the solution for the long term. However, in the short term, it is equally obvious nothing else can be done.

Transparency necessitates accepting and employing certain statistics to serve as a well-understood referent. Germany has had the International Monetary Fund (IMF) ask it to meet IMF standards. Even very well-known countries do not meet the IMF standards. Moreover, there is no real sanction on these countries if they do not meet the standard. This is true for advanced G7 countries such as Germany, as well as for those some refer to as "banana republics".[1]

The Financial Stability Forum

A very important institutional improvement came with the establishment of the Financial Stability Forum (FSF). Created by the German Central Bank President Hans Tietmeyer, the new body was accepted by the G7 in early 1999 as an informal forum to improve transparency and supervision. It is a council to co-ordinate a number of institutional actors; the Finance Ministers, the central bank presidents, the supervisory authorities of the G7 states, and international supervisory authorities such as the Bank for International Settlements (BIS). The major intergovernmental institutions; the World Bank, the IMF, and the Organisation for Economic Co-operation and Development (OECD), are represented as well.

This forum has certainly set the agenda for transparency and supervision. It has made it very clear that it is not just the task of government authorities to improve the situation. Rather, it is the responsibility of the private sector itself.

However, in the area of private sector burden sharing, matters have not advanced a great deal beyond these initial understandings. First, what is being proposed is that crisis prevention should be enhanced by a permanent dialogue between debtors and creditors. Those in financial markets in the private sector have learned that it is very helpful for mutual understanding if the investors have permanent contact, including permanent background information, from the issuers of equity. For that particular purpose, the private sector has analysts, who are the intermediaries between the two sides. These analysts aggressively question, on an ongoing basis, those who issue equity, to the benefit of both sides. Issuers are "grilled", and they must thus provide information. Those who wish to invest have better knowledge about the quality of the issues they are investing in.

It is now suggested that the same knowledge be provided in the relationship among sovereign authorities. They should indeed also be involved in a permanent grilling process. In such a situation, if one country's authorities are grilled, this does not provide an indication that something is wrong. It is, rather, merely a routine event. In contrast, at present, if one learns that some individuals are travelling to Brazil, for example, to ask questions about its financial system, it is very obvious to outsiders that one should "sell Brazil". Otherwise, one will be too late to exit that market without a major loss. Thus, in order to avoid that preemptive rush to the exits, there should be an ongoing permanent dialogue between creditors and debtors.

Who should be entitled to participate in this process? One cannot invite the entire world to participate, because the process would then become unmanageable. Yet if everyone is not included, there is a problem of insider information - some parties inside know what will happen, while others on the outside do not. Thus, it is important to ensure that there are intermediaries in this process, and that all the information gathered by these intermediaries is made public immediately.

However, whereas the concept is clear, it is not easy to implement it without arousing the doubts of all parties involved. At the technical level, it is not desirable to add 150 or 180 representatives at the table of the FSF in order to improve the financial architecture. In a technical way, the professionals should perform that job. Therefore, the number of experts at the table should be smaller rather than larger in order to produce a solution at an early stage.

Equity Ratios for Financial Institutions

More recently, a very important component of the new international financial architecture has been introduced into the debate. This is the call for the reconsideration of appropriate equity ratios for financial institutions. The BIS has introduced proposals for discussion, rather than presenting proposals that are close to final agreement. It is clear from these proposals that those involved in the process are not close to arriving at a conclusion. Yet it is obvious that the old equity ratios have not solved the current problem. Indeed, they have in part caused the problem. Therefore, there must be an adjustment. Over the last several years, several advisory authorities have seemed inclined to accept the private financial sector's own risk models as a reasonable basis for equity ratios. This now seems to be put into question.

But, again, how does one generate more flexible, more specialised, more individualised capital equity ratios? When discussing the issue along those lines, it becomes obvious that a considerable part of the problem stems from the fact that national financial institutions are by no means homogeneous. The current tendency is to treat such institutions as one. In fact, there is a much more complicated landscape. French banks, German banks, and English banks are a completely different breed one from one another. Their balance sheets look very different. Therefore, it seems rather arbitrary for a homogeneous standard to be applied to all of them. That is an issue that is now being examined. Here, the financial community again is in the early stages of a discussion rather than coming close to a conclusion. If solutions are found that consider the different kinds of banks, this does not mean that a fair treatment between banks on the one hand and non-banks on the other is assured. If they are forced to apply strict equity ratios, they have a competitive advantage.

Supervision

When considering supervisory authorities and their particular role, can one leave all supervisory functions to markets, or is supervisory authority needed? And if an authority is needed, which authorities should be used or created, and what rules should they oversee and apply? One cannot leave all tasks to the markets. Supervisory authority is required. Yet if one overburdens supervisory authorities, one is creating expectations that cannot be fulfilled.

The current structure of supervisory authority at the national and at the international level is very insufficient. Not even the United States would argue that the present structure is very effective. The U S has developed many creative derivatives markets, with a resulting inappropriateness of supervisory authority. Here the banks, the insurance companies, and the security houses and capital markets do not fit anymore into the segregated supervisory system, because derivatives have blurred the demarcation lines between the different financial institutions. Who is then regulating certain derivatives market? In many cases, derivatives were not allowed because it was impossible to identify the institutions truly responsible for the product. What then happened was predictable. In an international world, this product evaded the country where permission was not be granted. The result was an even less well-regulated system because the most modern instruments developed in jurisdictions where supervisory authorities were insufficient in general. That phenomenon is understood by the US Congress. It has plans to produce a much more comprehensive supervisory regulatory authority for financial institutions generally. But it will take a long time before a solution comes.

The G7 process is available to manage this challenge. Yet the G7 has now become "Snow White and the Seven Dwarfs". Moreover, the Europeans believe they can improve the G7 process by adding more "dwarfs" to the numbers, rather than by trying themselves to compete with the United States as a Snow White. The Europeans insist that more dwarfs be added because they want various councils from the European level to be added to the G7, rather than coming together as Europeans to speak with one voice within it. This latter route would mean an alternative Snow White would be added to the Snow White of the US Any reasonable international supervisory authority can only function if the only remaining superpower, the US, finally has a junior power to discuss issues with. Europe at this juncture is not functioning in this way. Thus prospects for an effective supervisory authority are anything but good.

Additional difficulties exist. The Europeans now have a common central bank. However this central bank does not even know what takes place in the financial markets of its territory. Certainly, it will know at a later stage. It is currently receiving its information mainly from the national central banks. Yet at present, in many of the countries such as Germany, even national central banks are not now the single supervisory authority for financial institutions. Having such a segmented supervisory landscape as currently exists in Europe is probably not the best arrangement for the future.

Additional Issues: Russia and Trade

Shaping the new international financial architecture requires confronting additional financial issues, such as Contingent Credit Lines (CCLs), and recent proposals for revised exchange rate regimes. Yet it further involves arriving at the proper approach to current challenges outside, but closely related to, the finance domain.

One such challenge is Russia. It is a special case. It should not be termed an "emerging market" nor a "developing country". It is a country that has more engineers and more raw material than any other member of the G7. Financial markets may believe that it is probable that at some point in the future Russia will be able to take care of itself and to bring some form of order into existence. Thus, the deferrals of its debt that have taken place mean that it will be able to pay something back to its creditors in the future. In contrast, if one were to force conditions on Russia immediately, in order to be safe, one would be left with empty nets.

There is a second incentive for private financial institutions to continue giving Russia the benefit of the doubt. That is their belief because, being asked by governments to lend to Russia in the 1980s, they would be rescued by those same governments in the 1990s. This is a poor basis on which to lend. There are no real hopes of a Russian recovery and repayment within the next ten years.

Rising oil prices will not provide a solution to Russia and its creditors. The quoted market oil prices and gas prices are not always the same as contract prices. The lack of revenues for the Russians, particularly in long-term contracts, will continue. Moreover, it cannot be assumed that the 1999 rise in oil prices will be the beginning of an increase of the real price of oil, because supply is very elastic in the medium term. Saudi Arabia, in particular, is not interested in having an oil price above US$20 in value, because it will then be confronted with American displeasure and a considerable increase in new oil supplies outside the OPEC cartel in the future.

Thus, anything well above US$20 a barrel for oil is not considered to be a sustainable price. The oil price is certainly a relevant factor for Russia's debt service capacities. Yet Russian solvency is based more on the nonexistence or nonfunctioning of the institutions in Russia, particularly those for establishing democracy and economic order. These are much more important than the revenue situation in a given year.

A second outstanding issue concerns the international trade system. It is important to move rapidly to launch a new round of multilateral trade liberalisation. It is tragic to have delayed the process due to an impasse over who should be selected as the new Director General of the World Trade Organization (WTO). The candidate from New Zealand, former Prime Minister Mike Moore, is very a talented and qualified person for the post. Yet, the equally qualified candidate from Thailand, Supachai Panitchpakdi, should have been selected as the head of this institution. His selection would have sent a very clear signal from the developed world that the WTO is indeed sensitive to developing countries' concerns. If the developed world continues to discuss a new international financial architecture at a time when the G7 does not allow trade to take place in a fair way, it does not make much sense to entertain any technical discussion about the improvement of the financial architecture.

Conclusion: The Need for a Bankruptcy Mechanism

In conclusion, the most important issues regarding the improvement of the international financial architecture are not now being discussed in a serious way. The first and most important factor is to allow bankruptcy to take place in the financial sector. This process should not be limited, as at present, to British institutions. It should also be allowed on the European continent and in other parts of the world. Moreover, institutions in the G7 countries must stand in the way of excessive recapitalisation. Such capitalisations do not help the consumer. They merely increase the problem of financial institutions becoming "too big to fail" through national mergers and acquisitions. The relevant cases in Europe are in Switzerland and France, and probably the Netherlands. Being "too big to fail" has become an important issue. More individual failures should be allowed to take place.

An additional problem is the existence of nontariff trade barriers for the financial sector generally. One such barrier is the *landesbanken* system. Another is the practice of co-determination. As a result, the German financial sector cannot be attacked from anywhere. The French market also has nontariff trade barriers. To create prudent banking, both bankruptcy and a government refusal to support more capitalisation of ailing institutions, plus an opening of "protected" financial institutions, are required.

Note

1 The term "banana republic" was used in reference to Germany when a German Bank management board member said that until 1995, Germany was a "banana republic", because private households spent more money on bananas than on shares. Only with the help of the privatization of Deutsche Telecom could Germany amend the situation.

References

Eichengreen, B. (1999), *Toward a New International Financial Architecture - A practical Post-Asia Agenda*, Washington DC.

Walter, N. (1999), "Again(st) the IMF", *Bulletins*, Deutsche Bank Research, No. 2, p. 3-4.

Walter, N. (1999), "Prävention statt Krise. Zukunftsentwürfe für eine globale Finanzarchitektur", *Internationale Politik*, 54(12), p. 19-26.

9 The Role of the International Monetary Fund as Lender of Last Resort

CURZIO GIANNINI[1]

Introduction

That we need to strengthen the institutional arrangements to deal more effectively with international financial instability is obvious. Less obvious is to what extent we can replicate internationally tools and practices that are well established at the national level. So the key issue to be confronted is: What kind of lender of last resort can we afford at the international level? Answering this question, it turns out, is no easy task, because of all the aspects of central banking, serving as lender of last resort is by far the most difficult to pin down. For one, the desirability and appropriate contours of the function cannot be identified independently of the monetary policy framework. Suppose bank deposits were not defined in nominal terms, much like mutual fund shares, or that monetary policy could be run in a purely discretionary manner without raising credibility problems. Would a lender of last resort still be needed? Many scholars on the subject would doubt it, to say the least.

But there is more. Providing emergency liquidity amounts to a suspension of market discipline, since it means lending in situations where no other lender in the market will. Hence, the very existence of a lender of last resort raises an enormous moral hazard problem, which can be kept within acceptable limits only by relying on the broader legal and institutional set-up-on regulation in the broadest sense of the word. In short, what the Tao Teh Ching says of the wheel could equally well be said of the lender-of-last-resort function: for all its complexity, what makes it work lies outside of it. Therefore, if we are to understand how a lender of last resort can address financial instability at the national level, as well as whether the notion of an international lender of last resort makes any sense, we must first look beyond the function's boundaries.

Now, at the time that Walter Bagehot, whose *Lombard Street* is still the *locus classicus* in this field, was writing, the monetary framework was pretty rigid, being based on the gold standard and on severe restrictions on the supply of currency, while the main financial centre in the world, the City of London, was run by a handful of financial institutions in a club-like fashion. This helps explain the Bagehot doctrine: when things turn bad, first expel - namely let go broke - the rotten apple from the club, then come to the rescue of the club as a whole by lending freely to all who can supply good collateral and can afford to pay a penalty rate.

The present situation at the national level is very different from the one Bagehot had before his eyes. For instance, in the industrial world, rigid monetary frameworks have been replaced with what may be called illuminated discretion, namely stability-oriented monetary policy under the responsibility of an independent central bank. Moreover, in most financial systems club-like behaviour is at most a vague memory of a distant past, having been swept away by financial liberalisation and heightened competition. As a consequence, the lender-of-last-resort function has also undergone momentous changes. The market-support operations to which Bagehot referred have now become extremely rare. In countries where they are still carried out, such as the United States, they take the form of open-market operations, which by definition cannot embody a penalty rate. By contrast, lender-of-last-resort operations directed at individual institutions - often even to those verging on insolvency - have become much more common. Under these circumstances, constructive ambiguity has become the main check on moral hazard. Since ambiguity means discretion, however, this way of containing moral hazard is subject, like all other forms of discretionary policy making, to a time-consistency problem. Its credibility rests on the availability of resources and high-quality information, as well as on sufficient technical autonomy and effective sanctioning powers. The latter are really key: if self-restraint is out of reach, then the lender of last resort must be in a position to inflict losses upon the management and shareholders of badly run institutions. If it was not, or if it never availed himself of such powers, constructive ambiguity would be just a rhetorical fiction. Total forbearance would be a more apt name.

Limitations on International Organisations

Under the Bretton Woods regime, extensive reliance on capital controls, the fragmentation of the regulatory set-up, and the room for flexibility implicit in the adjustable multilateral peg all conjured to keep the lender-of-last-resort function within national borders. Indeed, there is evidence that the architects of the post-war international monetary order consciously tried to avoid the International Monetary Fund (IMF) taking upon itself such a responsibility. But now, with nearly free capital mobility, an intense competitive climate in the financial system, many emerging countries still relying on exchange-rate pegs or even currency boards to "anchor" their economic policies, the issue of what can be done at the international level in this area has become inescapable. When addressing it, however, one should not forget that the international environment differs from the national one in at least three respects.

First, international organisations typically enjoy a lower degree of technical autonomy than comparable national institutions. National governments, especially the stronger ones, do not wish to surrender the power to handle emergencies - which are by definition situations whose pay-offs and costs are difficult to predict - but prefer to respond in ways they believe will further their national interest. If the IMF has enjoyed considerable autonomy in the first 50 years of its life, it is also thanks to the wisdom of its founders, who appropriately scaled down its tasks and ambitions, leaving in particular the lender-of-last-resort function out of the edifice. Moreover, international organisations deal with agents, i.e., national authorities, which are subject to domestic political constraints and agendas, and which, moreover, are largely responsible for the information on which any "objective" assessment of the need and desirability of emergency liquidity support. In such conditions, it is only rational that any lending be rationed, even in crisis times, and that conditionality should play such an important role in IMF programmes. Finally, and perhaps most importantly, to deter moral hazard on the creditors' side, international organisations can directly count neither on informal club-like norms of behaviour nor, lacking an international bankruptcy regime, on formal sanctioning powers.

Changes at the Margin

Things being so, any grand design to translate on an international plane the lender-of-last-resort function is to be regarded with suspicion. If we are to improve the international set-up for handling crises, we must work at the margins. The good news, however, is that such margins do exist.

A first margin concerns incentives for domestic policymakers in emerging market countries. The challenge here is to meet the demand for an external anchor coming from these countries, whose domestic institutions are insufficiently robust for the task, with as little reliance as possible on exchange rate pegs. What these countries need most is not money, since some enjoy high savings rates and a larger number can, under appropriate circumstances, tap international financial markets if they wish to speed up growth. What they need first of all is credibility. Here, the IMF is already doing its part. Few have noticed, on the one hand, that exchange rate pegs have in recent years become a less and less frequent component of IMF programmes, and, on the other, that while IMF programmes have never been so numerous, if measured by the ratio of countries with a programme to total membership, the actual reliance on IMF resources by countries which do have a programme has never been so low. That is, the IMF is already transforming itself from a lender to countries that have no easy access to world financial markets into that of credibility-enhancing device for those countries that do wish to rely on private foreign finance - in short, into the role of catalyser of other people's money. In the process, fixing the exchange rate is becoming less important and for a very simple reason: the better the credibility services of the IMF, the less the need to rely on highly visible but sometimes problematic tools, such as exchange rate pegs, to discipline domestic policy making.

So, no revolution is really needed in this area. One has only to appreciate more fully the scope and implications of trends that are already underway. The recent decision to establish the Contingent Credit Line (CCL) is a step in the right direction, since it shows that awareness of the need to strengthen the precautionary role of the IMF is increasing (although I share the view that the lack of a general ceiling on individual loans constitutes a serious weakness of the new facility). A further improvement upon current practices would be the explicit adoption within IMF programmes of monetary frameworks based on inflation targeting rather than on rigid exchange rate regimes. The IMF's staff has long resisted this shift of emphasis, fearing, on the one hand, that it would entail losing sight of the "balance of payments need" principle enshrined in the Articles of Agreement and, on the other hand, that it could prove too demanding, from an institutional standpoint, for many emerging market countries. But the notion of balance-of-payments need, as traditionally defined, has long since become obsolete, for the very same reasons that Article VI is now outdated, and there is little we can do about it.

At the same time, though, one must be aware that adopting inflation targeting means much more than setting a low target for the consumer price index. Pervasive institutional changes are needed to make it both effective and credible as a monetary framework. This is why we should not expect the approach to be applicable to all and sundry emerging market countries. But the bigger and more institutionally robust among them seem ready to meet the challenge. In this regard, the experiment underway in Brazil - where, after the recent crisis, inflation targeting has replaced, with the endorsement of the IMF, the crawling peg previously in place - should be followed with great attention. The less rigid the monetary framework becomes in emerging countries, the less we shall hear - provided the authorities' credibility is satisfactorily maintained by other means - of jumbo rescue packages of the kind that has filled the press over the last couple of years. The lender-of-last-resort function, as a consequence, will return once more to the wings, where it arguably belongs.

A second marginal improvement would be making creditors more sensitive to the risks they take. This is the area where confusion looms largest. In recent years, a big fuss has been made about "involving the private sector", "achieving a more equitable burden sharing", and the like. But reality is much simpler. Because of the characteristics of the international environment, rescue packages orchestrated to stem capital outflows tend to overprotect creditors. This would be no problem, if debtors could be made to pay the right premium for the insurance they get against the risk of a foreign exchange crisis and if this premium were fully factored into domestic policymakers' calculations. Unfortunately, things do not work out that way. Since institutions in developing countries are frequently less than robust, domestic policymaking often tends to be myopic. Moreover, when a crisis erupts, the international community has a vested interest in avoiding social unrest, because states, like big financial intermediaries, often have a going-concern value that is positive even when their "market" value is nil. Moral hazard, therefore, cannot effectively be checked acting on debtors alone. Hence, the lack of grip on international creditors amounts to a significant hole in the net; until this hole is filled, the whole international architecture will rest on shaky foundations.

Here, too, we do not start from scratch. Informal ways to deal with the problem have already been experimented in the course of the Asian crisis, especially in Korea. At the same time, without much publicity, over the years the IMF has developed an important tool, in the form of lending into arrears, to encourage recalcitrant creditors to negotiate debt restructuring. But moral suasion of the kind seen in Asia cannot be expected to work under all possible circumstances, as Brazil has in the meantime reminded us. As to lending into arrears, it has so far been relied upon only under rather favourable conditions, namely where bank lending accounted for the bulk of a country's foreign exposure. Clearly, more needs to be done in this area.

Conclusion

As experience with lenders of last resort in particular countries has shown, what is needed is a blend of carrot and stick - that is, of incentives and coercion. In this context, providing a carrot essentially means including among the conditions for granting access to IMF resources the existence of CCLs with the private sector of the type presently in place in Argentina and Mexico, as well as adherence to internationally agreed transparency and supervisory standards. By itself, however, this is not going to solve the problem, since foreign investors may hedge their exposure in crisis time, leaving the overall finance made available to debtor countries unaffected. Nor can good supervision *per se* entirely eliminate the risk of instability. Here is where the stick comes in. Investors must be confronted with a credible threat that they will be made to pay for their allocative choices in foreign markets. Since a coherent international bankruptcy regime is out of the question for the foreseeable future, in principle this can be done in either of two ways. It could be done *ex ante*, through improved regulation and supervision worldwide, so as to foster better risk assessment on the part of lenders. Or it could be done *ex post*, by expanding lending into arrears and the reach of Article VIII of the IMF's Articles of Agreement so as to make it more palatable for governments in emerging market countries (and less damaging to the IMF) to declare a moratorium on foreign debt, and possibly proceed to negotiated restructuring.

Both options have found their way into the authorities' agenda. With the establishment of the Forum on Financial Stability (FSF), however, the international community sent the market a strong signal that the regulatory option will be given top priority in the overall strategy. Concern that making moratoria easier to declare would push the balance of power too much in the direction of debtors - and possibly that it would also give too much leeway to international organisations - probably played an important part in this decision. But, whatever its motivation, the creation of the FSF is a far-reaching move. Internalising through regulation the consequences of a bad allocation of capital worldwide entails extending the reach of regulatory authorities to emerging market countries' banking systems, to all nonbank financial institutions, and to offshore financial centres. Ultimately, this means reducing the degree of competition in financial markets - the more so if creditors are to be "involved" in crisis management. It also means co-ordinating safety-net practices across countries, to avoid competitive distortions.

This is a daunting task, indeed. Will the world authorities live up to the standard they have set themselves? Let us hope they will, for historical experience shows that financial instability, if protracted and unchecked, tends to nurture protectionist pressures and inward-looking policies, neither of which are wealth creating in the long run. In the meantime, the IMF would be well advised to refine its role of provider of credibility services further, to insist on the need for smoother work-out procedures, and to avoid thinking of itself as a world central bank *in fieri*, since - as the experience of the last few years has shown - the world is definitely not yet ready to move in that direction.

Note

1 The views expressed here are entirely those of the author and should not be considered the views of the Banca d'Italia, nor the International Monetary Fund, where initial research for the topic was conducted.

Reference

Bagehot, Walter (1910), *Lombard Street,* Smith, Elder, London.

PART III
THE BROADER ISSUES

10 Practising Exchange Rate Flexibility

OLIVIER DAVANNE AND PIERRE JACQUET[1]

In the wake of the severe currency crises that have hit the world economy since the early 1990s, the debate between exchange rate "floaters" and "fixers" has, at least temporarily, narrowed down to a few options. Problems in emerging markets have clearly exposed the costs of excessive exchange rate rigidity. Similarly, in industrial countries, the experience with the European monetary system has lead to the obvious conclusion, in line with "Mundell's trilemma", that fixed but adjustable exchange rate systems could not be viable without effective capital controls. Over the last few years, then, a general consensus has emerged on how to manage the international monetary system. Specifically, countries are seen to face a limited menu of exchange rate policy options:

- Most large countries, including the most advanced emerging countries, are to embrace floating, with occasional *ad hoc* interventions, whether co-ordinated or not;
- Fixed exchange rate regimes should be ruled out, unless they take the extreme form of currency boards or full monetary union (which includes "dollarisation", that is, adopting a foreign currency as the only legal tender, and the type of multilateral, co-operative monetary union put in place by the European Union);
- Fixed but adjustable exchange rates may remain an option for poorer, less developed countries, under the condition that they be backed by capital controls.

This chapter reviews these options and argues that, although it marks indisputable progress as compared to earlier practices, the above menu is incomplete, unnecessarily restrictive, and can and should be substantially improved. The consensus rightly prescribes exchange rate flexibility but does not address the central question of how to practice it. This chapter explores why and how the Group of Three (G3) countries and emerging markets should monitor and manage exchange rate flexibility. The following section discusses the *raison d'être* of the consensus and reviews its main options. Sections 2 and 3 respectively explore ways to manage exchange rate flexibility usefully through a system of adjustable reference parities in emerging markets and through a mechanism of exchange rate monitoring in countries with a floating currency, especially in the G3. Section 4 discusses institutional implications and the role of the G7 and of the International Monetary Fund as far as the surveillance of markets and economic policies are concerned. A final section summarises the conclusions and recommendations.

The Consensus, Revisited

Recent experience has remarkably vindicated the inconsistency triangle originally exposed by Mundell (1968) among free capital mobility, fixed exchange rates, and national monetary policy autonomy. As a result, there has been a clear, consensual move away from fixed exchange rates, and, mostly, toward flexibility. The option of resorting to capital controls to back exchange rate stability does not receive much support. It is largely ruled out for industrial countries, and there is, insofar as emerging markets are concerned, a crucial distinction between controls on capital outflows, which receive little support, and on capital inflows, which seem more appropriate in view of the difficulties in these countries to manage large inflows of capital from abroad and the risk of their reversal. Except in less developed countries, capital controls are not seen in the current consensus as a desirable ingredient of exchange rate regimes.

This section documents the demise of fixed rates, before turning to some issues raised by exchange rate flexibility. It then discusses the alternative route of renouncing monetary sovereignty: while Europe was able to launch the European monetary union (EMU), this is not a likely option for other industrial countries for the time being; but some economists today argue that currency boards are the most attractive option for many developing countries.

The End of Fixed Rates

The crises of the 1990s have highlighted several difficulties with fixed exchange rates, especially when they are rigidly managed. First, the 1992-93 crisis of the exchange rate mechanism of the European Monetary System (EMS) illustrated the role of speculation. As major European countries gradually dismantled remaining capital controls, the EMS became vulnerable to speculative capital flows. As long as the *de facto* alignment of weak currency countries' monetary policies with that of the Bundesbank was deemed to be credible, notably anchored on the prospect of ultimate monetary union, the EMS remained stable. Indeed, it exhibited remarkable stability between 1987 and 1992. The Danish "no" to the referendum about monetary union membership in the spring of 1993, however, followed by the French clear lack of enthusiasm in the September referendum, together with legitimate questioning about the relevance of German monetary policy for countries confronted with recessionary forces and high interest rates, brutally restored uncertainty about the final outcome (EMU) and unleashed the triangular inconsistency. This opened a period of speculative attacks on weaker EMS currencies, and led to the eventual widening of fluctuation margins from 2.25 percent to 15 percent around the central parity on 2 August 1993.

The EMS crisis brought home one of the major implications of capital mobility, namely the role of private sector expectations. In this case, there was a presumption that, in the face of increased economic hardship, monetary authorities would find it difficult to stick to their preferred policy - shadowing the Bundesbank - and would sooner or later succumb to the option of autonomous behaviour. This belief was enough to feed speculation, even against currencies that were clearly not blatantly misaligned. In a world of free capital mobility, fixing the exchange rates invites pure speculation. Instead of assessing the current fundamentals, speculators speculate about the sustainability of current policies; the possibility also exists that they could anticipate that monetary authorities might give up when faced by the costs of fighting speculation. A speculative attack can then become self-fulfilling.

Second, crises in emerging countries also contributed to disqualify fixed exchange rate systems (even when they allowed for readjustments) or various forms of nominal anchoring (for example, through a fixed rate of monthly devaluation, chosen to less than compensate for the inflation differential with the anchor currency). These crises, from Mexico to Thailand, have illustrated the costs of real exchange rate overvaluation and the difficulty to react in time by an appropriate nominal devaluation before a speculative crisis plays havoc with the currency and the financial system. In countries where the exchange rate is used as an anchor to help reduce inflation, real overvaluation may be initially helpful as a constraining force, but it rapidly becomes a problem. Fixed exchange rates sooner or later turn out to be a credibility contest between monetary authorities and markets; short of timely parity changes, they lead to serious misalignments, finally setting the stage for speculative crises and devaluations. But timely parity changes cannot happen: so much credibility is staked on defending the parity that no government is ever willing to adjust it early enough, lest it be interpreted as a breach of resolve. Thailand, Mexico, or the United Kingdom before September 1992, among others, provide examples of this recurrent difficulty.[2]

The costs of preventing necessary exchange rate adjustments from taking place can be enormous. Real overvaluation helps import disinflation; but it is costly, unless it is wisely used as a subsidy to capital imports, speeding up development and translating into productivity gains than can alleviate the loss of competitiveness.[3] But even then, the accumulated misalignment must be corrected at some point, and correction never comes smoothly.

This is not the only problem with fixed exchange rates. They also create moral hazard to the extent that investors wrongly live under the illusion that there is no exchange rate risk and therefore are led to invest excessive amounts. In a context of high capital mobility, countries carelessly pile up short- term foreign debt denominated in hard currency. If and when the domestic currency becomes overvalued, the sheer size of the liabilities denominated in foreign currencies will play against a timely devaluation. But, eventually, the currency will have to be devalued and the debt burden skyrockets. A solution to this moral hazard could be found in a strict monitoring of the country's financial markets and economic policies by the international community, notably the IMF. But exchange rate rigidity is a strong impediment to effective monitoring, as amply illustrated in the case of Mexico in 1993, Thailand in 1997, and Brazil in 1998: a timely, critical assessment of national policies would interfere with the credibility of the exchange rate target and would extol a hefty risk premium to compensate for a risk of devaluation, thus contributing to economic duress and validating the initial critiques. As a result, IMF officials refrain from overtly critical assessments both through actual pressures and through self-restraint. Effective monitoring requires flexibility.

It is therefore one of the welcome features of the current consensus that fixed rate regimes have given way to increased flexibility. At the same time, there is a broad agreement that free floating is not the best option. The consensus therefore recognises the challenges of exchange rate flexibility, even though it has remained remarkably silent on how to address them.

The Challenges of Flexibility

Floating carries major defects. In developing countries, the exchange rate is a crucial price. Floating rates leave policymakers without an indicator and a constraint and leaves economic agents without any external anchor to their expectations. In countries which lack a strong institutional policy base, namely many developing countries, the option of anchoring the domestic economic policy on an internal anchor, such as an inflation target and central bank independence, simply does not exist, or is not credible. In such countries, floating accommodates the lack of policy discipline, but also by this very act makes it possible, thus maintaining the country in a sort of self-sustained "bad policy trap".[4] Floating, therefore, does little to contribute to develop policy proficiency and can even help sustain inappropriate policies. This is one of the reason why nominal exchange rate anchoring was resorted to by many developing countries in the 1980s. Now that the dangers of regimes with nominal exchange rate anchors, notwithstanding their contribution to disinflation, have been largely exposed, there is a need to devise a system that could combine the benefits of the nominal anchor and the requirements of flexibility. Free float, obviously, is not such a system for countries in which the institutional policy base is lacking.

Two further aspects deserve emphasis. First, a floating exchange rate leaves developing countries with unclear relative price signals that cannot but be detrimental to investment and development. For small, open developing countries that necessarily rely heavily on foreign trade and savings, flexible exchange rates are not an attractive option. Even for the larger ones, flexible rates expose them to wide swings in their real exchange rates and can bring undue costs to their economy, even if it is properly managed at the domestic level. Second, exchange rate instability in emerging countries can have a very negative and lasting impact on the availability of external finance as there is a need to compensate with a potentially hefty risk premium foreign investors or local investors relying on foreign finance for an increased exchange rate risk. Overall, the cost of capital and the level of investment are likely to be severely affected in emerging countries which do not try to limit exchange rate volatility.

In the more developed countries, including industrial countries and major emerging countries, the consensus rightly points out that what ultimately matters is the quality and credibility of domestic policies. Inflation targets and independent central banks are supposed to do more to stabilise exchange rates than any set of exchange rate policies. But even there, two factors also argue for still managing floating. First, as discussed below, foreign exchange markets are not efficient, exchange rates do not reflect fundamentals and there will be excessive nominal and real exchange rate volatility with potentially high costs for resource allocation due to erroneous signals even if national economic policies are "sound".[5] Unanticipated exchange rate movements abruptly change the conditions of price competition, this uncertainty may affect trade and investment decisions and lead to substantial resource misallocation.

Second, excessive fluctuations of the exchange rates of key currencies play havoc with economic and financial stability worldwide.[6] Preventing them should be seen as an international public good. This suggests that the management of key exchange rates should be considered as an important objective for multilateral action. Due to the *n*th-currency problem (with *n* currencies, there are *n-1* exchange rates), if all countries pursue their own exchange rate objective in a nonco-ordinated fashion, the chance is that conflict and instability will result. It opens the door to beggar-thy-neighbour policies, actual or imaginary, that may bear on the politics of international trade and investment and lead to protectionist pressures. Floating between major currencies also helps maintain the consistency between internationally unco-ordinated economic policies, but it also makes the lack of co-ordination more palatable, thus implicitly increasing the difficulty of such coordination and leading to a lesser perception of its usefulness. It is therefore hardly appropriate, as a policy response, for a globalising world that calls for increased co-ordination. The central point here is that managing the float is a problem of co-ordination, and that does not make it simpler.

These defects of floating exchange rates substantiate the case for more formal exchange rate arrangements, such as target zones, between major industrial countries. They have also recently led some leading economists to advocate the radical option of a renunciation of monetary sovereignty, either through a currency board or through the "dollarisation" of the economy.[7,8] A brief discussion of these options follows.

Is Monetary Sovereignty Still Relevant?

The option of unilaterally abandoning monetary sovereignty cannot be seriously envisioned for developed economies. It could not be accepted politically, and it would not make much sense economically in countries that have the necessary institutions for conducting monetary policy and that have to face idiosyncratic shocks. Monetary union, as a scheme through which countries do not abandon sovereignty but exert it at a higher level by sharing it, makes more sense, although it is open to the criticisms implied by the literature on optimum currency areas. But, for political reasons as well, the option is not open among the G3 countries. The success of the European monetary union was based on a very specific set of political characteristics, and crowned a process that had evolved over three decades. The EMU may expand over time, but it hardly provides a reproducible model for the rest of the world.

Various proposals for setting up target zones between major industrial countries have attracted attention and support as useful blueprints to manage exchange rates. Most of them, however, tend to ignore the constraint of political feasibility. If the target is left unspecified and the band too large, the target zone by itself is akin to floating and says little on management; in other variants, monetary authorities have to stake their credibility to a specific, visible commitment. The consensus view does not support the ambitious proposals for "hard bands", because by making the commitments explicit and by staking the government resolve to identifiable parity references and fluctuation bands, they sooner or later come down to a credibility contest between governments and markets. Hard bands require a strict commitment by governments to maintain exchange rates within agreed-upon margins around a specified parity. They are vulnerable to the weakness exposed by the EMS crisis and require a very tight and formalised co-operation of monetary policies. The time is not ripe to harness the kind of political support that would be needed for such a scheme to emerge. Hence, the consensual conclusion for G3 countries is that the best that can happen is more of the same, namely floating occasionally managed in a co-ordinated or unco-ordinated way through interventions or, rarely, through *ad hoc* co-ordination. The consensus reservations with hard bands are well grounded, but there is more to target zones than the hard band version (see below).

The menu is more open for developing countries. Here, the case for currency boards may look straightforward: capital mobility requires monetary policy credibility if the exchange rate is to remain stable. There is simply not enough institutional capacity in developing countries to provide the necessary credibility. Hence, it is worthwhile for them to abandon the pretense of autonomous policy making and rely, instead, on the credibility of foreign monetary policy. This leads to a substantial decline in the interest rate premium. The objection that foreign monetary policy may not be adapted to domestic circumstances is not convincing, because the lack of institutional maturity suggests that domestic monetary policy is not up to the task anyhow, and this is sanctioned on capital markets by hefty risk premiums.

While currency boards may work for some time in some countries (e.g., Argentina, Estonia, and others), they have inevitably imposed high costs and forced painful adjustment on banking sectors as lax domestic monetary policy was suddenly replaced by the binding constraint of foreign monetary policy. The important point is that a condition for currency boards to be successful and promote economic development is that financial restructuring and institution building take place. But as institutions strengthen, this may change the perception of the cost/benefit analysis of the currency board and lead to questions about the credibility of the commitment to maintain it over time. Currency boards should therefore be considered as useful, transitory devices, or, alternatively, as intermediate steps toward full monetary union with outside partners. For example, some Eastern European countries might try to anticipate EMU membership by setting up a currency board with Euroland. Premiums still occasionally imposed on the Argentinean peso demonstrate that the credibility of the currency board is not perfect. For a country like Brazil, one wonders how any move toward a currency board could be made credible. Sooner or later, even currency boards are bound to face a severe test of credibility, as long as the currency exists, its value can change and speculation can develop. Therefore, notwithstanding their possible transitory benefits and their role as possible intermediate steps toward full monetary integration, currency boards do not bring any systemic relief to the defects of excessive rigidity. To the contrary, they are but a fixed exchange rate system pushed to the limit, a huge gamble with uncertain long-term benefits, an invitation to ultimate brinkmanship both from monetary authorities and from market speculators.

Beyond the Consensus

The "consensus" thus leaves two major questions without an answer: First, how should a floating regime, if and when adopted by emerging countries, be managed? In the current consensus view, managed floating may well be for many the preferred option. But without a blueprint, the policy choice has little operational content. This is a central issue for countries looking at effective development strategies and in need of an external anchor to catalyse domestic change, institutional building, and sound economic policy making. The exchange rate regime matters in a very fundamental way; mistakes can be responsible for very costly setbacks.

Second, how does one address the double issue involved in floating among G3 countries, namely excess exchange rate volatility and insufficient economic policy co-ordination? These defects were noted above. It is useful, however, to also highlight the shortcomings of the current international macroeconomic environment.

Floating has left major countries without any collective discipline in terms of macroeconomic policy interaction, let alone co-ordination. Partly as a result, the sustainability of current exchange rates is very much in doubt, for the dollar, the yen, and the Euro. The recovery in Europe, in Japan, in Asia, the fate of the bubble on Wall Street are vulnerable to pronounced exchange rate instability. It is time to care about an effective monitoring of exchange rate movements. It will not solve the co-ordination problem, but it will raise the consciousness that the domestic economic policies of G3 countries are tightly interdependent and that the nonco-operative equilibrium can and should be improved upon.

Both for emerging markets and for industrial countries, the menu of options included in the consensus view is too limited. There is room for significant improvement, still taking on board the recent and valuable insights on which the consensus is based. For emerging markets, there is a fourth option to the exchange rate problem that could be attractive to some countries: it is possible to tie monetary policy through a sort of feedback rule that would make a system of Adjustable Reference Parities credible and viable. For G3 countries, more research on fundamentals and on equilibrium exchange rates, if properly conducted and used as a basis for debate and interaction between monetary authorities and the markets, can provide the basis for a mechanism of monitoring that could considerably help stabilise expectations in line with fundamentals. This is a first, modest, but promising, step toward managing G3 exchange rate flexibility. The following sections develop these ideas.[9]

The Fourth Option

As noted above, the international consensus is strongly critical of fixed-but-adjustable exchange rate regimes that have played such a prominent role in the financial crises of the 1990s. However, one can argue that recent problems had more to do with the way these systems were managed than with the stability of exchange rates *per se*.

Exchange rate crises in the 1990s, both within the EMS and in developing nations, have clearly sanctioned the failure of rigid, automatic policies used to ward off speculation, backed by the total use of exchange rate reserves and a massive increase in interest rates that could backfire into a recession. These policies are obviously unconvincing and fail to restore confidence in currencies, for speculators doubt their effectiveness and sustainability. They can even spell disaster when the measures fail (no more exchange reserves, loss of all monetary or even political credibility). It is, thus, very difficult in such conditions to prevent an exchange rate adjustment from happening under a speculative attack.

Elastic Flexibility as an Antidote Against Speculation

There are, however, subtler, and more effective ways to manage such systems and preserve exchange rate stability. The French exchange rate policy from the summer of 1993 to the spring of 1995 provides an interesting example of what could be called a sort of "elastic policy".

After the widening of the fluctuations margins of the EMS exchange rate mechanism on 2 August 1993, the French government, against market expectations, decided not to use the monetary policy autonomy thus restored to promote growth as a priority. Indirectly, through a series of coded messages, monetary authorities informed markets that French interest rates would be maintained significantly above German ones so long as the franc-mark parity did not return to the EMS central rate. The interest rate policy was thus aligned with that of Germany, maintaining a stable and reasonable risk premium destined to encourage the purchase of French francs. This monetary policy stance provided the kind of signal that markets respect questioning the authorities' exchange rate commitments were ready to heed. It was thus able to pull the franc back up to its pivotal rate within the EMS as early as late 1993. As a result, French monetary policy entered a period of calm after 12 months (September 1992-August1993) riddled with recurrent currency crises.

This elastic policy, terminated in the spring of 1995, was a remarkable success in terms of exchange rate management.[10] It succeeded because it responded to a so-called "second-generation crisis": the market did not question the middle or long-term sustainability of the franc to mark parity, but wondered whether French authorities could continue to pay for the costs in the short term.[11] The remarkable results of European central banks' post-1993 approach to exchange rate management has been highlighted by Bartoloni and Prati (1998). Their analysis "points to the usefulness of this policy for other countries that target their exchange rates". One of the lessons of this whole experience is that even sustainable parities may have to be defended against markets' speculation, and that defence, if properly orchestrated, can be successful.

Obviously, there were many specific factors behind the success of the elastic policy in the French case. Economic fundamentals were much stronger than in emerging countries and EMU prospects substantially enhanced the credibility of the French commitment in favour of stable exchange rates. Notwithstanding these differences, however, this example has a much broader significance and serves to illustrate some very general lessons on the feasibility and effective way to preserve relative exchange rate stability under the markets' fire. In particular, two distinct features of the elastic policy stand out in comparison with the traditional, unsuccessful approach to maintain exchange rate stability.

First of all, when confronting downward exchange rate pressure, authorities should assess whether the parity that comes under attack is really sustainable. If it was managed correctly in the past, there is in principle no reason for questioning it, unless a current, new, economic shock calls for a change. Any problem with sustainability, however, calls for timely readjustments. This is a major departure from current practices, in which monetary authorities stake so much in preserving the exchange rate target that they fail to take due and timely action with respect to necessary readjustments.

Second, a gradual, feedback-based, defence mechanism needs to be used to defend the sustainable parity. What was described as the elastic policy consists of defending the parity in a flexible way (no hikes in interest rates at unbearable levels, protection of exchange rate reserves), by resorting to something like the "French mechanism" as soon as the exchange rate has clearly overshot its target: interest rates can be pegged transparently to foreign rates, augmented with a significant and well-defined risk premium that takes into account the characteristics of the country concerned.[12] This risk premium is maintained or increased so long as the currency has not regained its target. If necessary, this defence mechanism can be backed by interventions on the exchange market. Now, there are obviously costs to the economy, in terms of interest rates that end up being higher than they should be: but these costs are due to market, rather than policy, failure, and giving in would result in letting the currency depreciate from a sustainable, equilibrium level, thus cautioning both costly misalignment and uncertainty.

A New Class of Fixed-But-Adjustable Rates: Adjustable Reference Parities

Such a system, called elsewhere a system of Adjustable Reference Parities, is clearly a member of the "fixed-but-adjustable" family of exchange rate regimes: exchange rates are allowed to fluctuate around a "reference parity" itself commonly subject to adjustment.[13] As analysed above, however, such a system avoids all the drawbacks of its more traditional cousins which lack flexibility and have failed so far. Here, two layers of flexibility deserve discussion: the nature and management of the reference parity, and the flexible response of monetary policy when the exchange rate departs from its reference parity.

A Reference Parity Defined as a Basket How does one choose the reference parity? A parity of reference must imperatively be defined as a basket of currencies that reflects the structure of external trade. The latter should at least include dollars, Euros, and yen.[14] One of the factors that triggered the Asian crisis was the loss of competitiveness for countries that had pegged their currencies to the single dollar between 1996 and 1997, a period during which the dollar had dramatically appreciated against the yen.

One aspect of flexibility is that parity readjustments are not ruled out by definition and should even be treated in a routine way. The possibility of a readjustment gives the market a clear incentive to closely monitor the fundamental economic position of the country and the compatibility of the current exchange rate with balanced economic growth in the medium to long term. Notwithstanding occasional changes, the reference parity should be adjusted as a flexible "crawling peg", and the gradual devaluation - or revaluation - should be known in advance. The goal would be to maintain the parity of reference at sustainable middle and long-term levels.[15]

Defining the exact terms of adjustment should be one of the key issues discussed at the IMF Article IV annual examination. General institutional issues and in particular the IMF's role with regard to exchange rate policies are dealt with below.

A Flexible, but Price-Stability-Oriented, Monetary Policy Response The defence of a parity judged as sustainable should be very progressive in order to avoid the trap of excessively high interest rates and the loss of international reserves. But there is a caveat: the capacity to tighten up the monetary conditions during economic overheating could be severely curtailed should stabilising exchange rates become too strong a priority. An incipient rise in interest rates is liable to lead to heavy capital inflows, which substantially limits the extent to which interest rates can rise, except for huge sterilised interventions in the foreign exchange market. In such a scenario, the appropriate response may be to let the currency appreciate against the reference parity. Should economic growth be too strong, a reference parity based exchange rate policy should not deter authorities from determining interest rates and keeping a lid on inflation. The optimal response in terms of currency appreciation will crucially depend on the economic context.

For example, if the risk of overheating is due to household consumption - the Mexican situation in the early 1990s- the best and most obvious response is a tighter fiscal policy that avoids both an increase in interest rates and an exchange rate appreciation. The latter would penalise the export sector even though it is not the source of the current difficulties and would contribute to an even greater increase in foreign debt. In many cases, however, fiscal policies cannot be used to address the source of the imbalance, and an interest rate rise and an exchange rate appreciation are preferable to letting inflation rise. Moreover, in such a situation, targeted controls on capital inflows, as with the by now famous "Chilean tax", can bring a useful contribution.

An Attractive Option for Emerging Countries

Which countries should use the fourth option of Adjustable Reference Parities? Such an option makes sense for many emerging countries in view of the costs of free-floating exchange rates discussed above. A system of Adjustable Reference Parities is not a "one fits all" solution. But, for some countries, such as Brazil in 1999, it may be considered as an attractive compromise between a currency board and a free float. In some ways, this system is a refinement of the target zone framework for emerging countries as discussed by Williamson (1998). The main difficulty with traditional crawling bands, however, is that, in general, monetary policy inside the band is not specified.[16] One view is that monetary policy should be used for internal stabilisation as long as the currency stays inside the band. This view is fraught with problems. Unless the fluctuation margin is very wide - at which time this can practically be referred to as a flexible exchange rate - margins for manoeuvring monetary policy should not be overestimated. If monetary authorities in emerging market countries want to use the entire fluctuation margin, without defending the central parity, market players are likely to react in advance, and exchange rates could bounce up or down against the margins before authorities are even willing or able to change interest rates. Indeed, most emerging market countries using crawling bands try to stabilise their currency close to the central rate. The Adjustable Reference Parities framework provides may be the best way to do so in a credible but flexible manner.

Learning How to Manage Floating Rates

The last 25 years have clearly highlighted how unstable free-floating rates can be. Excess volatility is a rather prevalent characteristic of asset prices, but the exchange rate market is probably one of the worst offenders in this respect.

As stressed by Blanchard (1999), there are two conceptually different kinds of bubbles in asset markets. Most real-life bubbles are a combination of these two pure types. First, investors may be grossly wrong, if judged with the benefit of hindsight, on market fundamentals. For example, they may overestimate the trend in firms' profits, as far as the equity market is concerned, or, in the foreign exchange (FX) market, the level of exchange rate that is sustainable in a long-term perspective, taking into account all the country's relevant characteristics (labour costs, productivity, savings, etc.). Second, the bubble can be speculative in the sense that investors may be broadly right on the fundamentals, but buy too high or sell too low in the expectation that in the short-term prices will continue to diverge from the level justified by the economic fundamentals.

The second type of bubbles is made possible by the fact that a large part of the investment community does not value financial assets from models based on fundamentals. Indeed, a well-documented fact is the diversity of the methodologies used by market participants to assess future asset prices and to make decisions about their investments. In general, the economic literature opposes the chartists and the fundamentalists, as in Frankel and Froot (1990), or the noise traders and the fundamentalists, as in Shleifer and Summers (1990). Noise traders comprise all the irrational investors, including but not limited to the chartists.

Obviously, second-type bubbles make it much more likely that first-type bubbles may occur. If people use valuation methodologies taking little account of the economic fundamentals, there are few incentives in the market place for thorough research efforts since prices tend to be disconnected from these fundamentals. Without such research, views on these fundamentals can become quite naive. On a more general note, one can argue that there is a general co-ordination problem in financial markets: one has few incentives to find the right model and study the real fundamentals if the other participants in the market do not care. To be successful, a short-term investor has to anticipate his or her colleagues' move rather than embarking on a thorough research effort.[17]

Overall, public authorities have an important role to play to limit the risks of these two kinds of bubbles and ensure an efficient working of the financial markets.[18] First, by being transparent themselves, by requiring the private sector to be transparent as well, and by directly or indirectly providing the necessary economic analysis, they may help market participants to have a better grasp of the fundamentals. In other words, they have a mission as information providers. Second, public authorities should do their best to avoid speculative bubbles, i.e., they should encourage the use of valuation methodologies based on fundamentals and react if and when destabilising behaviour drives prices far away from reasonable estimates of equilibrium values. Before discussing precisely what these two general orientations could mean specifically in the FX market, it is necessary first to be more specific about what is behind the concept of economic fundamentals as far as exchange rates are concerned.

Economic Fundamentals in the Foreign Exchange Market

In the medium to long term, the real economy has the final say and exchange rates cannot diverge forever from what is called their long-term equilibrium, i.e., the level consistent with balanced economic growth in the long term. This long-term equilibrium is a key economic fundamental of the FX market. How it can be estimated is dealt with below. However, one has first to reckon that there is no reason for the exchange rate to stay permanently at its long-term equilibrium.

Two factors may justify normal fluctuations of current, actual exchange rates around the sustainable, long-term equilibrium: discrepancies in real interest rates and risk premiums.

A positive real interest rate differential, for example, implies a real appreciation of the exchange rate relative to the long-term average. The reason is that it increases the attractiveness of investment in domestic financial assets. Such a differential can lead to a significant, albeit rational, real exchange rate appreciation. For example, if domestic real interest rates over a ten-year period are more than 1 percent higher than abroad, the domestic exchange rate could easily be overvalued by about 10 percent (in real terms); over a long period the investor would earn in interest (10 x 1 percent) what would be lost should the currency go back to the long-term exchange rate equilibrium (progressive elimination of the 10 percent overvaluation).

As a result, monetary policy is a key determinant of the fundamental value of a currency. As forcefully explained by Dornbusch (1976) more than 20 years ago, a loose monetary policy should have a strong negative impact on a currency since, on the one hand, its medium-term equilibrium value falls (in nominal terms, due to higher domestic prices in the future) and, on the other hand, in the short term it will fall even more (overshooting mechanism due to lower interest rates), because expectations of future appreciation are needed for investors to be willing to hold the currency at lower nominal interest rates. As a result, it is simply impossible to value correctly a currency when monetary policy is erratic and there is a complete lack of visibility on future inflation and real interest rates.

An independent central bank is often a rather useful first step to give more visibility on these key fundamentals. An independent central bank with an inflation target is even better, since the inflation target makes it easier to monitor its performance. Indeed, for countries with floating exchange rates, the lack of an external anchor makes it all the more necessary to have an internal anchor.

The natural link between exchange rates and spreads in different long-term interest rates assumes perfect asset substitutability, and will in general be affected by the existence of risk premiums. These can stem either from specific barriers to capital mobility that prevent assets from being perfectly substitutable, or from different assessments of risk. For example, a nation with a large external debt may have to serve its foreign creditors a return higher than what they can get in their own country. At given interest rates, risk premiums should therefore play a crucial role in exchange rate determination. If a given currency has to serve a positive risk premium, either the interest rates must increase by the size of the premium or the exchange rate must depreciate considerably in relation to the normal rate and reach a level at which investors will anticipate a future appreciation that will compensate them for the risk. For example, if they require an additional 1 percent return per year, their compensation over a ten-year period should be an initial currency undervaluation of about 10 percent. Exchange rate overshooting therefore responds to both the differences between domestic and foreign interest rates and relative risk premiums.

This simple analytical framework is rather useful for understanding the evolution of many currencies in the FX market over the last 20 years. Major shifts in exchange rates can sometimes be fully explained by substantial real interest rate differentials. For example, the long-term real interest rate differential between the United States and West Germany shifted from -6 percent to +4 percent between mid-1979 and early 1982, which on the basis of the previous analysis fully justifies the 100 percent real appreciation of the dollar over that period.

In fact, the most spectacular shifts in the dollar's value, at least relative to the mark, can clearly be traced back to the reversal in the US economic policy: an overly lax monetary policy in the late 1970s, followed by the Volcker-Reagan policy mix in the early 1980s, consisting of a tight, anti-inflationary monetary policy and a dramatic fiscal expansion through tax cuts and an increase in defence spending. The result was a spectacular growth in real interest rates and a brutal real appreciation of the dollar.

Figure 10.1 Real Dollar-Mark Exchange Rate (Base 100 in 1980, Left-Hand Scale) **and Real Interest Rate Differential** (in percent, Right Hand Scale)

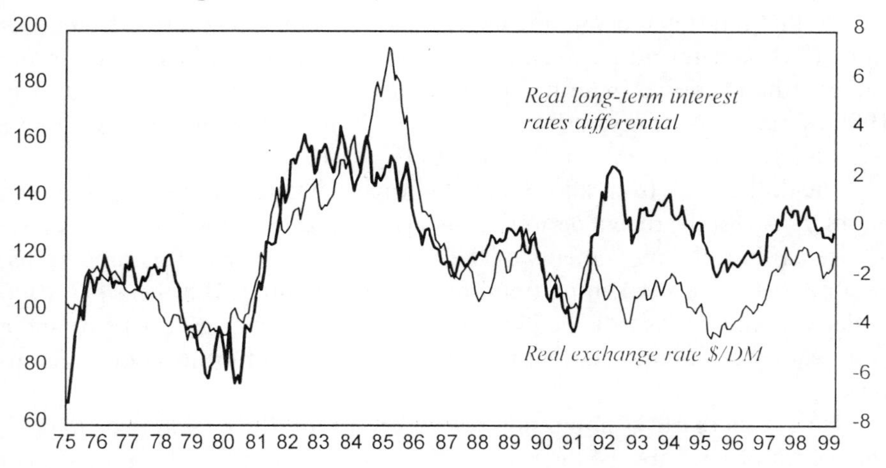

Most empirical work thus reveals a fairly close correlation between shifts in exchange rates and long-term real interest rate differentials for certain currencies.[19] Instability in exchange rates can often be traced back to vagaries in economic policies: an increase in inflation and an excessive drop in real interest rates (the United States in the late 1970s or France in the mid-1970s), an unbalanced policy mix, and a real interest rate hike in response to an overly expansionist fiscal policy (the United States in the early 1980s or Germany in the initial phase of unification at the end of the same decade). The chart below illustrates the correlation between the dollar-mark real exchange rate and the long-term real interest rate differential between the United States and Germany.[20]

This correlation sometimes comes as a surprise, such has been the influence of two papers published by Meese and Rogoff (1983, 1988). They maintained that exchange rates did not obey stable economic logic and followed what is referred to as a random walk. These papers are still quite influential and are among the most quoted in the exchange rate literature, despite the fact that they did not test correctly the existence of a strong relation for some currencies between real long-term interest rates and exchange rates.[21] The 1983 paper relied on short-term interest rates rather than long-term rates. In the 1988 paper, real long-term rates were calculated on the basis of the inflation rate of the last three months (annualised), which introduced a lot of noise into the data.[22]

In any case, while the correlation is generally rather strong, one has to reckon that a rational economic analysis based on interest rate differentials cannot account for all periods of instability. Thus, the sudden surge in the value of the US dollar in terms of European currencies in late 1984 and early 1985 remains rather mysterious, as does its drop in late 1987 or its relative weakness in 1993-1996 (see Figure 10.1).[23]

The dollar peak from late 1984 to February 1985 resembles a speculative bubble.[24] As for the recent period, shifts in risk premiums for American assets hardly explain the movements of the US currency: the ever rising external debt constitutes a weakening trend factor for the dollar. But the 1993-1996 dollar weakness was followed by a partial recovery over the past two and a half years, despite the fact that the American trade deficit has continued to surge.

Thus, Figure 10.1 should not been taken as an illustration that markets behave rationally most of the time and that private investors keep their eyes on fundamentals. Not only have excessive hikes or drops been recorded at times, but central banks have often had to intervene in order to stem panic situations. The market's relative apparent rationality is hardly a coincidence: it is for a large part due to the vigilance of major industrialised nations (in 1985 the dollar drop was accelerated by the intervention of central banks in the wake of the Plaza Agreement; in 1987 it was stabilised thanks to interventions as part of the Louvre accord; in 1994 it was once again stabilised thanks to interventions). The role of central banks has been even more important in the case of the dollar-yen rate, where major misalignments have been reduced only thanks to massive FX interventions (notably over the 1995-1998 period).

Indeed, one now knows that sterilised interventions proved to be very effective when properly orchestrated, especially when they were undertaken jointly.[25] There are a number of episodes where co-ordinated, sterilised interventions helped stabilise exchange rates in the past, but they often came very late, by lack of a systematic process that could help generate them.[26] Despite some success in the past, there is a clear lack of an international standard defining how the FX market should be monitored and when interventions should be decided. The following section discusses now some general guidelines before turning to institutional issues, i.e., how countries could collaborate together and with the IMF.

Monitoring the FX Market

An efficient monitoring of the FX market consists of explicitly assessing the position of various currencies on the basis of the three key fundamental variables highlighted above: their long-term equilibrium value, the long-term real interest rate and risks premium differentials.

More specifically, surveillance of the FX market consists of a two-step process.

Assessing how far currencies are away from a reasonable estimate of their long-run equilibrium An abundant literature exists on the subject. The dominant approach used in estimating a long-term exchange rate equilibrium consists of first defining a sustainable trade balance for the middle to long term, and then identifying the level of competitiveness that enables the trade balance to reach its sustainable level.[27]

The definition of a sustainable trade balance over the medium term will depend on the nature of the external financing constraint faced by the country. For a country without external financial constraints, the sustainable value is determined by the level of net savings (domestic savings minus domestic investment) that the country generates on a path of balanced growth (full employment and sustainable public debt).[28] For a country facing an external financial constraint, the sustainable trade (current account) balance is equal to the availability of funds.

Once the sustainable trade balance has been defined, the equilibrium real exchange rate is generally derived using external trade equations that link foreign trade, domestic demand, and external competitiveness. Interestingly, however, this process can lead to long-term equilibrium real exchange rate estimates that are rather far from traditional competitiveness indicators such as relative prices (purchasing power parities (PPP) - estimated by the Organisation for Economic Co-operation and Development (OECD), for instance), relative labour costs or average long-term real exchange rates. For example, as far as the Euro-dollar rate is concerned, most estimates put the long-term equilibrium between US$1.20 and US$1.30 dollar per Euro, while the OECD puts the PPP rate at US$1.06 (1998 figures) and most other traditional indicators on costs and prices put the normal rate at around US$1per Euro.[29]

As far as the currencies of major industrialised countries are concerned, the main explanation for such discrepancy rests in the very low price elasticity of trade volumes typically produced by traditional econometric trade equations. A large adjustment in relative prices is therefore necessary to engineer any required change in the volume of exports and imports. As far as the dollar is concerned, many observers relying on traditional trade equations believe that the dollar will have to become very weak, both relative to the euro and the yen, if the US is to cut down its external deficit to a sustainable level in the medium to long term.

But, the very low price elasticity found in authoritative empirical studies is somewhat puzzling, as thin export margins suggest a high degree of competition in most international markets. Moreover, export price elasticities below 1 for some countries are simply almost impossible to believe since they mean that on average exporters in these countries can raise their foreign sales in value terms simply by increasing their prices to whatever level they want. Common sense seems to point in the direction of much higher price elasticities in the medium to long term, and thus the need for less currency depreciation in countries with balance of payments problems. This suggests that applied economic research on what determines international trade volumes needs to be further encouraged and developed.[30]

As a result, while real equilibrium exchange rate quantification has made important headway in the recent past, one should probably not completely forget, for the time being, traditional competitiveness indicators based on costs and prices.

Discussing whether or not cyclical conditions and interest rates in various countries justify, from an investor perspective, the degree of undervaluation of some currencies In well-functioning financial markets, countries where economic activity is particularly weak should have lower real long-term interest rates and a relatively weak exchange rate. The consistency between real long-term interest rates and real exchange rates should be closely monitored. This implies an assessment of any risk premium imbedded in interest rates differentials: recall that a real long-term interest rate differential of 1 percent (for ten-year maturities) in favour of the foreign country and an adverse risk premium of 1 percent against the domestic currency imply a potential, rational real undervaluation of the domestic exchange rate of up to 20 percent.

A rather difficult part of the exercise is to estimate legitimate risk premiums. As far as G7 countries are concerned, especially G3 countries, political risks and inflation risks are absent and the major source of risk premium probably resides in differences in net external positions. A country with a large net foreign debt and deficits may have to pay a premium to receive the foreign finance it needs at given exchange rates. At the present time, however, there is no easy way to assess whether a country is already in a situation where its foreign debt is becoming too large to be easily financed. This is especially true for the US. There is very little detailed information on how easily supply and demands of various currencies match. In principle, it would be very useful to get more detailed insights into international investors' portfolios and expectations; there is no doubt a need for a risk premium on a currency issued by an indebted country when, on the basis of high expected returns, the average portfolio is distorted in favour of this currency.

Davanne (1999a) has looked at the way to get insights into investors' asset allocations and the level of risk premium, i.e., the expected excess return over short-term bills.[31] For most categories of investors, there is little that can be done to collect much more information on portfolio structures. However, there is a very important exception.

International banks have developed their own internal systems for measuring market risks. They are capable of studying their exposure to various currencies, notably on the Euro-dollar parity since 1 January 1999. Data regarding exposure to the main exchange rates risks could be grouped together by the bank supervisors on a monthly or quarterly basis, integrated by the Bank for International Settlements (BIS) and then circulated. Such a procedure would involve several difficulties, notably that of strictly protecting the confidentiality of individual data, but it would provide the monetary authorities and private investors with a much closer monitoring of the exchange market. Such a process already exists as far as international credit risks are concerned: the BIS and the community of bank supervisors collect data on credit to foreign counterparts and publish the aggregate results on a quarterly basis. An extension to exchange rate exposures might be conceivable.

Whatever the methodology employed, there is a need for a better monitoring of financial portfolios. The birth of the Euro makes it even more necessary in order to anticipate diversification strategies and get a better grasp of the factors likely to influence a potential excess demand for Euros and supply of dollars - at the level of the agreed long-term real exchange rate equilibrium. This analysis of supply and demand trends in the foreign exchange market should be an integral part of any surveillance process.

The Public Sphere as an Expectations Co-ordinator

This is not to suggest that this monitoring process should be confidential and univocally dedicated to the preparation of interventions in the FX market. Rather, it should be based on a permanent interaction with private investors and its actual ambition should be to make interventions unnecessary thanks to more stabilising behaviours in the private sector.

Monitoring authorities, whoever they are (an issue of international co-operation dealt with below), should not only form a view on the three key FX market fundamentals (equilibrium exchange rates, inflation and real long-term interest rates differentials, risk premiums) but should also monitor the private sector's consensus on these variables. Ideally, thanks to this dialogue, monitoring authorities and private investors should share a similar assessment of these fundamentals and the degree of uncertainty which inevitably surrounds any estimate.

At the present time, one could argue that pure fundamental analysis does not receive the weight it deserves in the foreign exchange market. Discussions among market participants seldom focus on notions like long-term equilibrium, risk premium, or, even, spreads of real long-term interest rates. Indeed, there is not even a consensus about the right valuation methodology to be used. As far as bonds and equities are concerned, market investors and the economists who advise them have a sound notion of the valuation model that should be used in theory (based on future profits, shifts in short-term interest rates, and risk premiums). This is not the case in the foreign exchange market.

A clear quest for value by the official sector, based on a transparent methodology and a permanent dialogue with the private sector, would help focus the mind of private investors on exchange rate fundamentals. More public guidance can help trigger a virtuous circle in which it pays to look at the fundamental economic variables, and in which the exchange rate ends up being more stable and predictable because everyone in the market agrees on the valuation methodology to be used.

The Institutional Setting: The Role of the IMF and the G7

The previous sections argued that emerging markets had more options with respect to exchange rate policies than suggested by the current consensus. They also contended that, for the G3 countries and countries opting for managed floating, a careful monitoring of fundamentals and exchange market behaviour was needed. These suggestions, however, are not directed at national governments alone. G3 exchange rate movements and policies clearly are crucial determinants of international interdependence and relate to the wider issue of the international co-ordination of economic policies. Emerging markets, exchange rate policies mainly matter because the interaction between these policies and international capital mobility can lead to severe misalignments and costly crises that have implications for the banking systems worldwide and that may call for foreign financial involvement, notably through the IMF and the G7. There are both negative externalities for the rest of the world, as well as an element of moral hazard that may yet compound the costs of misdirected policies.

This discussion suggests that, insofar as large countries are concerned, exchange rate management should have a multilateral dimension. The more important the currency, the bigger the multilateral concern. This section tentatively explores ways to organise multilateral surveillance. There are a number of possible routes. One is to build on the existing institutions already involved in surveillance and on past experience with managing exchange rates. In these tasks, the IMF and the G7 have played prominent roles. This section therefore concentrates on how they might jointly contribute to strengthening the current surveillance of exchange rates.

This discussion does not directly address the issue of exchange rate management in the poorest developing countries. They may have a wider menu of options, as they may at lesser cost resort to capital controls and maintain some autonomy in domestic policy making. They face, however, a crucial need to strengthen their economic policy institutions, and may thus resort to some nominal exchange rate targeting to import credibility and help build local institutions. While exchange rate mistakes, in these countries (as opposed to larger, emerging markets), will have a much lesser impact on the world economy, they still can carry high costs for the domestic economies. The latter therefore should benefit from some of the principles of multilateral surveillance highlighted below. The quasi-universal nature of the IMF and the World Bank suggest that the principles introduced below should also be extended to the surveillance of exchange rate policies in the poorer countries.

Multilateral Surveillance of Emerging Markets' Exchange Rate Policies

The role of inappropriate exchange rate policies in the dynamics and severity of the recent financial crises suggests that the emerging markets' exchange rate policies are a matter for multilateral surveillance, both in normal circumstances to contribute to crisis prevention and during balance of payments crises to help with crisis management. Crisis prevention calls for the international community to find ways to deter countries from following risky exchange rates policies. On the other hand, in times of crisis, it must be much more resolute in stabilising disorderly markets and in avoiding blatant exchange rate overshooting. A currency free fall generates risks of serious contagion and of creating a vicious circle of heavier debt burden, further loss of confidence, and further depreciation.

These two objectives assigned to multilateral surveillance are somewhat contradictory: a country has little incentive to follow cautious policies if it knows that it can rely on foreign support in case of trouble. Thus, monitoring of exchange rate policies and peer pressure, however necessary, are not enough; the international community must attach some form of conditionality to its intervention as "lender of last resort" in order to limit moral hazard.

Monitoring There are several reasons why the IMF should play a central role in exchange rate monitoring. First, the IMF already has a mandate to do so and this comes naturally as part of Article IV yearly consultations with individual countries. Second, the IMF has become a reservoir of economic and financial expertise. Such expertise could still be improved, but it must now be mobilised not as much to dictate what countries should do, but to assess the sustainability of current exchange rate and financial variables. Third, the IMF is on the front line to help bail out countries when there is a crisis and should therefore be very active in identifying pre-crisis situations, both in order to help prevent crises, and to mitigate any moral hazard associated with the expectation that, in a way or another, bail out will occur.

As noted above, a central issue, in the recent crises, was related to the difficulty of officially commenting on exchange rates: hinting at misalignment could precipitate an investor panic and a crisis. But this difficulty precisely rested on the excessive rigidity of exchange rate policies. When a lot of political capital has been invested in maintaining a fixed exchange rate, it is indeed hard to comment officially on that exchange rate being overvalued: governments cannot afford any doubt in the market about their commitment to the current rate, and the IMF cannot afford to comment on sustainability. Conversely, when some exchange rate flexibility becomes a general prescription, open dialogue on the level of the exchange rate becomes possible and desirable. Hence, surveillance demands flexibility. The post-Asian crisis is conducive to improving the efficiency of the surveillance process, not the least because the costs of excessive exchange rate rigidity in emerging markets have now been blatantly exposed. A consensus has now formed on the need to preserve and manage exchange rate flexibility.[32]

Crisis Management As a byproduct of more flexible exchange rate policies, the international community must be much more anxious and determined to avoid exchange rate overshooting. In this context, the function of lender of last resort deserves discussion: the international community, through the IMF or the G7, should be ready to engage a very large amount of money to avoid the panics and free falls in the exchange rate market. Panics should be interpreted as a sort of market failure which requires the intervention of the international community. There should be no confusion, however, on the role of the international community as a lender of last resort. Bringing some calm to disorderly markets could be a necessity, but lending massively to defend a rigid exchange rate is more often than not a loss of time and money. Indeed, one of the lessons of the recent exchange rate crises in emerging markets is that IMF financial assistance should not be used to artificially maintain ultimately unsustainable exchange rate policies. In general, countries should meet a number of conditions for eligibility for IMF and other international community money: (1) reach an agreement with the IMF on what is an appropriate level for the exchange rate in the medium term; (2) agree to use flexible a response to defend the jointly agreed reference level, (3) respect a number of more traditional elements of conditionality.[33]

Conditions (1) and (2) mean that the country facing a currency crisis relies on the adjustable reference parities framework introduced above, at least temporarily, to stabilise its currency and regain the market's confidence with the help of the international community. Overall, much progress is needed in terms of crisis management; having learnt that defending a rigid exchange rate may be a rather futile exercise, the IMF now has to reckon that free floating is not the only option for countries in the midst of a balance of payment crisis. Indeed, a country like Brazil paid a huge price in terms of interest rates, and thus high interest payments on the public debt, for having first tried to defend an unsustainable exchange rate and, second, allowed its currency to float without enough public guidance.

Other Forms of Conditionality Conditionality applies when members call on IMF resources. This is, therefore, *ex post* conditionality, attached to financial resources granted by the IMF once the problem has materialised. Traditional conditionality rest on principles of good economic governance, as developed through theoretical understanding and experience: best practices of fiscal and monetary policy making (price stability and long-term fiscal sustainability), and, since the Asian crisis, financial transparency and liberalisation. Here, the IMF has developed considerable expertise, and occasional timing mistakes are part of a necessary learning process on how to implement unquestionable principles in practice and over time. The key remaining issue consists of finding the best way to involve private sector investors in sharing the costs of rescue when the crisis is not a pure liquidity crisis, but comes partly from solvency problems, in the public or the banking sector.

The conditionality imposed on a country in crisis substantially reduces the moral hazard created by the readiness of the international community to help. Whether or not bail-out is finally forthcoming, the costs of crises are substantial for the countries where they take place. Even when external finance is available, it comes with delay and with unpopular strings attached to it through the IMF conditionality. One could even argue that the cost is generally too high when the crisis is related to contagion and has an element of market failure in it.

Indeed, one of the current challenges may be to define a new, *ex ante* conditionality. Respect of different codes for good conduct in the phase leading up to the crisis could give an implicit right to a much more favourable treatment and less stringent conditionality in case of crisis. Of prime importance for any such *ex ante* conditionality are questions related to exchange rate policy and banking supervision. Much more work is needed on the forms such *ex ante* conditionality might take. One of the weaknesses of the current surveillance system is that it is solely based on persuasion and discretion. *Ex ante* conditionality might substantially help with implementation.

G7 Exchange Rate Monitoring

Large industrialised countries are, of course, a case by themselves. First, their expertise in managing exchange rates is comparable to that of the IMF. Second, they have the financial resources to intervene in the market and, except for rare occasions, do not really need foreign help to fight the worst case of bubbles. Third, for large countries, co-operation is necessary because of the *n-1* problem: for example, the dollar-euro rate is both a matter of concern for the US and for Euro countries. In theory, one could imagine an independent monitoring of this exchange rate by the US and euro countries, and independent interventions in case of market turmoil, but such a decentralised process would clearly be much less efficient than a joint monitoring as part of the G7 general process of economic co-operation.

While the G7 should be the highest monitoring authority, it would make sense to charge the IMF with a secretariat responsibility, given its present role and its accumulated expertise. For each regular G7 meeting, the IMF could be asked to prepare a report presenting and discussing reasonable estimates of long-run exchange rate equilibrium, and assessing how far away major currencies are from these estimates. In the same report, or in a separate one, the IMF would also discuss whether observed departures from long-run equilibrium can be explained by cyclical conditions and interest rates, including risk premiums. The IMF report would present staff analyses, but also discuss other estimates and analyses available in the marketplace. Indeed, it would be extremely useful that the staff establishes on the issue of measurement of long-run exchange rate equilibrium a regular and open dialogue with both the academic world and private sector investors. In the current state of knowledge, competitive estimates are more likely than single estimates to convey the relevant information and act as a strong signal possibly anchoring expectations. The IMF is strongly advised to maintain an up-to-date database on the world major financial institutions' estimates of long-term exchange rate equilibrium. Many international bank research departments do not produce such estimates. Here the expectation is that an officially sanctioned focus on such estimates would at least provide some incentive for banks to do more work on this key issue. It is also to be hoped that a practice of dialogue and interaction between the private sector and the IMF staff might help expectations to converge toward reasonable estimates of "normal" exchange rates.

Knowledge of exchange rate equilibrium is, of course, imperfect and limited (see above). This is why the process recommended here is based on dialogue and interaction, rather than top-down communication. This is inevitably messier, but it is nevertheless necessary and more effective than simply relying on in-house estimates that would lack credibility. Moreover, both the IMF and the international community must strongly back research on producing reliable estimates of exchange rate equilibrium and of their time-line as a central input into this monitoring mechanism.

Such a process would not produce any true calculations. Its major contribution would be to help forge a consensus among policymakers about what is going on in the foreign exchange market. In normal times, attention would be limited to G7 currencies (the US dollar, Euro, yen, British pound, and Canadian dollar).

Some key advantages of such an enhanced monitoring process are its potential impact on private sector behaviour and in facilitating interventions in the market in cases of clear exchange rate overshooting. Moreover, the successful implementation of the monitoring process in the G7 countries could help emerging markets as well, both directly due to reduced volatility between world major currencies, but also indirectly if it helps the development, among private investors, of more fundamentally based valuation methodologies. In addition, emerging countries would certainly benefit from the experience gained by G7 practitioners in their enhanced surveillance process. The more advanced emerging countries that decide to pursue the demanding option of managed floating must be invited periodically to meet with G7 representatives to consult on modalities of surveillance and of mutual support. The markets would surely look favourably on such collaboration, which they might even interpret as a stabilising, implicit endorsement. This spill-over effect would considerably strengthen the effectiveness of the surveillance mechanisms reviewed above for emerging markets' exchange rate policies.

Beyond Monitoring

Clearly, simply monitoring exchange rate markets does not by itself solve the co-ordination problem and suppress all instability in exchange rates. When sharply diverging fiscal and monetary policies push interest rates far away in different countries, monitoring should not be expected to stop exchange rates from moving away from reasonable estimates of their long-term equilibrium. In other words, monitoring could suppress part of the volatility due to the inefficiency of the FX market, but it would not stop overshooting *à la* Dornbusch. But this approach has the merit of requiring a discussion of policies and of their interaction, which is the very first step of any coordination exercise. Co-ordination should be understood as a process, rather than a jump toward optimally co-ordinated policies that internalise economic interdependence. The experience of European integration serves to illustrate that, even in a favourable political context, the process of co-ordination requires much learning and much time.

Monitoring is an essential and realistic first step toward a deepening of international economic policy coordination. As such, it is both modest and realistic. It demands a substantial effort, but does not infringe much on national sovereignty while presenting clear benefits as compared to the current functioning of the international monetary system.

More ambitious schemes share two characteristics. First, authorities not only discuss plausible values for long-term equilibrium exchange rates, but now agree on a set of reference parities. Second, they decide on acceptable bands of fluctuation around these parities beyond which action is warranted. Such action may involve interventions in the market if the unwelcome movements in the parities have no real justifications or an effort to better co-ordinate the policy mix if the divergence finds its origin in a lack of economic policy co-ordination. Bergsten, Davanne, and Jacquet (1999) discuss various such schemes which differ on whether or not the agreement is made public and on the strength of the commitment to the band.

The option of flexible target zones makes much sense. In such a regime, there is no binding commitment to defend the zone, but rather a commitment to co-operate and co-ordinate economic policies in order to keep a reasonable degree of exchange rate stability. However, such a regime is not for the time being on the agenda for a mix of good and bad reasons. As far as the latter are concerned, many governments are reluctant to commit themselves to co-operate in an active way and prefer to keep maximum freedom despite the costs of large swings in exchange rates. Moreover, the sheer idea of target zones has a bad reputation due to the obvious drawbacks of hard bands which are clearly too rigid (see above). Many officials fail, honestly or not, to see the radical difference between flexible target zones and hard bands: the former is a device to encourage economic policy co-ordination while the latter may be a dangerous trap which forces countries to defend unsustainable exchange rates. As far as the good reasons are concerned, there is, as indicated repeatedly above, substantial uncertainty surrounding estimates of exchange rate long-term equilibrium. Ministers of finance are not yet ready, and perhaps rightly so, to put their stamp of approval behind the available estimates. However, a few years of successful monitoring can change this situation; once governments have worked out methods to discuss equilibrium exchange rates, the likelihood that they will agree on some plausible equilibrium value increases.[34]

Concluding Remarks

This chapter sends two broad messages. First, exchange rate flexibility is necessary and desirable. Never again should the world economy be held hostage by misplaced policies, sanctioned at the highest level, aiming at defending grossly misaligned exchange rates. While fixed-fixed exchange rate systems *à la* currency boards may be appropriate in some circumstances, such systems do present dangers and should be resorted to exceptionally and be managed very carefully. A currency board may make sense as an intermediate step toward a joining a regional monetary union. This may well be an option for some central and eastern European countries attracted by EMU.

Second, the current international monetary system blatantly lacks a doctrine of flexibility. As an alternative to fixed but adjustable exchange rate systems (that require capital controls and should appeal to the poorer developing countries), most countries are presented with a choice between losing monetary sovereignty or floating. And, should they chose floating, there is no good practice to follow in order to manage the exchange rate efficiently.

This chapter makes an initial contribution to thinking about what such a doctrine might look like. First, it argues that the menu of options has been too limited: even with substantial capital mobility, there is a variant of fixed but adjustable exchange rate regimes, labelled an Adjustable Reference Parity Regime, that can help those emerging markets that still wish to anchor domestic policies on an exchange rate target. Such a parity must be based on a basket of currencies, must be readily adjustable in a routine way, and must be defended by a flexible feedback-based monetary policy.

Second, there are ways to considerably improve international exchange rate monitoring as a first step toward a practice of regular co-ordination of economic policies. Monitoring would be based on tracking down the discrepancies between reasonable estimates of long-run exchange rate equilibrium and current exchange rates and checking them for valid explanations. This G7-based, IMF-supported, externally inclusive monitoring effort could help stabilise market expectations and exchange rates. It would also help develop methods of exchange rate valuation, in the markets, that are, at last, based on assessment of fundamentals.

These proposals provide no panacea to solve current problems. They require much work, notably on the very concept and calculation of equilibrium exchange rates and risk premiums. But such work is urgently necessary. The modest steps highlighted here can substantially contribute to exchange rate stability.

Notes

1. This chapter draws from a paper presented at the Tokyo Club, 28-29 October 1999 London Conference at the Royal Institute of International Affairs as part of the Tokyo Club 1999 research program.
2. In the exchange rate mechanism of the EMS, a decision to devalue the pound would have had to be a collective one and not only a British one.
3. This is what Spain did after joining the European Union.
4. Fixed exchange rates involve some moral hazard; one could also say that floating rates do as well albeit of a different sort, since they provide insurance against bad policies. The response to moral hazard is neither in fixed nor in floating rates, but in a mixture of flexibility and monitoring.
5. The overvaluation of the US dollar in 1984 and the first months of 1985 is a case in point.
6. Some even see in the fluctuations of the dollar/yen exchange rate the major factor behind the Asian crisis. See McKinnon (1998).
7. For example, Dornbusch (1999).
8. See the debate between Hausmann (1999) and Sachs and Larrain (1999) on the merits and mischiefs of dollarisation.
9. The proposals here expand on Bergsten, Davanne, and Jacquet (1999).
10. Of course, this does not address the question of whether the priority thus given to the exchange rate was appropriate in the first place, in a context - that of the summer 1993 - marked by hesitant growth and rising unemployment.
11. See Eichengreen, Rose and Wyplosz (1994) for a theoretical description of a "second generation" currency crisis.
12. For example, if the currency shifts more than 2 percent below its target.
13. See Davanne (1998), and Bergsten, Davanne, and Jacquet (1999).
14. The IMF might build representative indexes on currencies of emerging nations that could be taken into account in the baskets of reference, next to the dollar, the Euro, and the yen.
15. Such a crawling adjustment policy does not broaden margins for manoeuver for monetary policy. Planning a future exchange rate devaluation cannot be an effective response when faced with an economic slowdown. The favourable effect on competitiveness is deferred, while interest rates should progress initially so as to convince investors to keep a given currency despite a depreciating trend. In a first stage, monetary conditions are tightened. The export sector can, however, react favourably by anticipating the positive impact of the coming depreciation.
16. In a 1992 article, Svensson argues that the data available for the EMS, Nordic countries, the Bretton Woods system, and the gold standard point to an actual functioning of existing real world target zones very close to managed float with a target exchange rate level defended by frequent mean-reverting intra-marginal monetary policy intervention, i.e., a system that relies on the sort of elastic policy described in this chapter. His results suggest that more work should be devoted to formalising policy rules in such managed floats. Work on target zones, in particular,

should focus on specifying the behaviour of monetary policy inside the band.

17 Obviously, Keynes' (1936) metaphor on financial markets as special beauty contests can be seen as one of the first expression of this approach of financial markets. See Devenow and Welch (1996) for a survey of the literature on rational herding.

18 See Davanne (1999b) for an extended discussion of actual valuation methodologies, market efficiency, and the role of public authorities.

19 See notably Baxter (1994), Coe and Gloub (1986), Davanne (1990), and Sachs (1985).

20 Very similar charts used to interpret 25 years of floating exchange rates can be found in Blanchard (1997), Devanne (1990), and Dominguez and Frankel (1993).

21 For example, in a key survey of the literature on target zones, Svensson (1992) quoted Meese and Rogoff (1983) three times in support of the view that "a simple random walk usually out-performs other forecasting models".

22 In principle, real long-term interest rates should be estimated using the inflation expected by investors over the forthcoming 10 years. As a proxy, the chart uses the observed inflation differential over the last 12 months.

23 See also the synthesis by the IMF (1998) on links between the economic cycle, interest rates and exchange rates. *World Economic Outlook*, May 1998, chapter III: "The Business Cycle, International Linkages and Exchange Rates".

24 See also the comments by Krugman (1989).

25 See Dominguez (1990), Catte *et al.* (1994), and Dominguez and Frankel (1993). The latter offers some convincing evidence of the efficiency of most past co-ordinated interventions. It also clearly describes the various channels by which sterilised interventions can play a role: signalling on future monetary policy shifts, portfolio effect if foreign and domestic bonds are imperfect substitutes for each other from an investor perspective, bursting of a speculative signal.

26 However, over the last 15 years, interventions were decided only when governments reached the conclusion that the market was not fully reflecting the underlying economic fundamentals. Interventions would probably have proved much less efficient if they had been used in a systematic manner without due considerations for the conditions prevailing in the market. Indeed, the Jurgensen report (1983), submitted to the G7 Summit at Williamsburg in 1983, concluded that the effects of sterilised interventions could at most be minor and transitory, but the working group members were probably at that time influenced by their experience with badly devised interventions.

27 See IMF (1998), Williamson (1994) and Wren Lewis and Driver (1998).

28 The central open-economy national accounting identity states that net savings equal the current account balance. This can also be seen from the balance of payment identity that the current account equals net capital outflows, i.e., the net acquisition of foreign assets, identically equivalent to net national savings.

29 See Borowski and Couharde (1999).

30 Indeed, the power of traditional econometric tests to estimate the long-term price elasticities of exports seems rather weak and other approaches, e.g., case studies, might be used.

31 Report requested by Dominique Strauss-Kahn, French Minister of Finance, available in French and English at (www.finances.gouv.fr/pole_ecofin/politique_financiere/).

32 An alternative, discussed above, is to formally "abandon" the exchange rate, forgo national monetary policy, and create a currency board. For various reasons alluded to above, however, we believe that this course is not without danger. It should be restricted to countries looking for useful, intermediate steps to build credibility before formally entering a monetary union or before full dollarisation, if and when an appropriate judgement has been formed about the cost/benefit tradeoffs of such dramatic steps.

33 As with all rules, the last one could suffer a few exceptions, for example when a country is faced with hyperinflation, has lost all monetary credibility, and needs, at least temporarily, a very rigid external anchor. Moreover, low-income developing countries which have generally strong capital controls and are less vulnerable to speculative pressures are better positioned to defend strictly the jointly agreed parity.

34 The co-ordination of economic policies can also be improved without waiting for an explicit exchange rate target, as forcefully argued by Coeuré and Pisani-Ferry (1999), who have proposed a co-ordination process based on the joint endorsement by the G3 of a core set of broad macroeconomic principles.

References

Bartolini, L. and A. Prati (1998), *Soft Exchange Rates Bands and Speculative Attacks: Theory and Evidence from the ERM since August 1993*, IMF working Paper/98/156, International Monetary Fund, Washington DC.

Baxter, M. (1994), "Real Exchange Rates and Real Interest Differentials: Have We Missed the Business-Cycle Relationship?", *Journal of Monetary Economics*, Vol. 33.

Bergsten, F., O. Davanne and P. Jacquet (1999), "The Case for Joint Management of Exchange Rate Flexibility", Working Paper 99-9, Institute for International Economics, Washington DC.

Blanchard, O. (1997), *Macroeconomics*, Prentice Hall.

Blanchard, O. (1999), Comment on three reports to the French Conseil d'Analyse Economique, Report No. 18, Collection des Rapports du Conseil d'Analyse Economique, La Documentation Française, Paris.

Borowski, D. et C. Couharde (1999), "La Compétitivité Relative des Etats-Unis, du Japon et de la Zone Euro", annexe B, Report n° 18, Collection des Rapports du Conseil d'Analyse Economique, La Documentation Française, Paris.

Catte, P., G. Galli, and S. Rebecchini (1994), "Concerted interventions and the Dollar: An Analysis of Daily Data", In P. Kenen, F. Papadia and F. Saccomani, eds., *The International Monetary System*, Cambridge University Press, Cambridge.

Coe, D. and S. Golub (1986), "Exchange Rates and Real Long-term Differentials: Evidence for Eighteen OECD Countries", Document de travail de l'OCDE, Organisation for Economic Co-operation and Development, Paris.

Coeuré, B. and J. Pisani-Ferry (1999), "The Case Against Benign Neglect of Exchange Rate Stability", *Finance and Development*, September 1999, 36(3).

Davanne, O. (1990), "La Dynamique des Taux de Change", *Economie et Statistique* No. 236.

Davanne, O. (1998), *L'instabilité du Sytème Financier International*, Report to the French Prime Minister, Collection des Rapports du Conseil d'Analyse Economique, La Documentation Française, Paris.

Davanne, O. (1999a), "Transparency of Financial Portfolios and Control of Market Risks", available in French and English at www.finances.gouv.fr/pole_ecofin/politique_financiere.

Davanne, O. (1999b), "The Role of Transparency for a Better Pricing of Risks", mimeo.

Devenow, A. and I. Welch (1996), "Rational Herding in Financial Economics", *European Economic Review*, Vol 40.

Dominguez, K. (1990), "Market Responses to Coordinated Central Bank Intervention", *Carnegie-Rochester Series on Public Policy*, 32, pp.121-64.

Dominguez, K. and J. Frankel (1993), *Does Foreign Exchange Intervention Work?*, Institute For International Economics, Washington DC.

Dornbusch, R. (1976), "Expectations and Exchange Rate Dynamics", *Journal of Political Economy*, 84.

Dornbusch, R. (1999), "The Euro: Implications for Latin America", paper prepared for a policy research project of the World Bank, available at web.mit.edu/rudi/www.

Eichengreen, B., A. Rose and C. Wyplosz (1994), "Speculative Attacks on Pegged Exchange Rates: An Empirical Exploration with Special Reference to the European Monetary System", *NBER Working Paper, No. 4898*.

Frankel, J. and K. Froot (1990), "Chartists, Fundamentalists and Trading in the Foreign Exchange Market", *American Economic Review*, 80.

Hausmann, R. (1999), "Should There Be Five Currencies or One Hundred and Five?", *Foreign Policy*, fall, 65-79.

IMF (1998), *World Economic Outlook*, International Monetary Fund, Washington DC.

Jurgensen Report (1983), *Report of the Working Group on Exchange Market Intervention*, US Treasury Department, March, Washington DC.

Keynes, J.M. (1936), *The General Theory of Employment, Interest and Money*, Macmillan.

Krugman, P. (1989), *Exchange Rate Instability*, MIT Press, Cambridge.

McKinnon, R. (1998), "Exchange Rate Coordination for Surmounting the East Asian Currency Crisis", Paper presented at the Conference on *Financial Crises: Facts, Theories, and Policies*, International Monetary Fund, 18 November, Washington DC.

Meese, R. and K. Rogoff (1983), "Empirical Exchange Rate Models of the Seventies: Do They Fit Out of Sample?", *Journal of International Economics*, 14.

Meese, R. and K. Rogoff (1988), "Was It Real? The Exchange Rate-Interest Differential Relationship Over the Modern Floating-Rate Period", *The Journal of Finance*, 43.

Mundell, R. (1968), *International Economics*, Macmillan, New York.

Sachs, J. (1985), "The Dollar and the Policy Mix: 1985", *Brooking Papers on Economic Activity* 1.

Sachs, J. and F. Larrain (1999), "Why Dollarization Is More Straitjacket than Salvation", *Foreign Policy*, Fall, 80-93.

Shleifer A. and L. Summers (1990), "The Noise Trader Approach to Finance", *Journal of Economic Perspectives*, 4(2).

Svensson, L.E.O. (1992), "An Interpretation of Recent Research on Exchange Rate Target Zones", *Journal of Economic Perspectives*, 6(4), pp. 119-144.

Williamson, J. (1994), *Estimating Equilibrium Exchange Rates*, Institute for International Economics, Washington DC.

Williamson, J. (1998), "Crawling Bands or Monitoring Bands: How to Manage Exchange Rates in a World of Capital Mobility", *International Finance*, October.

Wren-Lewis, S. and R. Driver (1998), *Real Exchange Rates for the Year 2000*, Institute for International Economics, Washington DC.

11 Can Small Countries Keep Their Own Money and Floating Exchange Rates?

GEORGE M. VON FURSTENBERG

Introduction

What choice of exchange rate regime is left for small countries in the vicinity of a large country or group of countries with a currency that is in wide international use? Do such countries still really have a choice once they have fully opened up to international capital markets and free trade in financial services? This is the question discussed, and tentatively answered, in this chapter, looking well ahead.

A country's external exchange relations influence the efficiency of its adjustment to disturbances and its exposure to financial crises. Yet only one out of 60 sections of the G7 Finance Ministers' report to the Köln Economic Summit on *Strengthening the International Financial Architecture* was devoted to the important question of "exchange rate regimes in emerging economies". Except through incorporation by reference, the G7 Statement itself, issued 18 June 1999, did not contain any recommendations regarding the exchange rate system at all. The Finance Ministers were not quite so noncommital or unable to agree. Although they had noted in Section 33 of their report that the optimal exchange regime may well change, they at least gave some indication of what regime they considered most appropriate for the emerging economies at this time. Accommodating the positions of the International Monetary Fund (IMF), Canada, and the United Kingdom favouring floating exchange rates on one side, and the United States and one or two other G7 countries more open to the adoption of currency boards and dollarisation/eurosation on the other, the Finance Ministers agreed that:

> The international community should not provide large-scale official financing for a country intervening heavily to support a particular exchange rate, except where that level is judged sustainable and certain conditions have been met, such as

where the exchange rate policy is backed by a strong and credible commitment with supporting arrangements, and by consistent domestic policies.

In plain language similar to that which US Treasury Secretary Rubin had already used on 21 April 1999, the segment quoted above advises that exchange rates are no longer to be defended with large amounts of borrowed reserves and capital controls. Instead they should be left to float except when the commitment to fixed exchange rates is so deep that it dominates policy formation, as under some currency boards.

This conviction now is widely shared. Besides the G7 and other principals of the international financial system, a growing list of countries, so far still excluding most importantly mainland China, have lifted traditional capital controls designed to separate the domestic from the offshore capital markets. While price-based capital controls which implicitly or explicitly tax certain capital inflows (e.g., through unremunerated reserve requirements) or outflows, or direct measures that temporarily restrict short sales, domestic-currency loans to foreigners, or position taking in the futures market may be imposed to ward off or cope with acute crises, open international financial markets have become the rule in most countries.[1] As crisis after crisis has made clear, for all those countries a system of fixed but adjustable exchange rates is no longer tenable. Sachs, *et al.* (1996) have some strong words on the subject for Mexico 1994-95, which needed to be repeated for Asia 1997-98 (Radelet and Sachs, 1999) and for Brazil in 1998-99.

"For some time now, there have been only five countries [outside Euroland?] where the exchange rate has been fixed for more than five years – and the names of those five countries keep changing" (Hausmann 1999, p. 7). This leaves in the debate (1) floating exchange rates, (2) currency boards, and (3) monetary unions. I will argue that the first two of these, in small or medium-sized countries with low-credibility currencies, are plagued by both currency substitution and incomplete hedging to such an extent as to point to the safe haven of monetary union. However, monetary union can take the limited form of unilaterally adopting the strong international currency of a nearby country or group of countries as sole legal tender, as in Panama, or of deep financial integration on the basis of equality as in Euroland. Hence we recognise currency substitution and incomplete hedging as problems now afflicting small national exchange-rate systems and a variety of monetary unions as possible solutions.

What the G7 Finance Ministers did not say when they distanced themselves from maintaining fixed but adjustable exchange rates in emerging economies is that a system of flexible exchange rates, meaning (somewhat) managed floating, also has become very problematic for small countries that have opened up to international financial markets. By the same token, currency boards are proving to be stressful way-stations to unilateral (western hemisphere) or multilateral (Europe) monetary union. With both flexible exchange rates and currency boards appearing increasingly costly and beset by instability, high risk premia, and by substitution of internationally-used currencies, for purely national currencies, monetary union appears as the new endpoint of the exchange rate system in many regions. That means getting rid of a number of the lesser currencies and their exchange rates in a move toward regional currency consolidation. National monetary policies and exchange rates are becoming vectors, carriers of disease, and risks to economic health, which many small countries should dispense with.

Other researchers already have anticipated the growing deterritorialisation of money and the establishment of currency hierarchies. According to Cohen (1998), these are the characteristics which money, or claims denominated in it, must have to command a high rank in that hierarchy: confidence in its future purchasing power, exchange convenience, and free and assured capital-market negotiability, and a global presence promising widespread acceptability and transaction value. More recently the Chief Economist of the Inter-American Development Bank, Hausmann (1999, p. 1), has pointed to a growing search for new perspectives and arrangements by noting that "flexible regimes have been disappointing and fixed exchange rates are never fixed for long. Given this record, creative exchange rate arrangements are increasingly being discussed".

Floating Exchange Rates

Flexible rates once were advocated to allow even emerging economies to pursue an independent monetary policy and to obtain prompt and accurate delivery of the real exchange rate changes required by shocks when there are nominal rigidities. In practice, emerging economies, in the judgement of Frankel (1999, p. 4), "are not really able to use the tool of independent monetary policy effectively". Few now believe that the exchange-rate changes experienced under floating are predominantly stabilising for the course of the economy, with Ortiz (1999, p. 9), reflecting on Mexico's experience since 1995, being a prominent exception.

Exchange rate volatility under floating tends further to encourage currency substitution particularly in countries which lie adjacent to a country with an international currency, or country group with which they have progressively liberalised trade relations. A decline in currency protection of the inferior domestic brand of money allows the more liquid and less costly foreign brand to enter through both domestically-owned and foreign-owned banking channels.

Indeed, increasingly free trade in financial services and growing freedom of foreign establishment and foreign acquisition of domestic financial institutions have done more to foster currency competition than the absence of traditional capital controls alone. Attempts to reach a multilateral investment agreement (MAI) through the good offices of the OECD have been stalled for some years. But the growing international preoccupation with liberalising trade-related investment measures (TRIM) - first in the North American Free Trade Agreement (NAFTA) and then in its hemisphere-wide sequel, the Free Trade Area of the Americas (FTAA), as well as in the most recent (Uruguay) and forthcoming (WTO) rounds of multilateral trade negotiations - also serves to make the domestic currency monopoly increasingly contestable. Financial institutions that are based in countries with low-cost, high-efficiency domestic currency denominations thus are able to realise their external competitive advantage. They do so by offering deposit taking, lending, underwriting, insurance, and other financial services in countries with less useful currencies and less developed financial systems characterised by high costs of intermediation or large intermediation "spreads".

Currency risk premia must be paid and they are particularly large under floating. For 11 developing countries with alternating exchange rate regimes over the period 1960-98, Hausmann (1999, p. 8) reports that flexible regimes have averaged 9.2 percent real interest rates on deposits while fixed regimes have paid "only" 5.1 percent. Stein (1999, p. 4) has drawn attention to other risk-increasing features of flexible rates for those that hold financial assets denominated in domestic currency. He has pointed out that with a negative terms of trade shock, income declines and the exchange rate depreciates, reducing the real value of domestic-currency assets. Hence, "with local currency, people are playing double jeopardy; they either win big, or lose big. Given the risks, the public will shy away from holding domestic assets and prefer to hold dollars instead".

The resulting premia and wide spreads on domestic-currency financial business over dollar and other major currency interest rates tempt banks not fully to hedge all their foreign-currency liabilities. Unlike, for instance,

Eichengreen (1999, pp. 104-105), I do not expect the adoption of floating exchange rates to do much for the soundness of the banking system because such a step need not induce more hedging compared with a system of fixed but adjustable exchange rates. Such hedging can be accomplished through financial derivatives or directly by matching external liabilities with assets of equal value and availability on the balance sheet. When the benefits *and* costs of hedging both rise, there is no telling whether more or less hedging is going to be bought. Insufficiently cautious or desperate domestic financial institutions are likely to take a chance.

It may be useful to explain why the existence of a large risk premium in interest and exchange rate relations implies a correspondingly large temptation not to hedge foreign-exchange exposures fully. Covered interest parity is a consequence of arbitrage that is routinely used to derive the bilateral forward exchange rate at time $t+i$ from the corresponding spot rate at time t. All that are required are matching interest rates quoted in international markets at time t for term i in each of the two currencies. Now if there is a positive risk premium on one currency relative to the other (with the risk premium defined by what is technically known as the amount of violation of the Fisher-open condition of uncovered interest parity), the expected future spot price of foreign exchange is below the forward exchange rate. Indeed, the existence of a large risk premium - of the kind to be expected on a low-credibility, low-utility, and low-stability currency - implies that the odds are high that the foreign exchange short position can be covered at the end of the term i at a spot exchange rate more favorable than the forward rate quoted at time t for time t+i. In other words, financial operators will rightly regard it as a good, though not necessarily prudent, bet that the domestic currency will not depreciate as much as implied by the current level of the forward rate. Given that the cost of hedging is at least as high as the risk premium in effect at any one time, they may be tempted to leave part of their position uncovered. This deficiency may be revealed either by failing to hedge in financial markets or by creating doubtful dollar claims which incompletely match the dollar liabilities, particularly of banks.

The dollar assets of banks are doubtful if their loan clients do not have sufficient assured dollar cash flow from outside to service their dollar-denominated debts without having to go to the exchange market. If there is a gap, the quality of US-dollar-denominated bank assets fluctuates with the prevailing exchange rate and hence does not afford a true hedge against banks' noncontingent US dollar liabilities. This hidden currency risk explains why the borrower would be charged much more than on an otherwise comparable US-dollar-denominated claim in the United States. An even larger risk premium is required on domestic-currency deposits and hence on loan claims with banks. The excessively high costs of using the local currency then will create pressure for reducing its use in the domestic banking system relative to banking business done in the dominant international currency of the region. This process of currency substitution, which has already gone very far in Argentina, is now gaining momentum in Mexico where the peso floats unsteadily and with declining market share against the US dollar. Incomplete hedging and currency substitution are both reactions and factors contributing to the high risk premiums on financial investments booked in a small country that has not relinquished its currency.

Currency Boards

Contrary to the promise of discouraging speculative attack by virtue of being difficult to overturn, US dollar-based currency-board arrangements have not been able to prevent the emergence of occasionally high and variable risk premia.

- The average monthly treasury bill rate in Hong Kong, whose current status is that of a monetarily independent province of China, was 10.00 percent on the HK dollar at the end of a brief period of speculative attack cresting in October 1997 compared with a US Treasury bill rate of 4.95 percent. Hong Kong is about 40 percent US-dollarised judging by the share of deposits (more precisely, of M3 in 1998) denominated in that currency. Because of the intensity of intermediate goods trade with mainland China, Hong Kong's trade-weighted real exchange rate with the rest of the world can diverge from the US path of that rate.

- The three-month Buenos Aires Interbank Offered Rate (BAIBOR) ranged from 8 percent to 17 percent in pesos and from 7 percent to 12 percent in US dollars in the first half of 1999, compared with a three-month US dollar London Interbank Offered Rate (LIBOR) of 5 percent. Argentina already has been 75 percent dollarised (Ize and Levy-Yeyati, 1998, pp. 20, 26). Because Brazil started floating under pressure in January 1999 and its currency, the real, initially depreciated by about 30 percent in real terms, the maintenance of

> Argentina's parity with the US dollar over the medium term is obviously being questioned in the market.

While Hong Kong's currency board arrangement appeared solid in the summer of 1999, the economic stability and growth benefits of Argentina's continued adherence to such an arrangement with a faraway country, and hence political support, have declined. There is strong pressure either to abrogate some of its Common Market commitments or to stabilise the exchange rate with its Mercosur partners, particularly Brazil, after a devaluation of the peso, at levels all members can live with. This shows once again that maintaining adjustable or floating, and in either case unreliable, exchange rates among the members of a common market ultimately cannot be reconciled with completion of that common market and the achievement of deep economic integration of its member countries. Rather, once one country depreciates, the other members are pressed.

Argentina may not be able to escape its predicament without major harm on account of the widespread dollarisation of its economy. If it were to match Brazil's real devaluation through exchange rate flexibility of its own, it would gravely damage those of Argentinian corporations whose service obligations on dollar liabilities exceed the dollar portion of their net cash flow. The quality of bank assets thus would deteriorate. In addition, there would be a growing discrepancy between the realisable value of US dollar assets and the face value of liquid dollar liabilities on the books of banks. For instance, a mortgagor in the suburbs of Buenos Aires who opts for a dollar-denominated over a peso-denominated mortgage because it saves 300 basis points interest, cannot be a credible dollar mortgagor with a salary set in peso. The reason is that the risk characteristics of the mortgage, as judged for instance by the ratio of mortgage payment to income and the US dollar value of the security property, fail to be independent of the peso-dollar exchange rate. Hence any devaluation, with or without maintaining the trappings of the currency-board arrangement, will be highly contractionary initially. It will bring on an immediate intermediation and economic crisis that will only gradually permit a return to macroeconomic balance through a revival of exports. For this reason, formal dollarisation may be more suitable than devaluation to get rid of the currency board and the credibility problems that now plague it.

Bimonetarism and the Way Out of Transition Problems

The joint circulation of two or more moneys at fixed exchange rates within a country, bimonetarism, just like bimetallism in an earlier century, has often been viewed as a prescription for disaster. When market conditions require a change in relative prices but the authorities resist, the about-to-be-depreciated metal would drive out the "strong" metal as a means of payment, as in Gresham's Law. When countries allow banks to accept interest-bearing US dollar deposits along with deposits in their own national currency at an officially fixed exchange rate, pressure on that exchange rate is processed differently: the good deposit money now threatens to drive out the bad as a store of value. When anticipating a depreciation of the local currency, there will be a tendency to rush into US dollars, unless that tendency is credibly restrained by sufficiently high and politically sustainable interest rates on local-currency claims, as it rarely is, or can be. Whenever countries far away from the United States and largely outside its economic orbit, such as Argentina and Hong Kong, fix their exchange rate with the US dollar in currency-board arrangements while their major trading partners (Brazil, China) follow a different exchange rate regime, they are heading for trouble. Hong Kong had trouble on account of the devaluation of surrounding currencies for over a year prior to September 1998 and is not out of the woods yet. Argentina was traumatised in early 1999 by Brazil's sharp real depreciation, much of which has stuck so far. The aggressive promotion of currency board arrangements with the US dollar in places as remote as Indonesia, and not just in its own neighbourhood, clearly is unsafe.

The national monetary and exchange arrangements of most of the smaller countries may no longer be sustainable, no matter what the nature of such arrangements. The realisation is growing that national monetary sovereignty is becoming increasingly obsolete and dysfunctional for many of the financially smaller and less developed countries of the world. Once these countries have opened their financial sectors both regionally and globally at least to the extent implied by the absence of capital and foreign-investment controls coupled with the principle of national treatment, then pressures to do away with restrictions on payments, financial investments, and foreign-currency deposit taking will be overwhelming. Unless a particular small country is a strong international competitor in the provision of financial services and a net exporter of such services, and unless it has a long tradition of managing a hard and internationally competitive currency like the Swiss franc, pound sterling, or the Canadian dollar, its currency may not be able to survive unprotected. Even then some nationals of these countries (e.g., Holle 1999) have expressed doubts about the desirability of keeping their own money indefinitely. Elsewhere, too, currency protection is becoming ever more difficult to arrange and to defend in a liberal trading regime. Hence, even if the IMF's capital account amendment remains shelved, capital controls and national currency protection are doomed in practice.

With currencies and currency denominations then chosen so as to yield maximum liquidity service at the lowest cost, the currencies of most of the smaller countries inevitably will be destabilised by currency substitution. Indeed, these currencies eventually will be swept under in countries that adjoin an area already equipped with a low-cost, high-utility international currency. This is beginning to happen, for instance in Poland, the Czech Republic, and Hungary - not to mention currency-board countries like Estonia and Bosnia - with regard to the DM/Euro, and in Mexico with respect to the US dollar.

The process of currency substitution, rather than leading to deep financial integration that would allow banks and other financial institutions in the region to deal confidently with each other, tends to destabilise the indigenous banking systems of small countries. Since banks from the adjoining international-money area have lower funding costs in that currency, they likely can out-compete indigenous banking institutions in the business denominated in the international currency such as Euro or US dollar. To be willing to hold some of their deposits in a local currency that is clearly becoming less useful and far more risky than the international currency, depositors will require systematically higher real rates of return on deposits denominated in local than in international currency. These higher real rates in turn have to be paid, after adding a large spread for bank overhead and default risk, by those marginal borrowers who are still in the market for local-currency loans because they have no other financing options. Depending on the coverage of deposit insurance, the adverse selection and deterioration of bank balance sheets will further contribute to the vicious cycle by which the local currency is gradually eliminated from the market. This process of elimination is punctuated by crises of the local banks and by almost continuous strains on the intermediation system and on traditional banking relationships.

Instead of lauding spontaneous, and consequently disruptive, dollarisation, as even luminaries such as Barro (1999) have done, thought should be given to the hard institutional work of extending or developing monetary unions in the major regions: Here Europe, and not the United States, has led the way in building a more stable financial system from the ground up. This is a system in which all members, and their banking and finance institutions, can participate with roughly equal opportunity and proportional benefit, instead of one country claiming all the say-so and seigniorage profit. The United States already obtains more than twice as much cash-equivalent benefit annually from the use of at least 60 percent of its noninterest bearing currency in other countries than it provides for international development and foreign aid. Dollarisation without representation would extend the pattern of winner-take-all, to the rest of the world's displeasure.

Forms of Monetary Union

Monetary union is the capstone of economic integration. However, as the many recent applications of the gravity model (see Frankel, 1997) have demonstrated conclusively, even in this day and age, the international integration both of production and of trade are much closer regionally than globally. Such integration is marked by a deep supplier network fostering intermediate-goods or components trade within and between firms, and co-production arrangements throughout the region. The result is that countries may well conduct two-thirds or more of their entire international trade with their common-market or free-trade-area partners. Because multiple links imply mutual dependence, a supply disturbance affecting, say, the supplier of an essential part in one country soon affects assembly operations throughout the region. Similarly, the economic effects of a downturn in demand in one country are quickly shared with neighbouring countries which are its major source of imports.

Technically, therefore, it is becoming ever clearer that economic integration strengthens the symmetry of shock exposure, as Frankel and Rose (1998) provide recent evidence. This increased symmetry should then extend also to policy, particularly monetary policy. As a recent OECD study (1999, pp. 12-16) has qualified carefully, if equal aversion to inflation and similar transmission mechanisms of monetary policy to the economy are added to the symmetry of exogenous disturbances themselves, the optimal policy response would be the same for all countries in the integrated region.

Another factor promoting the move toward monetary union is that exchange rates function less like shock absorbers facilitating adjustment and more like unpredictable disturbances that upset production arrangements and industry location patterns within economically integrated regions. Buiter

(1997) has emphasised that having more types of financial claims and hence more relative asset prices is not costless. The price behaviour, for instance of exchange rates, tends to be endogenously determined only in (small) part, while also being an independent conveyor of disturbances to the rest of the economic system. Cooper (1999, p. 122) has elaborated on the self-justifying expectations that give exchange rates a fundamentally unstable dynamic. Certainly monetary union is the perfect cure for money demand disturbances originating in the small country, as it makes the supply of money to such a country very nearly perfectly elastic at the unionwide (interbank or money-market) interest rate.

Monetary union not only helps avoid disruptions from certain quarters but also generates new opportunities for those countries which can accede to a union that is based on an international currency native to the region. Differential currency risk premia with the country issuing such an international currency are eliminated for the small country. Its differential country risk premium is much diminished also as national monetary and exchange rate policy is relinquished and fiscal affairs are submitted to the judgement of both government peer groups and the market. Further reasons for interest-rate convergence within the monetary union are that comparable standards are achieved throughout the financial services industry of the region, so that financial markets can be integrated confidently and without reference to nationality across all member countries. In the run-up to monetary union, this involves institutional and regulatory overhaul and market-driven adoption of best practices throughout the region. The resulting race to the top benefits, in particular, those small countries which start out at lower levels of economic and financial developments more than their neighbours already in the union.

Monetary Union is for the Economically Integrated Countries of a Region

As Fontagné and Freudenberg (1999) have documented, the case for monetary union grows with the intensity of regional integration to which it itself contributes. However, monetary union should follow, not precede, deep integration. Without such prior integration, the shock exposure of countries will be far too asymmetric to allow them to march to the same monetary tune, sharing the union's external exchange rate and internal financial system and interest rates.

Thus, if they could start over, economically not deeply integrated, distant countries, such as Argentina and the United States, should not aim for monetary union or its inferior realisation, unilateral dollarisation, which now appears as the endpoint of Argentina's currency board. Hemisphere-wide monetary union may become optimal once economic integration has spread through the chain of countries between the United States and Argentina to the principal trading partners, such as Brazil, in between. Until then, however, countries that are not yet locked into suboptimal arrangements, such as unnatural currency boards with high exit or conversion costs, have only Hobson's choice: They will have to float against the international currencies. They can do so either alone or in combination with neighbouring countries with purely national currencies until a deep connection is forged to a country or group of countries with an international money. It is worth recalling that Alexandre Kafka, the Dean of the IMF's Executive Board for decades and to this day its single most important non-US member, provided an assessment of the extent to which Latin American countries approach the conditions of optimum currency areas already in 1973.

Obviously, being economically and geographically close to an international-money zone is good for Eastern Europe, North Africa, and parts of the Middle East with regard first to unilateral eurosation and then to eventual accession to European Monetary Union. It is also good for countries first immediately to the South and Southeast of the United States and then throughout the FTAA. But while the existing monetary union is set to spread in Europe and dollarisation is spreading in the western hemisphere, it is difficult to see how one or more unions with an international currency could safely emerge in Asia although the US dollar is already widely used there. Even currency board arrangements with the US dollar in Asia are likely to be quite unsuitable for maintenance of equilibrium in trade and capital flows, given the lack of effective integration achieved under the Asian-Pacific Economic Cooperation Forum (APEC) by the countries of the Pacific Rim.

Conclusion

Monetary unions are set to spread in some regions. If they cover areas that are already deeply integrated economically and do at least two-thirds of their international trade internally, they offer significant advantages over a system of floating exchange rates as well as over currency boards. Both of these national systems suffer from currency substitution and an almost irresistible temptation to keep hedging incomplete when they apply to countries which can not call an internationally-used currency denomination their own. These deficiencies contribute to vulnerability of the domestic financial system and provide a natural opening for foreign banks. Ultimately much or all of the deposit and loan business conducted in small and purely national currencies becomes uncompetitive, being weighed down by high risks and costs compared with business conducted in the dominant currency denominations or international money brands.

International currencies thus increasingly will assert themselves in the world. The inevitable currency consolidation can be achieved either on a fairly equal and equitable basis through negotiation and gradual implementation of a deep monetary union, or unilaterally. If the country with the dominant international currency in the region is unwilling to negotiate a multilateral union with its neighbours, the competitive forces of currency substitution can eventually force currency consolidation in free financial markets nonetheless. This process involves passing through high-risk stages of bimonetarism to the complete unilateral displacement of the local currency by an international currency without necessarily achieving a deep and confident integration of financial and banking systems or gaining access to a lender of last resort.

It appears that much of the international financial community, including the IMF, has become convinced that exchange rates pegged in a narrow band must yield to floating just when floating has outlived its usefulness for small currencies. These currencies are being superseded by market forces as the foundations for an independent monetary policy have begun to crumble. In several parts of the world, small and purely national currencies now are up against an international currency with less and less regulatory protection. The twin blades of free trade in financial services and freedom of foreign establishment snip away at the business that can usefully be conducted in the low-credibility and high-cost domestic currency denomination.

The IMF deals with ministries, central banking institutions, and other agencies of national governments; it has more independent authority, though not necessarily more effect, the smaller and more backward a country. Hence it is predisposed to advise small countries on the exercise of *national* policy and on the management of *national* exchange rates. It is not well suited for counselling them on how best to adapt to market forces and to achieve monetary union with an international currency over a wide region. Yet this is where many of these countries will be heading. On a personal basis, the IMF's First Deputy Managing Director has expressed similar views, though there is a question whether financial market shocks more than countries' policies move exchange rates:

> It is also likely that if the Euro succeeds – and it will succeed – that we will see fewer and fewer national currencies. The Argentine dollarization move and the quiet Mexican dollarization now under way are likely to make progress in the years ahead.... When you have watched what countries do with their floating exchange rates over long periods, you become much more concerned about the damage they can do by having their own exchange rate to manipulate. - Fischer, 1999, 2-3.

In the western hemisphere, for instance, achievement of the FTAA among 34 countries by the year 2005, as currently planned, surely is not compatible with having anything like that number of currencies ultimately surviving, not even in the shelter of a currency board. However, carrying the ongoing unilateral dollarisation to its logical conclusion of making the US dollar sole legal tender throughout the hemisphere would be a politically presumptuous, unco-operative - and hence at least initially half-baked - form of monetary and financial union. It offers far less to joiners than the multilateral model exemplified by the European Monetary Union (EMU).

The EMU is the type of model which the countries in this hemisphere should be demanding not just to obtain their fair share of seigniorage profits and a modicum of co-determination, but also to achieve deep financial integration. Such integration would not impose harmonisation in advance but would be based on mutual recognition of financial-adequacy and regulatory standards while meeting strict minimum requirements such as those proposed under the auspices of the BIS. Differing with Summers' surmise (1999, pp. 13-14) that "European economic and monetary union may be the exception that proves the rule about challenges of integrating national monies", I submit that currency consolidation has caught the wave of the future. Following an EMU-type model to such consolidation would allow the smaller currency systems an opportunity to arrange a friendly merger with surrounding currency, exchange, and financial systems, rather than being hopelessly tossed about, crowded out, and washed under.

Note

1 See Cooper (1999) and Ulan (2000) for descriptions and analysis.

References

Barro, R.J. (1999), "Let the Dollar Reign from Seattle to Santiago", *Wall Street Journal*, Midwest edition (March 8), p. A18.

Buiter, W. (1997), "The Economic Case for Monetary Union in the European Union", *Review of International Economics, Special Supplement*, 5(4), pp. 10-35.

Cohen, B.J. (1998), *The Geography of Money*, Cornell University Press, Ithaca NY.

Cooper, R.N. (1999), "Should Capital Controls be Banished?", *Brookings Papers on Economic Activity*, No. 1, pp. 89-125.

Eichengreen, B. (1999), *Toward a New International Financial Architecture: A Practical Post-Asia Agenda*, Institute for International Economics, Washington DC.

Fischer, S. (1999), "The Financial Crisis in Emerging Markets: Some Lessons", Outline of comments prepared for delivery at the conference of the Economic Strategy Institute, Washington DC (April 28), pp. 1-4.

Fontagné, L. and M. Freudenberg (1999), "Endogenous Symmetry of Shocks in a Monetary Union", *Open Economies Review*, 10(3), pp. 263-288.

Frankel, J.A. (1999), in International Monetary Fund Economic Forum, "Dollarization: Fad or Future for Latin America?", http://www.imf.org/external/np/tr/1999/TR990624.HTM, pp. 2-6.

Frankel, J.A. (1997), *Regional Trading Blocs In the World Economic System*, Institute for International Economics, Washington DC.

Frankel, J.A. and A.K. Rose (1998), "The Endogeneity of the Optimum Currency Area Criteria", *Economic Journal*, vol. (449), pp. 1109-1025.

G7 (1999), *G7 Statement*, Cologne, 18-20 June.

G7 Finance Ministers (1999), *Strengthening the International Financial Architecture: Report of the G7 Finance Ministers to the Köln Economic Summit*, Cologne, 18-20 June.

Hausmann, R. (1999), "Exchange Rate Debate" and other short articles, *Latin American Economic Policies*, vol. 7 (Second Quarter), pp. 1-2, 6-8.

Holle, P. (1999), "Canadians Wonder Whether the Loonie is for the Birds", *Wall Street Journal*, August 6, p. A11.

Ize, A. and E. Levy-Yeyati (1998), "Dollarization of Financial Intermediation: Causes and Policy Implications", International Monetary Fund Working Paper, WP/98/28.

Kafka, A. (1973), "Optimum Currency Areas and Latin America", in H.G. Johnson and A.K. Swoboda, eds., *The Economics of Common Currencies*, George Allen & Unwin, London, pp. 210-218.

OECD (1999), *EMU Facts, Challenges and Policies*, Paris, Organisation for Economic Co-operation and Development.

Ortiz, G. (1999), 6-10 in IMF Economic Forum, "Dollarization: Fad or Future for Latin America?", http://www.imf.org/external/np/tr/1999/TR990624.HTM.

Radelet, S. and J. Sachs (1999), "What Have We Learned, So Far, from the Asian Financial Crisis?", Unpublished paper, (January 4), pp. 1-24.

Sachs, J., A. Tornell and A. Velasco (1996), "The Collapse of the Mexican Peso: What Have We Learned?", *Economic Policy*, (22), pp. 15-56.

Stein, E. (1999), "Financial Systems and Exchange Rates: Losing Interest in Flexibility", *Latin American Economic Policies*, vol. 7, pp. 2, 8.

Summers, L.H. (1999), "Distinguished Lecture on Economics in Government: Reflections on Managing Global Integration", *The Journal of Economic Perspectives*, 13(2), (Spring), pp. 3-18.

Ulan, M.K. (2000), "Is a Chilean-Style Tax on Short-Term Capital Flows Stabilizing? A Review Essay", *Open Economies Review*, forthcoming.

12 From Globalisation to Regionalism: The Foreign Direct Investment Dimension of International Finance

ALAN M. RUGMAN

Introduction

With the collapse of Asian economic growth in 1997 and the ensuing worldwide recession of 1998-99, the world may well be witnessing the end of globalisation. In the wake of the crisis, with the backlash in the affected economies against unrestrained portfolio capital and lending flows, and the defeat of efforts to liberalise foreign direct investment (FDI), and international trade more at the Organisation for Economic Co-operation and Development (OECD) (Rugman 1999) and at the World Trade Organisation (WTO) at its 1999 ministerial meeting in Seattle respectively, the momentum of, and enthusiasm for, globalisation has been halted or even reversed.

Globalisation has thus developed a bad name, partly as a result of the Asian financial crisis and its infection of the rest of the world. The perceived failure of global market-based capitalism is leading to calls for tighter financial regulation and capital controls. Yet globalisation has relatively little to do with recent world financial turmoil, which has been caused by short-term investors in financial capital. Instead, the correct focus of globalisation is on the activities of multinational enterprises (MNEs) and the FDI they represent and generate.

The health of the new international financial architecture depends crucially not on short-term capital flows and their management, but on the inextricably interlinked but often overlooked issue of long-term capital flows through foreign direct investment. It thus depends ultimately on the operations and calculations of the multinational corporations that conduct this activity.

A close analysis of this deep foundation of the international financial system suggests that much of the current controversy and concern about the post-crisis challenge to financial globalisation and its management by firms and governments is misplaced. For in the realm of foreign direct investment and multinational corporation behaviour, globalisation never really occurred at all.

The vast majority of the world's manufacturing and service activity is organised regionally, not globally. Multinational enterprises, the engines of international business, think regionally and act locally. They operate from the triad-based home bases of the United States, European Union (EU), or Japan, at the hub of business networks in which clusters of value-added activities are organised. The process of globalisation is therefore a triad and management-driven one.

Today the world's 500 largest MNEs, based in the triad of the United States, the European Union, and Japan, account for more than 90 percent of the world's volume of FDI and about half of world trade. Yet these MNEs are not really "global". Instead they operate on a triad-regional basis. Most FDI is intra-regional, rather than inter-regional.

For example, more than 90 percent of all the automobiles consumed in North America are built in North American factories owned by Japanese and European MNEs as well as by General Motors, Ford, and Daimler-Chrysler (Weintraub and Sands 1998). In Europe, the situation is similar, as it is in Japan. In the specialty chemicals sector, over 90 percent of all paint is made and used regionally by triad-based MNEs. The same is true in steel, heavy electrical equipment, and much of the rest of the manufacturing sector. Only consumer electronics and high-value added goods with low transport costs are really global. Similarly, in the service sector, which now employs 70 percent of people in North America, Western Europe, and Japan, MNEs operate in local clusters in their home-based economies (Porter 1990).

From this vantage point, the current crisis of globalisation is exposed not as an historic period of instability or shift in the structure of the global economy and its management, but merely as a temporary disequilibrium. It arose as the Japanese/Asian side of the triad was experiencing poor corporate and poor financial market performance. In contrast, US and European MNEs were performing relatively better.

Recent research on some 200 of the world's largest MNEs found that between 1996 and 1998 Japanese MNEs had an average return on foreign assets of 1.25 percent. That return is dismal compared with 6.24 percent for MNEs based in the United States and 5.49 percent for European MNEs, including 7.78 percent for British ones. These key data from the Templeton Global Performance Index are shown in Table 12.1. These data reflect the slower pace of trade and investment liberalisation in Japan compared with the other two parts of the triad. As a result of liberalisation and deregulation the North American and European-based MNEs have been more successful.

Table 12.1 Average Annual Returns on Foreign Assets (ROFAs) by MNEs 1996-1997

Home Country of MNE	Average ROFAs
Britain	7.78
United States	6.24
Rest of Europe	5.11
Canada	3.16
Germany	2.95
France	2.75
China	2.10
Japan	1.25
Australia	0.31

Source: Michael Gestrin, Rory Knight, and Alan M Rugman (1998), *The Templeton Global Performance Index*, Templeton College, University of Oxford, Oxford.

Competing Conceptions of Globalisation

The term "globalisation" is much abused and diversely defined by scholars who conceive of it from the viewpoint of their own discipline. For economists and those in management studies, globalisation can be defined as the activities of multinational enterprises engaging in foreign direct investment to create foreign subsidiaries which add value across national borders. In contrast, sociologists argue that globalisation is a multidimensional phenomenon, best "understood in terms of simultaneous, complex related processes in the realms of economy, politics, culture, technology and so forth" (Tomlinson 1992, p.16). From this vantage point two major themes emerge.

The first is that global modernity leads to the social and cultural aspects of the process of the lived experience of the complex connectivity of global modernity. This builds on the argument that, with globalisation, social relations are no longer local but stretch across time and space. The linkage of global modernity to global culture contrasts the power of multinational enterprises to distribute a global capitalist monoculture with a more sceptical realist viewpoint about the highly regulated and divided world system in place today. Tomlinson concludes that "there is little here to support the view that a single, unified global culture in any conventional sense is about to emerge" (p. 105), with culture defined as "the social production of existentially significant meaning" (p. 21).

The second theme is that a deterritorialisation of culture is occurring due to the hybridisation of cultures. This process is being speeded up by global mass media and communications technologies. Tomlinson's conclusion is that the global culture which is emerging is complex and deterritorialised rather than simplistic and monolithic. This complexity exists because culture is not linked to local nation states but is deterritorialised, which, in turn, links to a cultural process of enforced proximity and cosmopolitan politics.

In this very broad perspective the key driver of globalisation, the multinational enterprise, no longer takes centre stage. Yet it is not international trade (which has existed for two millennia) or even flows of short-term portfolio finance that have created the modern social, cultural, and political problems of the world. Rather, it is the power and influence of modern multinational enterprises operating their businesses within different countries that are the perceived cause of global harmonisation in areas such as culture.

The Role of Multinational Enterprises

The standard definition of globalisation, based on economics and business strategy, is the worldwide production and marketing of goods and services by multinational enterprises. An MNE is defined in turn as a firm with production and/or distribution facilities in two or more countries. With this type of globalisation, MNEs can realise economies of scale and build dispersed production networks. They are able to produce and sell goods and products across national borders, often within their own internal networks of subsidiaries, or in close alliances with partner firms (Rugman 1996).

Using these definitions, it is clear that the world is dominated by the activities of triad-based MNEs which operate "regionally" rather than globally. MNEs are neither globally monolithic nor excessively powerful in political terms. The largest 500 of them are evenly based in the triad economies of the United States, the European Union, and Japan. Across a wide variety of industrial sectors and traded services, these triad-based MNEs compete for global market shares and profits. Yet the process of regional competition itself erodes any possibility of sustainable long-term rents for these MNEs. Research shows that the world's largest 500 MNEs do not earn excess profits over time and that economic efficiency is enhanced by their activities (Rugman 1996).

In turn, the nature of triad-based competition faced by these MNEs limits their ability to pursue political goals, since they are forced to concentrate on their day-to-day operational efficiency and strategic planning in order to survive. It is a common mistake to associate the very large economic size of MNEs with political power, as does Strange (1988, 1996, 1998). While many of the largest 500 MNEs have total revenues greater than the gross national products of mid- to small-sized countries, they act within the parameters of regulations and rules set by governments and international organisations. These enterprises are preoccupied with survival, profitability, and growth. In general, they are far too busy to deal in any meaningful way with the social, cultural, and related non-economic areas of government activity.

Some political scientists critical of globalisation and market forces neglect these phenomena. They argue that MNEs operate in a system of global free trade policed by a powerful WTO (Gray 1998). In fact, the WTO has a small secretariat of around 300 professionals. Its role is merely to be an appeal court for trade disputes between member countries. It is basically a reactive quasi-judicial body rather than a policy-making and enforcement mechanism for free trade. Indeed, most of the disputes arise from the closing of markets by the misuse of trade remedy laws, rather than from market opening issues.

Where there is some conflict between MNEs and government is in the area of international political economy, defined as the ability of MNEs to lobby and otherwise influence the policies of national (and sub-national) governments. This occurs in areas such as trade, investment, science, and technology, and in the administration by bureaucracies of these policies. Yet, even here, the interests of MNEs are largely triad-based. For example, Japanese MNEs will mainly help to develop Japanese competitiveness in their home base, and only contribute peripherally to the public policies of the host countries in which they have subsidiaries. In summary, groups of MNEs can help to develop their home economies, but the nature of triad competition erodes any sustainable global market power of individual MNEs.

Triad-Based Production

Multinational enterprises dominate international production across major industries such as automobiles, consumer electronics, chemicals and petrochemicals, petroleum, and pharmaceuticals. In these sectors there is a very large amount of intra-industry, indeed, intra-firm trade and investment. The United Nations annual *World Investment Report* estimates that as much as 60 percent of trade and investment in these sectors is intra-firm. Of that, well over 90 percent of the world's stock of FDI and over half of its trade is conducted by the very largest MNEs listed in Table 12.2.

Table 12.2 The World's 500 Largest MNEs

Country/Block	Number of MNEs in 1996
United States	185
European Community	156
Japan	100
Switzerland	11
South Korea	9
Canada	12
Brazil	4
Australia	7
China	6
Other	10
Total	500

Source: Adapted from "The Fortune Global 500", *Fortune*, 4 August, 1997.

Advances in technology intensify the concentration of economic power in the hands of MNEs. It is not so much in the creation of new knowledge (as here smaller, innovating firms can do well) but in the application to mass production that the MNE has an advantage. Most of the manufacturing productivity advances in Japanese MNEs have occurred in incremental process improvements reflecting efficient organisational structures. Pure research, when needed, can be bought from abroad, as the Japanese MNEs have done through their activities in California's Silicon Valley and other US-based research centres. It is the proprietary internalisation of technology that gives MNEs the edge in their worldwide production and marketing (Rugman 1996).

A second mistake in much of the current thinking about globalisation is to equate the innovative production and intensive global marketing of MNEs with the development of a homogenised global culture. While the success of MNEs in producing goods and services increases worldwide consumption (or materialism) there is little evidence that the end result of triad-based MNEs is a global culture. Rather, an increase in standards of living offers consumers greater choice, as MNEs respond to the growth of divergent tastes with niche products and services.

Many MNEs are "nationally responsive" and/or are both scale economy driven and nationally responsive at the same time (Bartlett and Ghoshal 1989). In other words, MNEs do not all pursue global low cost or differentiation strategies, which could, perhaps, lead to a homogenisation of culture. Some are in a strategic space where they need to adapt their products and services to the different political, cultural, and religious systems all too pervasive in the world today.

The homogenisation argument is correct to the point that it suggests there may be strong "regional" effects, i.e., each of the triads may be spreading influence regionally rather than globally. In North America, the US influence is apparent in Canada and Mexico (although the language difference in Quebec and Mexico is a strongly mitigating factor). In Asia, Japanese influence is widespread. Yet in Europe there is relatively little cultural homogenisation as strong national differences persist despite the success of the Brussels bureaucracy in developing EU-wide economic policies with common legal standards and practices.

Regional Production and Marketing

The MNEs in Table 12.1 are the vehicles for increasing global interdependence. Yet they are also strongly based in the triad of North America, the EU, and Japan, with 442 of the world's largest 500 coming from these regions. These triad blocs are in some danger of becoming even more protectionist since all of them adopt nontariff barriers to trade and investment to limit access to their internal markets and/or give preferential access to certain partners in return for reciprocal advantages. Examples of nontariff barriers include rules of origin, discriminatory health and safety codes used to keep out agricultural products, new environmental regulations in the EU and NAFTA, exempted sectors from the principle of national treatment (such as culture, education, health, etc.), and poorly administered anti-dumping and countervailing duty laws.

The extent of nontariff barriers in the triad serves to limit access to their home base markets. Many US restrictions are aimed at Japanese and European competitors, and vice versa. Three strong "regional" trading and investment blocs have developed. For example, the world automobile industry is not really globalised; instead, well over 90 percent of production and sales take place in each of the three separate triad markets, using intra-bloc networks of suppliers and distributors. Agreements like NAFTA build on over 30 years of US-Canadian automobile managed trade (Weintraub and Sands 1998). The regional nature of the auto industry is replicated in chemicals, petrochemicals, steel, and other major industrial sectors. The focus is on market access on a regional, rather than a global, basis. While this is good news for triad-based MNEs, it makes life difficult for MNEs from nontriad economies, since they need access to a triad market even to start a global strategy.

This point is reconfirmed in Table 12.3, which reports the 20 most transnational MNEs, defined as those with over two-thirds of their activities outside their home base. The index of transnationality is a simple mean of the ratio of foreign to total activities for three indexes, sales, assets, and employees. To some extent Table 12.3 is the inverse of the strong home-base triad argument of Table 12.1. In this new table, the MNEs are usually from smaller, nontriad countries such as Switzerland or Canada, and they need foreign sales to obtain globalisation status. For example, Canada has a small market, only one-tenth the economic size of the United States and EU. Thus Seagram, Alcan, and Thompson will realise the great majority of their sales outside their home country. Even the MNEs in Table 12.3 that are in the EU are from countries such as the United Kingdom, Holland, Sweden, i.e. they are MNEs whose home country market is small relative to the large market of the EU. For these MNEs from smaller economies, access to the triad market is central to their success. They have all developed such regional market access strategies, sometimes in accord with regional trade and investment agreements like the EU and the North American Free Trade Agreement (NAFTA).

Table 12.3 World's Leading Multinational Enterprises, 1997

Rank	Company Name	Home Country	Index of Transnationality
1	Seagram Co.	Canada	97.6
2	Asea Brown Boveri	Switzerland	95.7
3	Thomson Corporation	Canada	95.1
4	Nestle SA	Switzerland	93.2
5	Unilever N.V.	Netherlands	92.4
6	Solvay	Belgium	92.3
7	Electrolux AB	Sweden	89.4
8	Philips Electronics N.V.	Netherlands	86.4
9	Bayer AG	Germany	82.7
10	Roche Holding AG	Switzerland	82.2
11	Holderbank Financiere Glarus AG	Switzerland	80.8
12	Akzo Nobel N.V.	Netherlands	79.5
13	BTR	UK	78.2
14	Glaxo Wellcome Plc	UK	78.2
15	L'Air Liquide Group	France	78.1
16	Hoechst AG	Germany	76.5
17	Imperial Chemical Industries	UK	75.0
18	Cable and Wireless Plc	UK	74.7
19	Novartis	Switzerland	74.4
20	Total SA	France	73.2

Source: Adapted from United Nations (1999), *World Investment Report*, UN Publications, Geneva.

Regionalisation

One of the paradoxes of globalisation is that, in the world of FDI and MNEs, it never really occurred. Instead, the vast majority of MNE manufacturing and service activity is organised regionally, not globally. While MNEs are the engines of international business, their strategies are regional. Political factors and institutional organisations reinforce business at a regional level rather than at the multilateral level required for full globalisation. The dominant world manufacturing MNEs operate in each others' triad markets, giving a "regional" set of activities which is commonly confused with globalisation.

Ford, General Motors, IBM, GE, and Dupont all have hundreds of thousands of employees in dozens of country subsidiaries across the triad. Toyota, Matsushita, Sony, and NEC have outsourced much of their component production to Southeast Asia and employ thousands of Americans and Europeans. European firms such as Unilever, Shell, Nestlé, ABB, and Phillips are even more decentralised across the triad with a large degree of autonomy for subsidiary managers (Bartlett and Ghoshal 1989).

Large MNEs often serve as flagships in regional business networks. Many other firms have roles as network partners, as key suppliers, key customers, and so on (Rugman and D'Cruz 1997). Small and medium-sized businesses are partners in business networks led by the largest MNEs. Government can also be a partner in successful business networks (as in Japan), but by acting as a facilitator to help improve competitiveness, rather than as a regulator.

As a result of what is sometimes called globalisation, various writers have argued that there is an emerging homogenisation of world products and services (Ohmae 1990). The collapse of communism and the triumph of market-based democracies has reinforced this viewpoint that Western-based (including Japanese) consumerism is the dominant force behind the success of the MNEs. This "end of history" thesis has been advanced by Fukuyama (1992).

In some sectors, such as consumer electronics, this view of globalisation is correct. Yet in many others it is not. In both automobiles and chemicals, over 90 percent of products produced in each of the triad regions is sold within that region. There is no global car. Instead, there are US, European, and Japanese bases for automobile production, supported by the paints and plastics business of the chemicals sector and regional triad-based steel producers. Indeed, most manufacturing activity is regional, not global. In terms of output (goods and services produced and sold) and input (number of employees and financing) well over 90 percent of MNE manufacturing is intra-regional rather than global (Rugman and Hodgetts 1995).

In the service sectors, the lack of pure globalisation is even more apparent. Except for professional service providers (such as consultants, film stars, and business school professors) well over 95 percent of all employees in the service sector are local, not global. For example, virtually all workers in the health care sector are local, being location-bound by either national or regional professional regulatory and accreditation bodies. Regions have cultural attributes and political borders which are stronger than the economic forces of globalisation. There are no global prescription drugs. Instead, MNEs have to engage in FDI and satisfy national state regulations in order to sell locally. Centralised production and worldwide distribution are not possible for pharmaceutical MNEs.

Managers of MNEs are likely to make major mistakes if they believe their business is global when it is regional. The managerial consequences of the lack of pure globalisation has led to the need for regional, triad-based strategies by MNEs.

The influential home country "diamond" model of international competitiveness, (Porter 1990) is fully consistent with this triad/regional dynamic. An MNE will build upon the strong home-base diamond characteristics of the United States, EU, or Japan, and use the appropriate triad market as a staging ground for activities in other markets. But the great majority of production and sales of the MNE will be concentrated in its home region. This is especially true for US and Japanese MNEs, and perhaps less so for British ones, although most European, for example German, MNEs sell mainly within the EU. Smaller firms, such as the German Mittelstand, make virtually all their sales within the EU.

In the successor "double diamond" model (Rugman 1996), the role of the triad is again dominant. Smaller economies can develop MNEs only if these firms have access to a neighbouring regional market. For example, Canadian MNEs such as Northern Telecom, Alcan, and Bombardier have developed double diamond relationships with the United States. Korean chaebols sell both to Japan and the United States, using two double-diamonds. Mexico is developing MNEs within NAFTA, using a Mexico-US double diamond approach. The double- and single-diamond theories do not support any pure globalisation strategies of MNEs. Rather, they help explain the reality of regional/triad production and sales.

The work of international institutions such as the General Agreement on Tariffs and Trade (GATT)/WTO reinforces regional, rather than fostering global, production. Most tariff cuts and investment liberalisation are agreed upon bilaterally and thus regionally, rather than in a generic multilateral manner. The voluntary "club" membership of the GATT/WTO leads to mutual accommodations by trade partners, rather than agreement to sweeping new free market principles (Ostry 1997). The failure of the OECD's multilateral agreement on investment and of the WTO's effort to launch a new millennium round of multilateral trade liberalisation negotiations at its Seattle ministerial meeting in December 1999 is the latest sign that the trade and investment liberalisation required for globalisation are slowing down and even going into reverse, promoting regionalisation (Rugman 1999).

The imperfect nature of global markets has been reinforced by political developments and new institutional structures. The emergence of the NAFTA is a mixed blessing. While tariffs are eliminated and the national treatment principle is applied to foreign direct investment these benefits of liberalisation are offset by the erection of new nontariff barriers to trade. These include restrictive rules of origin affecting automobile and textile production in Mexico, which effectively deny entry to the US market (Rugman 1994). In addition, many service sectors, including health, social services, education, transportation, and financial services, are exempted from national treatment, leading to the institutionalisation of discriminatory investment measures. The domestic laws protecting Canada's medicare system are listed in the NAFTA Annexes as exemptions from the principle of national treatment, thereby retaining national sovereignty in the administration of health care. Using this analysis, NAFTA has emerged as a relatively closed regional bloc, though not as closed as the EU. In particular, the local service sector (including health care) is now protected regionally as well as nationally against the forces of globalisation and free markets.

The EU single-market measures of 1992 and the single currency of 1999 signal an increase in inter-regional trade and investment in Europe, rather than a movement towards globalisation. The continued use of anti-dumping trade remedy law by the EU, examined by Ostry (1997), plus protectionist trade measures in the form of, for example newsprint quotes against Canada and the discriminatory application of health and environmental regulations against "outsiders" is further evidence of the closing of the EU bloc due to the political lobbying of "insider" firms and organisations. Indeed, the use of environmental regulations and health codes as a trade-related barrier to entry is one of the major anchors of regional (EU, NAFTA) policy (Rugman, Kirton, and Soloway 1999, Rugman and Kirton 1999).

The Asian financial crisis has slowed down the emergence of an Asian triad bloc led by Japan and put the Association of Southeast Asian Nations (ASEAN) off the rails. ASEAN started as a political security group but has moved steadily toward an economic bloc. The biggest problem is the lack of progress in the transregional Asian Pacific Economic Co-operation (APEC) forum. The failed leaders meeting in Malaysia in 1998 and the largely technical one in New Zealand in September 1999 indicate a lack of commitment to free trade and investment liberalisation. Only if APEC moves ahead will globalisation prosper. Without it, regional blocs will persist.

Support for this regionalisation thesis comes from several modern political scientists The "new" regionalism is defined by Hettne *et al.* (1999) "as a multidimensional form of integration which includes economic, political, social and cultural aspects..." It goes beyond the "old" regionalism of 25 years ago which was concerned only with the economics of free trade regimes and customs unions or the politics of security alliances. However, the new regionalism is a complement to globalisation, not a substitute for it. It complements the mostly economic aspects of globalisation by adopting a broader, multidimensional challenge to the Westphalian nation state. In this new regionalism there are multiple stakeholders and a multipolar global order.

The EU is the only core region with a robust formal political organisation, since North America (with NAFTA) and the APEC forum lack a strong regional political organisation although they are pursuing increased economic integration. Intermediate regions are being drawn into these three core regions. In some cases (US-Canada in NAFTA) the new regionalism is replacing bilateralism; in others (South Asia) it is not. Hettne *et al.* (1999) argue that the new regionalism is supposed to contribute to the three preferred outcomes of peace, development, and ecological substantiality and that new regionalism can support a new multilateralism. The new regionalism is a big tent. It can accommodate these more moderate liberal views with the extremist rhetoric of Samir Amin (who defines globalisation as the five monopolies over technology, finance, resources, media, and weapons of mass destruction) and Richard Falk's long list of aspects of "negative globalism".

MNEs as Flagship Firms

The leading role of multinational enterprises in regional triad development is even greater as the very large MNEs in Table 12.1 usually serve as flagship firms. A flagship firm is an MNE operating at the hub of an extensive business network, or cluster. Usually the flagship has long-term relational contracts with a set of four other partners, key suppliers, key customers, key competitors, and the nonbusiness infrastructure. This generates the "five partners" model, where the flagship firm is the core or hub of a business network with the other four partners.

The nonbusiness infrastructure includes network partners in research and educational institutes. It can also include efficiency-related aspects of government (rather than the regulatory and redistributional function of government). An example of a network relationship with a university business school would be a customised executive course developed with an external organisation in which the business school faculty develop new and specialised materials to improve the skills and/or strategic thinking of the organisation's managers. An example of a non-network relationship is the MBA programme, which is general and not customised.

Flagship relationships exist, to some degree, across the major triad-based industrial sectors such as automobiles, chemicals, telecommunications, the agri-food business, and in some of the service sectors such as banking. In these sectors, the large 500 MNEs are flagship firms, competing globally. They now have strong linkages to independent key supplier firms (which, in turn, are sometimes MNEs). For example, Dupont is a key supplier of paint to General Motors, while Nortel is a key supplier to Bell Canada/Stentor, as is Alcatel to France Telecom (Rugman and D'Cruz 1997).

Large MNEs also have similar long-term relationships with key customers and distributors. These organisations usually have skills in dealing with final consumers in foreign markets. With a successful key customer relationship the MNE need not internalise the sales and distribution functions and can forgo the costly development of skills in learning about foreign cultures and languages. Other MNEs are a fourth partner of MNEs today, driven into key competitor relationships by the high costs of research and development, and the difficulty of securing access to new markets. These strategic alliances are more unstable than the key supplier/key customer linkages.

The key supplier relationship is built on both performance and trust. The key suppliers in the automobile sector are those that have been the quickest to adopt the quality standards of the automobile MNEs. There now exists a much smaller set of key suppliers (with a large part of the value added in the component market) than the large number of other suppliers that still interact with automobile assemblers on a more variable and strictly price-driven basis. The key suppliers and flagship MNEs are mutually dependent and exhibit more trust in their long-term managerial relationships than would be normal between suppliers and MNEs.

The fifth and final set of partners is in the nonbusiness infrastructure, usually service organisations. Today over 70 percent of people in the Western economies work in the service sector, compared to 30 percent in manufacturing. The productivity of these service sector organisations (which include health, social services, education, cultural industries as well as transportation, and financial services) can be a major influence on competitiveness. The MNE serves as a vehicle to build bridges to the service sector, which includes government. The logic of the flagship/five partners framework of international competitiveness is that various units of government (such as research groups, industry, and agriculture specialists) can have efficiency-related linkages to the business sector, and, by interacting with MNEs, gain a regional triad perspective, with better competitive benchmarks.

The implication is that MNEs provide the triad-based strategic perspective for the five partners and that each true partner does not need a separate international strategy except to be a "key" partner of the MNE. This is, of course, difficult for governments to accept, but it clarifies their role as a facilitator (but not a determinant) of competitiveness. The Western flagship/five partner system is, of course, similar in many respects to the Japanese *keiretsu* and, to a smaller extent, the Korean *chaebols*. Even the Chinese family/clan system which is a much looser network has strong elements of the tacit trust relationships at the heart of the flagship/five partners system. In all four types of business systems, the MNE adopts a flagship role and has strong partners, including a more active role by governments and banks in the Asian networks.

Conclusion: Key Implications for Managers

The multinational enterprise is the key actor on the stage of international business. It is the organisation which leads globalisation and which operates as the flagship firm for sets of regionally based business networks and clusters. The MNE interacts with governments but is not powerful enough to pursue a separate agenda of world economic domination. Instead, the reality of regional triad power is that MNEs need to compete for market share and profits. The energies of their top managers are devoted to operational efficiency and the successful implementation of strategy decisions, and not to global political issues.

Much of the literature dealing with globalisation is far too simplistic. While there are some economic drivers of globalisation, there are extremely strong cultural and political barriers preventing the development of a single world market. Only in a few sectors, such as consumer electronics, is there a successful firm-level strategy of globalisation, with homogeneous products being sold on price and quality worldwide For most other manufacturing sectors, and all service sectors, regionalisation is much more prevalent than globalisation. The triad regions are characterised by heterogeneity more than homogeneity.

Managers thus need to change their thinking as the "end of globalisation" is here. They must:

- design strategies to take account of regional trade and investment agreements (such as NAFTA, the single market of the EU, Mercosur, etc.) rather than multilateral agreements (such as the GATT/WTO, and MAI);
- design organisational structures which develop triad-based internal know-how capabilities and organisational competencies rather than use international divisions or unworkable global organisational structures;
- develop new thinking and knowledge about regional business networks and triad-based clusters, and assess the similar attributes of triad competitors, rather than develop so-called global strategies;
- develop analytical methods to assess regional drivers of success, rather than globalisation drivers;
- think regional, act local; forget global.

References

Bartlett, Christopher A., and Ghoshal, Sumantra (1989) *Managing Across Borders: The Transnational Solution*, Harvard Business School Press, Boston.

Fukuyama, Francis (1992), *The End of History and the Last Man*, Free Press, New York.

Gray, John (1998), *False Dawn: The Delusions of Global Capitalism*, Granta Books, London.

Hettne, Björn, András Inotai and Osvaldo Sunkel, eds. (1999), *Globalization and the New Regionalism*, Macmillan, London.

Ohmae, Kenichi (1990), *The Borderless World*, Harper Collins, New York.

Ostry, Sylvia (1997), *The Post-Cold War Trading System: Who's on First?* University of Chicago Press, Chicago.

Porter, Michael E. (1990), *The Competitive Advantage of Nations*, Free Press, New York.

Rugman, A. (1999), "Negotiating Multilateral Rules to Promote Investment", in M. Hodges, J. Kirton and J. Daniels, eds., *The G8's Role in the New Millennium*, Ashgate, Aldershot, pp. 143-158.

Rugman, Alan M. (1996), Selected Papers. *Volume 1: The Theory of Multinational Enterprises; Volume 2: Multinationals and Trade Policy*, Edward Elgar, Cheltenham.

Rugman, Alan M., ed. (1994), *Foreign Investment and NAFTA*, University of South Carolina Press, Columbia, SC.

Rugman, Alan M. and Joseph R. D'Cruz (1997), "The Theory of the Flagship Firm", *European Management Review*, 15(4), pp. 403-411.

Rugman, Alan M. and Richard Hodgetts (1995), *International Business: A Strategic Management Approach*, McGraw-Hill, New York.

Rugman, Alan M., John Kirton and Julie A. Soloway (1999), *Environmental Regulations and Corporate Strategy*, Oxford University Press, forthcoming, Oxford.

Rugman, Alan M. and John Kirton (1999), "NAFTA, Environmental Regulations and International Business Strategies", 11(4).

Strange, Susan (1998), *Mad Money*, Manchester University Press, Manchester.

Strange, Susan (1996), *The Retreat of the State*, Cambridge University Press, Cambridge.
Strange, Susan (1988), *States and Markets*, Pinter, London.
Tomlinson, John (1999), *Globalization and Culture*, Polity Press, Cambridge.
United Nations Conference on Trade and Development (UNCTAD) (1997), *World Investment Report*, United Nations, New York.
Weintraub, S. and C. Sands, eds. (1998), *The North American Auto Industry Under NAFTA*, CSIS Press, Washington DC.

13 Challenges and Contributions to the Conventional Wisdom

KARL KAISER, JOHN J. KIRTON, AND JOSEPH P. DANIELS

Introduction

Reform of the international financial architecture is a dynamic and rapidly changing problem that by nature does not have a definitive answer. Hence, one would expect substantial disagreement on reform measures among the contributors herein. Remarkably, there is a strong consensus that emerges here. This consensus stands in stark contrast to the often "contradictory and mutually incompatible" (Eichengreen, 1999, p. 1) proposals offered elsewhere, primarily by economists and members of the policy community based in the United States.

This concluding chapter considers the views of some of the leading, U.S.-based authorities in the current debate on strengthening the international financial system, to identify their areas of overlap and divergence. The resulting, lengthy list of recommendations they provide is incrementalist in nature. It offers a baseline point of comparison for the evaluations assembled here. There is a general acceptance among these established authorities of the conventional wisdom on reforming the international financial architecture. The scholars and practitioners assembled in this volume, however, with their additional perspectives from Europe and Asia and North America beyond the United States, call for a bolder approach. They challenge the presumed effectiveness of many of the proposed reforms, offer new insights on encouraging stabilising behaviour of financial market participants, and add much-needed perspectives on the political process that is required for the development, acceptance, and monitoring of said reforms.

This chapter begins with a brief overview of the perspectives of some of the leading scholars on the international financial system. It then summarises the perspectives in the context of the core issue areas identified in the introduction to this text. Finally, it highlights the views offered in this volume, indicating the points of overlap and divergence with the conventional wisdom previously offered.

The Conventional Wisdom: A Brief Survey

Arguably the best-known contribution to the current debate is Barry Eichengreen's book, *Toward a New Financial Architecture: A Practical Post-Asia Agenda* (1999). A prolific writer on the history of the international monetary system, Eichengreen is well positioned to assemble and assess the views and proposals on reform that have been advanced by many prominent individuals and authorities.[1]

Eichengreen argues that most of the favoured proposals are incompatible with one another because different people view the problem of financial instability from divergent perspectives. His own proposals are advanced, in contrast, on the basis of five clear assumptions, as follows. First, financial liberalisation allows market to allocate capital in the most efficient manner and, therefore, has significant benefits. Secondly, and in contrast to others (such as Harold James 1999), integration of financial markets is irreversible. Thirdly, information asymmetries are pervasive in financial markets and, therefore, financial safety nets are needed in light of the instability generated by these asymmetries. Fourthly, bankruptcy codes are needed, as information and transactions costs prevent markets from promptly resolving financial crises. Finally, political considerations will influence economic reform.

Eichengreen chooses, as do the other established scholars reviewed here, to offer "recommendations [that] may seem unambitious ... but have a chance of being implemented" (1999, p. 4). His approach is to offer proposals that are practical in light of the fact that though financial markets are ever-increasingly global, they continue to be regulated at the national level. His recommendations form the benchmark for this brief review and are summarised as follows.

Because of the problem of asymmetric information in financial markets, accounting and auditing standards should be advanced and adopted. The adoption of standards, and the monitoring of compliance will require a co-ordinated effort among international, national, and private sector bodies and should be addressed within the context of reforming the International Monetary Fund. In regard to improved information, Eichengreen specifically calls for:

Better information on businesses, banks, and sovereign nations, including:

- rigorous disclosure requirements;
- the use of internationally recognised auditing and accounting standards;

- improved corporate governance standards so that claimants can monitor and control; financial decisions;
- international monitoring of compliance and its public dissemination.

The pace of financial market liberalisation has been much more rapid than increases in supervision and regulation, particularly in emerging economies. What is needed, therefore, is:

Improved supervision and regulation of financial markets and market participants, such as:

- improved risk-management techniques of banks;
- improved regulation and supervision;
- limiting or taxing bank (principally foreign currency denominated) borrowing abroad, specifically Chilean-style capital-inflow taxes.

In regard to debt clauses, Eichengreen admits that no single country would pursue this alone as it might send an unfortunate signal to the markets. Hence, actions of this type can be accomplished only on a co-ordinated basis. His recommendation here is:

International Debt Restructuring, such as:

- adding majority voting and shareholding clauses to loan contracts;
- collective-representation clauses, including; provisions for a representative to coordinate creditors in the case of sovereign debt, and clauses providing that a minimum percentage of bondholders must agree for legal action to be taken;
- the creation of standing committees of creditors;
- IMF lending in arrears, when appropriate.

Eichengreen argues that the IMF must realise that it cannot solve all the problems of the international financial system by itself. The IMF must work with appropriate private sector organisations and international committees. In addition, the IMF should promote exchange rate flexibility as this will encourage agents to hedge foreign exchange exposures, reducing insolvency that results from unexpected exchange rate changes and Chilean-style capital controls. Hence, he calls for:

Reform of the IMF, to include:

- working with appropriate bodies to establish standards;

- monitoring member country compliance with these standards;
- becoming a pro-active coordinator of debt restructuring;
- enhancing its legitimacy through greater disclosure and transparency, forming a new consensus of appropriate macroeconomic policies in light of today's integrated financial markets, promoting Chilean-style capital controls, and encouraging flexible exchange rates.

Shortly after Eichengreen's analysis, Alan Blinder offered his own *Eight Steps to a New Financial Order* (1999). Both his theme and recommendations echo those of Eichengreen. Blinder maintains that financial instability cannot be eliminated, but sees the current situation of numerous and severe crises as unacceptable. Blinder also concurs that ostentatious proposals are a dead-end and that it is "Better to stick with more modest plans that require little or no institution-building. The world's poor cannot wait for grand edifices to be built" (1999, p. 53).

Five of the eight steps recommended by Blinder are in clear agreement with the proposals of Eichengreen: Flexible exchange rates, restricting excessive short-term borrowing in foreign currency, sound macroeconomic and financial policies (particularly improved bank supervision and accounting and auditing standards), reconsideration of IMF austerity programs in light of the modern international economy, and establishing procedures for debt settlement, including collective action clauses. In addition, Blinder argues for a proper sequencing of capital market liberalisation. This includes consideration of Chilean-style control on short-term capital inflows and tempering the IMF's encouragement of premature liberalisation. Blinder argues that the IMF pays too much attention to creditors and too little to the innocent bystanders in a financial crises. Hence, he argues that more resources should be devoted to protecting the social safety nets of nations from experiencing a financial meltdown. Finally, he argues for preventative funds, such as the IMF's Contingent Credit Line, to be available for countries that follow sound policies, in order to keep spectators at bay. He does not, however, go as far as to recommend regional agreements, though he does not address these explicitly or rule them out.

A third set of proposals has come from the Council on Foreign Relations, which in 1998 sponsored the Independent Task Force of the International Financial Architecture. Its report was authored by Morris Goldstein (Council on Foreign Relations 1999). The basic principles of the report is that the burden of reform is on the emerging economies and their creditors, but that participation is required by the industrialised economies as is reform and redirection of the IMF and the World Bank. The Council offers seven recommendations. Five of these parallel those of Eichengreen (who was a member of the Task Force) and Blinder, though the context is slightly different.

The Task Force recommends that countries that practice "good housekeeping", (which includes sound macroeconomic policy, a strong and well-regulated banking system, compliance with international standards for disclosure, and avoidance of excessive short-term borrowing) be rewarded with more favourable IMF lending terms and lower regulatory capital requirements for banks lending to these countries. In addition, it proposes avoidance of excessive short-term capital flows with Chilean-style capital controls, flexible exchange rates, private sector burden sharing, and collective action clauses, and reform and refocusing of IMF and World Bank responsibilities.

The Task Force also suggests less IMF lending, specifically a return to normal lending limits of 100 to 300 percent of country quota. The belief here is that less lending will change private agents' expectations about future lending and reduce the moral hazard problem. Lending should focus on smoothing operations in currency markets, help finance bank restructuring, and provide for social safety nets, as advocated by Blinder. Finally, the Task Forces advocates greater political support of reform measures. As with Eichengreen, there is an admission that political considerations and will power will drive or stymie reform efforts. The Council urges greater involvement of the emerging economies in the process. They call on the Interim Committee, the Financial Stability Forum (FSF), and the presidents of the regional developments banks to convene a meeting of the finance ministers to set an agenda and time line.

A fourth major set of proposals comes from a symposium whose results were reported in the *Journal of Economic Perspectives* and summarised by Fredric Mishkin (1999). Though the symposium covered a great deal of territory, three issue areas found in all of the proposals above are treated in greater detail. These are the role of international institutions, banking stability, and capital controls. Mishkin and Rogoff (1999) concur with the Council on Foreign Relations that an international lender of last resort is needed, but argue it is not practical to envision one with "deep pockets". Mishkin's argument is based on the moral hazard problem that is created with such an institution while Rogoff focusses on the amount of resources that would be required. Rogoff reaches further, examining many other proposals for international institution formation and reformation, including the establishment of a financial crisis manager and an international bankruptcy court. He concludes that none of these proposals are feasible at this time.

In this symposium, Caprio and Honohan (1999) deal with the problem of banking stability in emerging countries. They initially assert that capital requirements are not sufficient for dealing with banks in emerging nations, as in many of these nations financial liberalisation occurred faster than the establishment of adequate regulation and supervision of intermediaries. Hence, what is needed is better and increased supervision of intermediaries in these nations. As they see it, a principle problem that policymakers must grasp is that the solutions that work in industrialised economies may not work in emerging economies because of differences in market volatility and the institutional setting. Oppressive regulation, however, is not the solution. An environment that provides a framework of incentives that encourages diversification and balancing of loans and competition is one that enhance the efficiency and stability of these banking systems.

Sebastian Edwards' (1999) task is to consider the capital controls recommended in all of the proposals noted above. He argues that the evidence shows that controls on capital outflows are ineffective while the benefits of controls on the inflow of capital, such as those used by Chile, are overrated. Nonetheless, controls on short-term capital inflows may extend the maturity of debt and, therefore, be a useful *temporary stopgap* measure. Ultimately, what is needed is the obvious medley of prudent macroeconomic policies, banking regulation and supervision, and flexible exchange rates.

The Consensus of the Conventional Wisdom

The authors reviewed above agree that the worst of the Asian crisis is now past, but that similar financial failures are inevitable in the future, given the current environment. Liberalised financial markets will always be prone to seizing up. No reform effort, no matter how comprehensive it might be, can completely eliminate this aspect. Liberalised financial markets are certainly beneficial, as they direct capital to its most productive function. Yet when markets are liberalised prior to necessary microeconomic and macroeconomic reforms (such as proper monetary, fiscal, and exchange rate policies, and appropriate banking and domestic financial market regulation and supervision), large and sudden inflows and outflows of short-term capital can overwhelm an emerging nation's system of intermediaries, leading to a financial melt-down. It appears that this is precisely what happened in East Asia from 1997 onward.

Though financial markets are becoming more globally integrated, they remain regulated at the domestic level. For emerging nations that rely heavily on their domestic banking system for the allocation of capital, and that have less than sufficient competition, regulation and supervision, liberalisation has proved to be a risky process. A great deal needs to be done here. The industrialised nations need to set the example for the emerging nations through the approval and adoption of accounting, disclosure, and auditing standards. Much is now being done in generating such standards. The difficult task that lies ahead will be ensuring their acceptance and monitoring compliance with them. The G7, IMF, and the committees of national regulators must co-ordinate their efforts in this regard. They must further devise a system of incentives that encourages market participants and the governments of the emerging and developing nations to comply.

There is no question that informational asymmetries pervade financial markets and that this type of market failure is amplified in international transactions. Improvements in transparency and surveillance are important, but in and of themselves will not accomplish much. Rather, there is a need for more draconian measures such as capital controls on short-term inflows. This type of measure is offered with trepidation, but offered nonetheless. The purpose is to extend the average maturity of debt and reduce the reliance on bank borrowing from abroad.

Private sector involvement is certainly a common element of all the proposals above. Each collection has called for shareholder clauses on loans and collective-representation clauses on debt. These types of measure have the potential to reduce the quality of debt issued by sending the wrong type of message to market participants. As a result, no nation would unilaterally adopt these measures. A coordinated effort is required. The prospect of a co-ordinated effort, however, seems unlikely as long as the United States remains firm in its opposition to reform in this area.

The area that receives virtually no attention at all is the role of the G7 in the overall process. This is quite unfortunate as the G7, both at the leaders, and Finance Ministers level, represent the critical political force necessary for any reform to take place. While earlier G7 action may have proven disappointing in its foresight, timeliness, and content (Daniels 1999), as the Council on Foreign Relations Task Force rightly argues, greater political support of reform efforts is needed. The G7, and the extended fora of the G7, are essential in coordinating the activities of the various bodies at work on the formation of standards, the promulgation of such standards, and the encouragement of their adoption.

Challenges and Contributions to the Conventional Wisdom

The analyses offered in this volume contain a number of points of convergence with the views presented above. However on the whole they mount a challenge to the conventional wisdom by adding a more diverse and often bolder view on the origin of recent crises, the specific direction to be taken, and the political process that will steer the entire operation.

There is a consensus on the benefits of globalisation of financial markets that is driven home in the works of Rugman and Daniels. These authors also agree that short-term capital flows can be destabilising, whereas foreign direct investment is not. Rugman goes further on this issue by pointing out that the process of integration is in fact driven by foreign direct investment activities of multinational enterprises. The authors diverge from the conventional wisdom by shifting away from the focus on short-term flows, as capital controls on short-term inflows are, at best, second best policies. In addition to the obvious reforms needed in banking and financial market supervision and regulation, what is called for is a regional system of incentives that encourages long-term investment, as opposed to schemes that discourage short-term capital. Indeed, Rugman argues that the lack of such a strategy is a central explanation of the East Asian crisis.

There is also much agree on the proper role of the IMF. Giannini concurs that there is a role for a lender of last resort. He leads the debate in a new direction by arguing that the IMF is already heading away from being an *international* lender of last resort and toward becoming a lender of credibility. That is, the IMF can provide credibility to otherwise sound economies that have experienced a crisis by lending into arrears and by enabling them to access private capital courses. Von Furstenberg adds, building on Goodhart (1999), that borrowed money should not be used to defend exchange rate pegs. What von Furstenberg also brings to the debate is the realisation that most of the crisis countries have abandoned pegged regimes and the challenge now remains one of finding the appropriate regime. It appears that regional arrangements are inevitable with many national currencies disappearing in the process.

That reform of banking supervision and regulation is essential to successful financial market regulation is unarguable. Kiuchi, however, points out that a critical element missing in the debate over reform is how politicians compound the problem by overriding banking officials and regulators. No reform, regardless of how well intentioned it might be, can be successful without proper political backing. There is a need, therefore, to develop alternatives to domestic banking systems that allow for direct financing. Hence, Kiuchi argues for the development of an Asian bond market which would replace some of the short-term bank borrowing abroad, and also extend the maturity of debt.

A lack of the type of transparency that is called for in the conventional wisdom had little to do with the outbreak of the East Asian crisis, as argued by von Furstenberg. Information asymmetries are an important element in such crises, but the measures currently envisioned will do little to prevent similar crises from occurring in the future. What von Furstenberg brings to the debate is the importance of *political* transparency. That is, being clear as to motives and to whom the benefits of reform will accrue, will do much to enhance the credibility of the reform process itself. Walter echoes this scepticism about the impact of transparency and argues that much more needs to be done in the way of bank capital requirements. Walter concurs with the conventional wisdom that a new mechanism is needed to allow bankruptcy and that the recapitalisation of failing financial institutions should be halted.

The Role of the G7

Among all the authors in this volume, there is a widespread consensus about the central role the G7 plays in responding to international financial crises, and strengthening the international financial system to reduce the massive economic, political and social costs which such crisis can exact upon so many. This consensus embraces the relevance and leadership role of the G7 in these issues, its relationship to the other bodies charged with their management, the effectiveness of its performance in crisis response and system/reconstruction, and where and how it should concentrate its efforts in the future.

The Relevance and Leadership Role of the G7

There is overwhelming agreement that the G7 and its leadership have been, and should be, central in the process of responding to international financial crises and constructing a new system to meet the needs of a now globalised world. Bayne shows how responding to crisis and reconstructing the international financial system in its various dimensions has recurrently been the central tasks of the G7, and that it have been critical in solving differences that have persisted at lower levels, keeping up the pressure to ensure what members have agreed is properly carried out, and in explaining and justifying their actions to outside countries and the broader public. Kirton regards it, rather than the IMF or US alone, as playing the central part during the crisis of 1997-99. Daniels argues that the G7's performance in coordination and implementation will determine the ultimate success or failure of the effort to reform the international financial system.

Even those with more critical views admit its relevance. Kiuchi, amidst his sympathy for regional solutions, views the 7 as having an important leadership role in catalyzing needed action at an early stage, and in helping Asian nations develop guidelines to help them develop their financial systems. Wood sees the G7 as central to the global coordination of economic policies, even though he argues it has now become an "anachronism" given the rising weight of developing countries, shifts in trade competitiveness, and the new vulnerability among all nations brought by globalisation. Von Furstenberg admits the useful role the G7 played in endorsing IMF incubated codes and in strengthening the IMF's Interim Committee, even while recognising the limited relevance of such an emphasis. Walter suggests, in keeping with the American leadership model of international co-operation and G7 effectiveness (Putnam and Bayne 1987), that the G7 can play a key role in providing the United States with the junior partner it needs to work with, in a world of "Snow White and the Seven Dwarfs". Gianini approves of the G7-inspired informal ways devised to deal with the Asian crisis and Korea, and the G7's creation of the Financial Stability Forum. Only Rugman, with his emphasis on the role of foreign direct investment, multinational enterprise's regionalism and regional institutions, implicitly casts doubt in the relevance of the G7 itself in the broader scheme.

The G7's Relationship to the Other Financial Institutions

At the same time, there is an equally strong conviction that the G7 can act perform its needed role if it works in tandem with the established multilateral organisations regional bodies, in ways that incorporate more fully the work of outside countries and private sector forums. Bayne underscores the need to ground G7's decision in the formal constitutional and institutional structure of established international organisation such as the IMF if they are to be effective in the long run. Kirton shows, consistent with the model of democratic institutionalism for explaining G8 performance (Kirton and

Daniels 1999, Kokotsis and Daniels 1999), how the G7 needed the IMF, International Bank for Reconstruction and Development (IRBD), and regional development banks as a nest for catalysing co-operation and for securing resources to help stem crisis of 1997-9. For Daniels, it is the G7 that can help provide the badly needed clarification of the roles of the IMF and IBRD. Kiuchi calls for an enhancement of the IMF's authority to deal with capital account liberalisation. For von Furstenberg, and Walter the IMF and BIS were central in generating the standards to secure greater transparency, with the G7 endorsing their work, although the former sees the IMF as poorly positioned to engender the needed moves away from floating exchange rate regimes and into the world of regional monetary union. For Rugman, in contrast, multilateral and plurilateral bodies such as the Organisation for Economic Co-operation and Development (OECD) and General Agreement on Trade and Tariffs (GATT) and the World Trade Organisation (WTO) have failed to provide the needed rules for investment liberalisation, while regional bodies are busy generating results.

The need to involve outsiders in the work of the G7 is underscored by many of the analyses in this volume. Kiuchi points to the need for regional arrangements such as an Asian Monetary Fund (AMF) and regional policy co-ordination, or bilateral plans such as the New Miyazawa Initiative. Wood applauds the Cologne G7's decision to enlarge the FSF and give new responsibilities to the IMF's renamed International Finance and Monetary Committee, as the start of a much-needed process of greater inclusion. Kirton notes how the G7 broadened to include others through the FSF and G22 in devising the new system. Daniels echoes this plea to include large developing countries. Bayne, expanding on his earlier call (Bayne 1999) and noting the success of the process leading to the Cologne debt initiative, points to the importance, especially in the wake of the failed Seattle WTO meeting, of better communication with public and civil society actors.

The Effectiveness of G7 Action in Crisis Response and System Reconstruction

All the authors point further to the wisdom and effectiveness of G7 action in crisis response and system reform, although most also identify instances when G7 agreement and action was poorly conceived, insufficient, or badly executed. Bayne's review of the G7's four major efforts during its first 25 years reveals a variable record, ranging from a highly but not totally effective response in 1975, through to a much delayed impact on middle income debt relief from 1982 onward, relief of debt of the poorest from 1988 onward, and crisis response and system reconstruction from 1994 to the present. Wood believes the Cologne communiqué makes a significant contribution to strengthening the international financial architecture, but gives the report a very cautious evaluation, and one that expresses skepticism about the ability of the G7 to implement it effectively in the absence of broader participation from the developing countries themselves. He further judges the G7 in general to be highly effective in macroeconomic co-ordination, but notes its *ad hoc*, cases by case approach to developing country debt relief in the 1980s left the system highly vulnerable to the crises of the 1990s. The highest marks come from Kirton, who concludes the G7 beat markets in South Korea, Brazil, and over private sector burden sharing, and successfully contained Asian and global financial crises, if through the provision of "just in time" "just enough" leadership. He concurs with Bayne that it was ultimately action by the G7 leaders themselves that was needed, and that the G7 leaders were much better at responding to crises than at foreseeing and preventing them.

The economists in this volume substantially agree with this portrait, although offer more harsh judgements about the market rationality of many of the particular decisions the G7 produces. Kiuchi suggests the G7 has been effective in its *de facto* task of surveillance and coordination of exchange rates. Daniels sees the G7 Finance minister's report to the leaders at the Cologne Summit as a comprehensive, high quality document that reflects well the work being done by the G7 and others since the Halifax Summit of 1995, and one that does an excellent task of framing the current situation. He does, however, note the G7 at Cologne provided little detail on private sector involvement in crisis prevention, and was not firm enough in its conclusions on exchange rate regimes. Walter, while implicitly approving the FSF, points to the need to address more basic and hitherto neglected issues. Von Furstenberg remains the most critical, declaring that its HIPC initiative is a debt trap, that its approach to transparency only helps those at the top of the hierarchy, that this approach will do very little to reduce the risk of financial crises occurring in the future, and that the G7 Report underplayed the role of exchange rate regimes in emerging economies in the overall architectural effort.

The G7's Focus for the Future

Finally, many authors in this volume have clear views as to how the G7 should proceed in the future. Bayne calls for a broadening and shift of attention, through the G7 correcting their neglect of the trade system as their first priority for Okinawa 2000. This involves resolve their internal differences on trade liberalisation, restoring the authority of the WTO, making their own policies and the WTO more responsive to the requirements of developing countries, especially small and poor ones, and getting the Millennium Round successfully launched. Wood argues with equal conviction that in the future G7 decision making will have to be more inclusive of the views of certain large developing countries, and that G7 countries should give technical assistance to LDC's to help them develop mechanisms to reduce systemic risk. Kiuchi suggests the G7 should provide leadership to secure a *de facto* target zone mechanism for exchange rates among the big three, give the IMF authority for capital account management, and look with favour on regional co-operation on macroeconomics policy and the development of Asian bond market.

It is Daniels who provided the boldest vision of the G7's required role in the future. He declares that the G7 must play the essential task of managing the many bodies at work in reforming the international financial architecture. To do so it must co-ordinate the overall process, serve as a driving force for the implementation of agreements, and act as the leading advocate of benefits of capital account liberalisation. It is thus clear that, despite the substantial steps forward made by the G7 at Cologne, their central role and formidable challenge in strengthening the international financial system to meet the needs of the new millennium will remain active in the years to come.

Note

1 Of course the literature on financial crises and reforms to the international financial architecture is substantial, as evident in the collective references to this text. We focus only a few of the most widely-distributed publications here so as to derive a concise summary. For an excellent symposium on the Tequila Crisis of 1994-95, we refer the reader to volume 23 of the *Journal of Banking and Finance* (1999).

References

Bayne, N. (1999), "Continuity and Leadership in an Age of Globalization", in M. Hodges, *et al.*, *The G8's Role in the New Millennium*, Ashgate, Aldershot, pp. 21-44.

Blinder, Alan (1999), "Eight Steps to a New Financial Order", *Foreign Affairs*, 78(5), pp. 50-63.

Caprio, Gerald and Patrick Honohan (1999), "Restoring Banking Stability: Beyond Supervised Capital Requirements", *Journal of Economic Perspectives*, 13(4), pp. 43-64.

Council on Foreign Relations (1999), "The Future of the International Financial Architecture: A Council on Foreign Relations Task Force", *Foreign Affairs*, 78(6), pp. 169-184.

Daniels, J. (1999), "Supervising the International Financial System", in M. Hodges, *et al.*, *The G8's Role in the New Millennium*, Ashgate, Aldershot, pp. 107-118.

Edwards, Sebastian (1999), "How Effective are Capital Controls?", *Journal of Economic Perspectives*, 13(4), pp. 65-84.

Eichengreen, Barry (1999), *Toward a New International Financial Architecture: A Practical Post-Asia Agenda*, Institute for International Economics, Washington DC.

Goodhart, C, (1999), "Managing the Global Economy", in M. Hodges, *et al.*, *The G8's Role in the New Millennium*, Ashgate, Aldershot, pp. 135-140.

James, Harold, (1999), "Is Liberalization Reversible?", International Monetary Fund, *Finance and Development*, pp. 11-14.

Kirton, J. and Daniels, J. (1999), "The Role of the G8 in the New Millennium", in M. Hodges, *et al.*, *The G8's Role in the New Millennium*, Ashgate, Aldershot, pp. 3-18.

Kokotsis, E. and Daniels, J. (1999), "G8 Summits and Compliance", in M. Hodges, J. Kirton and J. Daniels, *The G8's Role in the New Millennium*, Ashgate, Aldershot, pp. 69-74.

Mishkin, Fredric S. (1999), "Global Financial Instability: Framework, Events, Issues", *Journal of Economic Perspectives*, 13(4), pp. 3-20.

Putnam, R. and Bayne, N. (1987), *Hanging Together: The Seven Power Summits*, Harvard University Press, Cambridge.

Rogoff, Kenneth (1999), "International Institutions for Reducing Global Financial Instability", *Journal of Economic Perspectives*, *13*(4), pp. 21-42.

Appendix

STRENGTHENING THE INTERNATIONAL FINANCIAL ARCHITECTURE

Report of G7 Finance Ministers to the Köln Economic Summit
18 - 20 June, 1999

Introduction

1. A well-functioning international financial system is essential to allow an efficient allocation of global savings and investment, and provide the conditions needed to improve world-wide growth and living standards in all countries. Recent events in the world economy have demonstrated that a strengthening of the system is needed to maximize the benefits of, and reduce the risks posed by, global economic and financial integration.

2. Reform of the international financial architecture will also reinforce the open multilateral trading system. Keeping markets open for goods and capital will make the global economy more resilient to shocks. The benefits and economic opportunities derived from open markets have led to a significant improvement in living standards in industrialized and emerging economies. We believe the process of globalization offers great additional potential to create wealth and employment.

3. As Finance Ministers of the major economies, we are aware of our special responsibility for improving the conditions for a proper functioning of the international financial and monetary system and, in particular, enhancing sound fundamentals necessary for exchange rate stability. To this end we will maintain strong cooperation to promote stability of the international monetary system and exchange rates among major currencies that are in line with fundamentals.

4. Following the remit from last year's Birmingham Summit, we have proposed in co-operation with other countries a number of important reforms to the architecture of the international financial system. We believe the

initiatives and reforms that have been agreed will make a significant contribution to the stability of the world financial system.

5. In this increasingly integrated global economy, in which policy responsibility still lies mainly with sovereign states, the challenge is to promote global financial stability through national action as well as through enhanced international cooperation. All countries, together with the international financial institutions and private sector financial institutions, must share this responsibility.

6. This does not require new international organizations. It requires that all countries assume their responsibility for global stability by pursuing sound macroeconomic and sustainable exchange rate policies and establishing strong and resilient financial systems. It requires the adoption and implementation of internationally-agreed standards and rules in these and other areas. It requires the existing institutions to adapt their roles to meet the demands of today's global financial system: in particular to put in place effective mechanisms for devising standards, monitoring their implementation and making public the results; to have the right tools to help countries to manage crises; and to take steps to enhance their effectiveness, accountability and legitimacy. It also requires the right structure of incentives for all participants in the international financial system - national authorities as well as the private sector.

7. Our overall strategy is to identify and put in place policies to help markets work properly and to provide the public goods necessary to achieve this objective. This requires public authorities to provide for enhanced transparency and disclosure, improved regulation and supervision of financial institutions and markets, and policies to protect the most vulnerable. It also requires that private creditors and investors bear responsibility for the risks that they take, and are involved appropriately in crisis prevention and crisis management. In these respects, the establishment of internationally-agreed codes and standards for policy-makers serves both as an incentive for better governance and as a yardstick against which to measure country risk.

8. Last autumn, we identified for our Leaders the need for concrete actions to strengthen the international financial architecture. This report recommends specific reforms in six priority areas:

a. Strengthening and reforming the international financial institutions and arrangements;

b. Enhancing transparency and promoting best practices;

c. Strengthening financial regulation in industrialized countries;

d. Strengthening macroeconomic policies and financial systems in emerging markets;

e. Improving crisis prevention and management, and involving the private sector;

f. Promoting social policies to protect the poor and most vulnerable.

9. We believe these proposals will reduce the risk of, and help better manage, future financial crises. We are committed to, and will monitor closely, their implementation, and will continue to report on progress as necessary. Of course, financial markets will continue to evolve and this is likely to require further adaptations of the international financial system in the years ahead.

A. Strengthening and reforming the international financial institutions and arrangements

10. The development of global economic and financial arrangements to reflect the changing nature of the world economy is a continuous process. Our aim is to promote more efficient international financial institutions and arrangements, in which all relevant interests can be effectively represented.

11. We agree on a set of principles which should guide this process:

a. The IMF and the World Bank have the central role in the international economic and financial system, and in facilitating cooperation among countries in these fields.

b. The international supervisory and regulatory bodies have a crucial role to play in making the international financial system more robust.

c. The accountability and transparency of these bodies and of the IFIs should be strengthened.

d. A broad range of countries should be involved in discussions on how to adapt the international financial system to the changing global environment.

e. A system based on constituencies is appropriate for the governance of the institutions.

12. A number of steps have been taken to widen the ongoing dialogue on the

international financial system to a broader range of countries, including the establishment of the New Arrangements to Borrow (NAB) comprising 25 participants; the special meetings involving Ministers and Governors of systemically significant economies that occurred during 1998; the seminars involving 33 industrial and emerging economies held this Spring in Bonn and Washington; and this year's Spring meeting of the IMF Interim Committee which was prepared for the first time by a special meeting of deputies.

13. The new Financial Stability Forum was created to enhance international cooperation and coordination in the area of financial market supervision and surveillance. The Forum met for the first time in April, and agreed to focus initially on three issues: the implications of highly leveraged institutions, off-shore centres and short-term capital flows. This process will include participants from other industrial and emerging economies. We agree that the Forum should, by the time of the September meeting, be broadened to include significant financial centres, in a format that provides for effective dialogue.

14. A number of proposals have been discussed for institutional reform, including the proposal for transformation of the Interim Committee into a Council. At this time, recognising our special responsibility as major shareholders in the Bretton Woods institutions we have agreed to support the following important steps towards institutional reform.

a. The Interim Committee would be given a permanent standing - as the "International Financial and Monetary Committee". The Committee's mandate should be consistent with the principle, which we reaffirm, that the IMF must play a prominent role in facilitating cooperation among all countries, especially in the area of macroeconomic and monetary issues that are at the center of the IMF's mandate, as stated in Article 1 of its Articles of Agreement.

- Deputy-level meetings of the new Committee would be held twice a year shortly before the Ministerial meetings, building on the successful meeting of the Interim Committee Deputies this April.
- The President of the World Bank would play a privileged role in the new Committee; the Chairman of the Financial Stability Forum would be given observer status.
- Joint sessions of the International Financial and Monetary Committee and the Development Committee would be held when appropriate on issues where there is a clear overlap of responsibilities.

b. We will work together to establish an informal mechanism for dialogue among systemically important countries within the framework of the Bretton Woods institutional system.

We continue to review these arrangements, taking account of the proposals which have been put forward to strengthen the institutional arrangements, including the proposal to transform the Interim Committee into a Council.

15. We have also agreed to take steps to improve the effectiveness of the IMF and other IFIs, including by:

a. pursuing enhanced monitoring of policy commitments while drawings on the Fund remain outstanding but after program conditionality has ended, in order to reinforce incentives for good performance;
b. sharpening the focus of the IFIs on sectors where they have a comparative advantage, and broadening their dialogue with other international fora and with the private sector. Special attention needs to be paid to the specific circumstances of the country concerned aiming at encouraging direct ownership of the programs;
c. building upon the experience of IMF-supported programmes in the financial crisis, the IMF should explore ways further to improve IMF surveillance and programmes so that they better reflect the changes in the world economy, in particular potentially abrupt large-scale cross border capital movements.
d. enhancing the accountability of the IMF by improving transparency, the decision-making procedures and the timely flow of information.
e. encouraging the IMF to continue undertaking systematic evaluations both internal and external of the effectiveness of selected operations programmes, policies and procedures.

B. Enhancing Transparency and Promoting Best Practices

16. The availability of accurate and timely information is an essential ingredient for well-functioning financial markets and market economies. Such information is necessary for market participants and should be used by them to make good decisions. It also provides greater incentives for policy-makers to implement sound economic policies. Improved information will help markets to adjust more smoothly to economic developments, minimise contagion and reduce volatility.

17. Significant progress has been achieved in a number of areas. The IMF has made substantial progress in promoting enhanced disclosure of economic statistics and indicators, and in developing voluntary codes of good practice and standards to ensure appropriate transparency of the processes by which governments formulate macroeconomic and financial policies:

a. The IMF Executive Board approved in March 1999 an expansion of the Special Data Dissemination Standard (SDDS) to provide for a more comprehensive and timely disclosure of data on countries' international reserve positions. The expanded SDDS, which will go into effect in April 2000, addresses gaps in the original standard established in 1996. Efforts are also being taken through the Inter-Agency Task Force on Financial Statistics to harmonize the statistics published on developing and transition countries' external debt by the BIS, IMF, OECD, and the World Bank, and quarterly publication has begun.

b. The IMF' s Code of Good Practices on Fiscal Transparency has been approved by the Executive Board and was endorsed by the Interim Committee in April 1998. An implementation manual, questionnaire, and self-evaluation report have been prepared and are being disseminated.

c. A draft Code of Good Practices on Transparency in Monetary and Financial Policies has been published for comment and should be completed by the 1999 IMF Annual Meetings.

18. The IMF has also approved a number of measures to increase transparency in member countries' economic policies as well as its own operations, including: (i) greater use of Public Information Notices to provide information on IMF policy issues; (ii) procedures for the release of Letters of Intent, Memoranda of Economic and Financial Policies, and Policy Framework Papers that underpin IMF-supported programs; (iii) publication of the Chairman's statement following Board approval or review of members' programs; and (iv) a pilot project for the voluntary public release of Article IV staff reports. In the World Bank, Country Assistance Strategies, which set out the major development challenges of individual countries and guide the Bank's lending programme, will in principle be made public as of July 1999.

19. Transparency of the private sector is of particular importance to the orderly and efficient functioning of financial markets. The Basle Committee, IOSCO, and the IAIS have established Core Principles for supervision in their respective areas of responsibility. Valuable actions in this area also include IOSCO's issuance of Disclosure Standards to Facilitate Cross-Border

Offerings and Initial Listings by Multinational Issuers. The BIS-Committee on the Global Financial System (CGFS) is reviewing ways to improve market disclosure, including a model template for public disclosure of their exposures and risk profile by institutions engaged in trading, investment and lending activity, both regulated and unregulated. Further work on this issue, involving other relevant authorities, was supported in the Financial Stability Forum.

20. We support and commend the efforts being taken by private sector bodies to enhance transparency. We welcome the completion by the International Accounting Standards Committee of its core set of international accounting standards, and we look forward to IOSCO, IAIS and the Basle Committee completing their reviews. We urge all those involved in setting accounting standards to work together so that high quality accounting standards can continue to be developed and agreed internationally.

21. With considerable progress already having been made in the development of standards and codes of good practice, the key challenge now facing the international community is to encourage implementation. We attach high priority to the following steps:

a. Wider compliance with the SDDS by countries with access to the international capital markets, wider agreement on specific SDDS standards for reporting of external debt, addition of indicators of financial sector soundness, and efforts to promote greater public awareness of, and use of, the information conveyed by the SDDS.

b. Steps further to increase transparency in the IMF's own operation and its member countries' economic policies, including the greater release of Board documents.

c. Developing a system for surveillance of implementation of the codes and standards, built on the Article IV process of the IMF, involving close collaboration with the World Bank and the standard setting bodies. To this end, we call on the Fund to develop a mechanism for coordinating this liaison, and to report on the effectiveness of the Article IV process as a means of monitoring and encouraging adherence to standards. Country adherence to standards should also be used in determining Fund conditionality.

d. Systematic incorporation of information on a country's observance of transparency standards in the Fund's regular Article IV surveillance reports, as well as in special reports on country transparency practices prepared by the staff. We are encouraged in this respect that experimental transparency reports have already been prepared by the Fund staff, and that countries have engaged in pilot self-assessments of their own transparency practices. We look to these reports to be extended to form an integral part of the Article IV surveillance process.

e. Continued efforts towards implementation of the Core Principles established by the Basle Committee, IOSCO, and IAIS, including in the context of the Core Principles Methodology Working Group and with appropriate involvement by the IMF and World Bank.

f. Moves by our regulators to consider a country's adherence to the range of relevant international standards, including international standards for banking supervision, as part of the prudential criteria used when considering market entry by foreign banks.

g. Recognising the importance of providing a sufficient degree of transparency by all market participants, steps should be taken to improve transparency by all market participants, including steps to improve the quality and timeliness of public disclosure of direct material exposure to highly leveraged financial institutions, and of relevant information by highly leveraged institutions. We look forward to the work of the Financial Stability Forum on this issue.

h. The ongoing efforts by IOSCO to review the advisability and feasibility of imposing transparency and disclosure requirements on highly leveraged institutions.

i. Completion of the work of the CGFS on reporting of aggregate positions and transactions in foreign exchange markets.

j. Measures to induce off-shore centres to comply with internationally agreed standards and codes in the area of transparency and supervision. We look forward to the work of the Financial Stability Forum on this issue.

k. The OECD's recently-approved core principles on corporate governance, and the World Bank's continuing work with the OECD and other international institutions to encourage their broadest possible adoption and implementation in emerging market and industrial countries.

l. Compilation of the various financial and economic policy standards and best practices into a common reference such as a compendium on international financial and economic policy standards, through which countries could articulate their intention to implement the various standards and best practices.

C. Strengthening Financial Regulation in Industrial Countries

22. The past two years have reminded us that investors and creditors often tend to underestimate risks as they reach for higher yields. In periods of market euphoria, market participants can make credit and investment decisions that might not otherwise have been made. In hindsight, the failures on the part of lenders and supervisors in the major countries include poor risk management practices, inadequate information as well as inadequate attention to available information, and capital standards that provide unintended incentives to lend to risky borrowers. Such excessive risk taking, combined with high degrees of leverage, can magnify the negative effects of any event or series of events.

23. Measures to induce creditors and investors to act with greater discipline (i.e., to analyse and weigh risks appropriately in their lending and investment decisions), should aim at avoiding excessive leverage and encouraging more prudent assessment of the risks associated with lending to emerging markets. In addition to the measures on transparency set out above, we have identified three critical areas that should be addressed by industrial countries:

a. Improving risk assessment and risk management. Measures to induce creditors and investors in industrial countries to act with greater discipline can dampen investors' tendency to underestimate risks in good times and exaggerate them in bad times. These measures can take the form of increased supervisory oversight of firms' risk management practices, and strengthened capital adequacy.

b. Assessing the implications for supervisors and regulators of Highly Leveraged Institutions (HLIs). Leverage can play a positive role, but problems can arise when excessive leverage is accompanied by excessive concentration of risk. In addition, concerns have been expressed about the activities of HLIs with respect to their impact on market dynamics generally and vulnerable economies in particular.

c. Encouraging offshore financial centres (OFCs) to comply with international standards. Financial market participants need to compete on a level playing field. Therefore, as we continue to strengthen our own regulatory standards, it will be important for OFCs to strengthen their supervisory systems and standards.

24. A substantial amount of work has already been undertaken. In particular, in January 1999, the Basle Committee promulgated guidance on sound

practices for banks in relation to HLIs, including credit analysis practices, and the development of more accurate exposure measures. The sound practices also include setting meaningful overall credit limits for HLIs, and monitoring credit exposures relating to HLIs.

25. Special requirements are demanded by the supervision of complex, internationally active financial organisations. The Joint Forum on Financial Conglomerates has done valuable work on the development of principles, regulatory techniques and other guidance for meeting some of the most significant regulatory challenges arising from the emergence of inter-nationally active financial conglomerates. In February 1999 its parent organisations, the Basle Committee, IOSCO and IAIS endorsed and released a package of papers dealing with, among other things, techniques for:

a. assessing the capital adequacy of conglomerates,

b. facilitating the exchange of information among supervisors, including the identification of co-ordinators,

c. facilitating co-ordination among supervisors, and

d. testing the fitness and propriety of managers, directors and major shareholders of conglomerates.

26. On risk assessment and risk management, the existing work of the Basle Committee provides a useful start for further work in this area. More work is now required:

a. We welcome the Basle Committee's recent agreement on proposed revisions to the Capital Accord to make it more sensitive to risk, including credit risk involved in lending to emerging markets and in short-term lending, and reflecting compliance with international standards such as the SDDS and Basle Core Principles. We welcome the Basle Committee's intention to consider broader revisions to the existing system of risk-based capital regulation, taking into account changing market practices.

b. We encourage private firms to strengthen their own risk management practices. In this regard, we note that the Counterparty Risk Management Policy Group will soon issue a report on strengthened risk management practices. Once issued, we call on national authorities to consider whether to endorse these recommendations.

c. National authorities should ensure that banking institutions in their countries implement adequate risk management practices in accordance with the recommendations set forth in the Basle Committee's January 1999 papers on HLIs.

d. We welcome the efforts of IOSCO to strengthen risk management practices for securities firms in relation to HLIs and to consider other measures to limit counterparty risk in dealings with HLIs.

27. On Highly Leveraged Institutions, we look forward to the work of the new Financial Stability Forum on a number of issues, including systemic issues relating to market dynamics generally and vulnerable economies in particular. Considerations should be broadly based and encompass the whole range of available measures, including of the pros and cons of indirect and direct supervisory approaches as well as of enhancing transparency by improving reporting and disclosure.

28. Some offshore centres have already taken measures to enhance home country supervision. However, not all countries have yet taken such measures. Moving forward, we hope the following will occur:

a. Countries with close relations with OFCs should exert pressure on those jurisdictions to comply with international standards.
b. As noted above, the Basle Committee should link risk weights to compliance with international standards.
c. IOSCO and Basle-sponsored working groups should make membership in their bodies contingent on progress towards implementation of international standards.
d. The Financial Action Task Force should take concrete steps to bring OFCs, and under-regulated and non-cooperating jurisdictions, into compliance with the 40 recommendations against money laundering and to protect the international financial community from the adverse impact of those that do not comply.
e. More generally, we look forward to the work of the Financial Stability Forum on OFCs.

29. In writing this report we took account of the reports of the G7 Financial Experts Group on Supervision and Regulation in the Financial Sector and the G7 Working Group on Financial Crime.

D. Strengthening Macroeconomic Policies and Financial Systems in Emerging Markets

30. Recent financial crises have demonstrated the need to strengthen

economic fundamentals and financial systems in emerging economies. This is essential not only to improve economic welfare in these countries, but also to help create an environment conducive to international economic and financial stability. While large-scale international capital flows have provided an important contribution to the development of emerging economies, they have also changed the nature of risks facing those countries: weak macro-economic policies and financial infrastructures can be penalised more severely and more suddenly by investors. A broad international consensus has recently been formed on a number of issues:

a. Countries need to pursue sound macroeconomic policies, including sustainable exchange rate regimes and prudent fiscal policies. They should adhere to sound principles of debt management. A high priority should also be given to strengthening emerging economies' financial sectors and supervisory regimes.

b. Some emerging economies have sought to achieve exchange rate stability by adopting peg regimes against a single currency or a basket of currencies, often in the same region, of countries with which they have the closest trade and investment links. Countries choosing fixed rates must be willing, as necessary, to subordinate other policy goals to that of fixing the exchange rate. If countries choose fixed rates, recent history suggests that arrangements institutionalising that policy can be useful to sustaining a credible commitment to fixed rates.

c. There are particular risks and vulnerabilities associated with excessive short-term borrowing, particularly in foreign currencies. Where problems have developed, there have often been important and unwise policy biases in favour of short term capital flows. Countries should avoid excessive accumulation of short-term debt, maintain an appropriate structure of liabilities, and seek to eliminate biases in favour of short-term borrowing.

d. Capital account liberalisation should be carried out in a careful and well-sequenced manner, accompanied by a sound and well-regulated financial sector and by a consistent macroeconomic policy framework.

e. The use of controls on capital inflows may be justified for a transitional period as countries strengthen the institutional and regulatory environment in their domestic financial systems. Where financial sectors and supervisory regimes are weak, safeguards may be appropriate to limit foreign currency exposure of the banking system. More comprehensive controls on inflows have been employed by some countries as a means to shield themselves from market pressures. Such steps may carry costs and should not in any case be used as a substitute for reform. In addition to these considerations, controls on capital outflows can carry even greater long term costs. They have not been a very effective policy instrument and should not be a substitute for policy reform, although they may be necessary in certain exceptional circumstances.

31. We agree that emerging economies themselves must take the lead in strengthening their economies and financial systems. In addition:

a. It is our objective to help emerging economies adapt their policies and organisations to those required to participate fully in the world economy.

b. The IFIs and other international bodies should enhance their cooperation in terms of giving useful advice and assistance to emerging economies.

32. Numerous countries will need technical assistance if standards of best practice are to be implemented without delay and effective supervision is to be achieved. As there is only a limited number of experts available both in national authorities and in international organisations, we call on the Financial Stability Forum to consider methods to improve the coordination of technical assistance, including the possibility of establishing a clearing mechanism for this purpose at the international level to ensure that technical assistance is co-ordinated and to make best use of all available resources.

Exchange Rate Regimes in Emerging Economies

33. Further work is needed on appropriate exchange rate regimes for emerging market economies. The choice of exchange rate regime is critical for emerging economies to achieve sustainable economic development, and also has important implications for the world economy, including in the context of large-scale official financing. In this context:

a. We agree that the most appropriate regime for any given economy may differ, depending on particular economic circumstances, such as the degree of integration with its trading partners. Since economic circumstances vary over time, the most appropriate regime for any given country may also vary. In any case, stability depends on the exchange rate regime being backed by consistent macroeconomic policies and supported by robust financial systems.

b. We agree that the international community should not provide large-scale official financing for a country intervening heavily to support a particular exchange rate level, except where that level is judged sustainable and certain conditions have been met, such as where the exchange rate policy is backed by a strong and credible commitment with supporting arrangements, and by consistent domestic policies.

c. We encourage the IMF to continue its work in this area and to enhance the attention it gives to exchange rate sustainability in the context of its surveillance activities. The IMF should encourage countries to adapt their policies by giving them advice, and support when appropriate, in order to help avoid moves towards unsustainable positions.

Financial Systems

34. Further efforts are needed to strengthen financial systems in emerging markets:

a. We commit ourselves to enhancing our cooperation, together with the IFIs and relevant international regulatory bodies, to promote improved financial supervision in emerging economies.

b. The IMF and the World Bank should coordinate their advice to emerging economies, in particular in the area of financial sector reforms. As part of policy reviews, they should enhance surveillance over the broad range of policies now understood to be crucial to financial stability. Countries should be encouraged to demonstrate their commitment to making rapid progress towards full compliance with existing international codes as part of IMF and World Bank conditionality when the IFIs extend loans or credits.

c. We welcome the establishment of the Financial Sector Liaison Committee (FSLC) in September 1998, and the IMF-World Bank Financial Sector Assessment Programme (FSAP), to enhance effective collaboration between the Fund and Bank in this area. The breadth and pace of these efforts need to be increased, by more effectively integrating the efforts and operations of the two institutions in the financial sector, also drawing on relevant expertise in national and international regulatory and supervisory bodies. We call upon the Fund and the Bank to prepare a joint report on their progress and on proposals to meet these objectives by the time of the Annual Meetings in September. These proposals should aim to provide more effective organisation and deployment of resources to improve crisis response, the design and delivery of financial-sector programmes, and technical assistance for member countries.

d. We welcome commitments given by the emerging economies of Asia and Latin America in various fora to take the necessary steps towards implementation of the Basle Core Principles for effective banking supervision. We call upon the governments of other countries to make every effort to ensure that by 2001 plans are in place to implement the Core Principles. The core principles of IOSCO and IAIS should also be implemented by all countries without delay.

e. Governments should narrow the scope of their guarantees of private obligations so as to make sure that creditors do not lend to private entities with the expectation that they will be protected from adverse outcomes. Those guarantees that are provided should be clear and transparent: non-bank financial institutions that fall outside the scope of such regulation should not be covered by explicit or implicit government guarantees created for the banking sector.

Capital Flows

35. We encourage the IMF to continue its work on the appropriate pace and sequencing of capital account liberalisation, and to explore further issues related to the Fund's role in facilitating an orderly approach to such liberalisation. In this context, particular attention should be paid to eliminating policy biases in favour of short-term capital flows, particularly in foreign currencies, and promoting sound debt management policies. The IMF should also further refine its analysis of the experience of countries with the use of capital controls. In this regard, there is a strong case for further studying the benefits and costs of market-based prudential measures aimed at curbing excessive capital inflows, including those used by the Chilean authorities in the recent past.

36. We call on the IMF and other relevant institutions to cooperate with national authorities to create a better system for monitoring cross-border capital flows:

a. We note the importance of timely and comprehensive data on capital flows, and encourage the IMF and national authorities, with the assistance of relevant institutions such as the BIS, to create more detailed data on inflows and outflows of capital by maturity, currency, type, and borrower. In this context, we welcome the agreement to improve data on short-term liabilities of the official sector in the context of strengthening the Special Data Dissemination Standard (SDDS).

b. We encourage the use of high-frequency debt monitoring systems which can be used to verify the sustainability of debt structures, especially

of foreign short-term exposures, and encourage the IMF to intensify its work with member governments in this area.
c. We look forward to the work of the Financial Stability Forum on short-term capital flows.

Debt Management

37. We will work with emerging market economies and the IFIs to promote best practices in debt management, which should:
a. encourage greater reliance on long-maturity, and if possible domestic-currency denominated, debt to maintain a debt profile that provides substantial protection against temporary market disruption; avoid transforming long-term debt into short-term debt;
b. remove biases which encourage short-term private borrowing;
c. encourage the creation of deeper domestic bond markets to facilitate long-term domestic currency debt financing;
d. encourage governments that are heavily dependent on commodities revenue to hedge their exposure to commodity price volatility, and promote arrangements that provide greater contractual risk-sharing between creditors and debtors;
e. promote debt management that minimises exposure to liquidity risk, including rollover risk, rather than minimises short-term borrowing costs. Provisions in sovereign debt contracts that can augment balance of payments pressure in a crisis should be avoided; and
f. promote the use of contractual provisions in offshore sovereign bond documentation that facilitate orderly restructuring, as described in section E below.

E. Improving Crisis Prevention and Management, and Involving the Private Sector

38. Recent crises have emphasised the need to improve the approach of the international community to financial crisis prevention and resolution, and adapt it to a world of open capital markets. We need to shape expectations so that private creditors know that they will bear the consequences of their investment decisions, and to identify ways to reduce the risk of contagion.

Crisis Prevention

39. Prevention of financial crises is key. The measures that we have outlined in the sections above provide important ways to improve crisis prevention. In addition, new clear principles and new tools are needed to limit contagion and to fully recognise the crucial role private investors play in today's integrated financial markets.

40. The new IMF contingent credit line (CCL) will play an important part in promoting international financial stability. This facility aims at protecting from contagion countries with reasonable debt structures, sound macro-economic and structural policies, and which are also engaged in an appropriate process of consultation with private creditors. The facility should encourage the IMF towards an increasing focus on crisis prevention, and will provide further incentives for countries to take early measures to avoid the risk of financial crisis. The CCL provides an additional mechanism for encouraging countries to implement standards.

41. Countries should take ex ante steps to strengthen the framework for the market-based, cooperative and orderly resolution of the debt payment difficulties that do arise. We have agreed on the following measures:

a. Appropriate communication between debtors and creditors is important in both crisis prevention and resolution. We encourage emerging economies to develop mechanisms for more systematic dialogue with their main creditors. We also support strengthened contacts between the international financial institutions, notably the IMF, and the private sector.

b. We encourage the use of market based tools aimed at preventing crises and facilitating adjustment to shocks, including through the use of innovative financial arrangements, including private market-based contingent credit lines in emerging countries and roll-over options in debt instruments. These measures would facilitate access to the international markets in times of instability for emerging countries, and, in the context of a sound debt management framework, can thus help prevent liquidity crises and give countries a breathing space to make decisive macro-economic or structural adjustments.

42. We have agreed on the importance of stronger efforts to encourage progress in broadening the use of collective action clauses in sovereign debt

contracts, along with other provisions that facilitate creditor coordination and discourage disruptive legal action. We recommend:

a. making the use of such provisions a component of international best practices in debt management, and a consideration in determining access to the IMF's Contingent Credit Line;

b. focusing attention on the use of these provisions in international surveillance, and making such provisions a consideration in IMF conditionality, as appropriate;

c. considering incorporating these provisions into sovereign debt that is enhanced by the multilateral development banks;

d. Further considering the possible inclusion of such provisions in our own debt instruments, and otherwise encouraging the use of such provisions in the debt instruments issued by other sovereigns in our markets.

43. We also encourage efforts to establish sound and efficient bankruptcy procedures and strong judicial systems. We support the work of the international financial institutions to help countries to improve the transparency, predictability, and equity of their insolvency and debtor-creditor regimes.

A Framework for Private Sector Involvement in Crisis Resolution

44. In addition to crisis prevention measures addressed above, we are agreed that the international financial community needs to set out in advance a broad framework of principles and tools for involving the private sector in the resolution of crises. The following framework should help to promote more orderly crisis resolution and therefore be of mutual benefit to debtors and creditors in finding cooperative solutions. It should also help to promote cooperative solutions between borrowing countries and the private sector and to shape expectations in a way which reduces the risk that investors believe they will be protected from adverse outcomes. Developing a framework of this kind which facilitates debtor/creditor cooperation should minimise the incidence and intensity of crises and also minimise the time before debtor countries can expect to regain market access.

Principles

45. We agree that this framework should comprise the following key

principles:

a. The approach to crisis resolution must not undermine the obligation of countries to meet their debts in full and on time. Otherwise, private investment and financial flows that are crucial for growth could be adversely affected and the risk of contagion increase.
b. Market discipline will work only if creditors bear the consequences of the risks that they take. Private credit decisions need to be based on an assessment of the potential risk and return associated with a particular investment, not on the expectation that creditors will be protected from adverse outcomes by the official sector.
c. In a crisis, reducing net debt payments to the private sector can potentially contribute to meeting a country's immediate financing needs and reducing the amount of finance to be provided by the official sector. It can also contribute to maintaining appropriate incentives for prudent credit and investment decisions going forward. These potential gains must be balanced against the impact that such measures may have on the country's own ability to attract new private capital flows, as well as the potential impact on other countries and the system in general through contagion.
d. No one category of private creditors should be regarded as inherently privileged relative to others in a similar position. When both are material, claims of bondholders should not be viewed as senior to claims of banks.
e. The aim of crisis management wherever possible should be to achieve co-operative solutions negotiated between the debtor country and its creditors, building on effective dialogues established in advance.

Considerations

46. The principles outlined above, and the tools we propose below, should help establish a broad framework for making judgements about the policy response appropriate to a given case. The appropriate role for private creditors, if any, and the policy approaches needed to induce private creditors to play this role will vary depending on the circumstances of the particular case. There are advantages to making clear in advance the basic considerations that will guide our actions and specific approaches we will employ. The principles and tools we propose should help provide a degree of predictability for investors, without sacrificing the flexibility required to address effectively each particular financial crisis.

47. There is a variety of circumstances where countries might face external financing pressures There are circumstances where we believe emphasis might best be placed on market-based, voluntary solutions to resolve the country's financial difficulties. There are also cases where more comprehensive approaches may be appropriate to provide a more sustainable future payments path. In practice, there will be a spectrum of cases between hese two extremes. Where a country falls on this spectrum, will help to determine the policy approach best suited to its particular circumstances. Relevant considerations include the country's underlying capacity to pay and its access to the markets.

48. In addition, the feasibility of different policy approaches will depend on the nature of outstanding debt instruments. These will influence assessments of which claims need to be addressed to resolve the country's financing difficulties, the magnitude of possible concerns about equitable treatment among various categories of creditors, and the scope for voluntary versus more coercive solutions. The nature of the relevant debt obligations can differ along many axes, including whether the debt obligations are principally private or public; foreign or local currency; short-term or long-term; payment of principal or interest; offshore or onshore; secured or unsecured; held narrowly or held by a diffuse group of creditors.

49. It is important to put into place incentives that would encourage a country to take strong steps at the early stages of its financial difficulties to prevent a deepening crisis.

Tools

50. To address effectively a wide range of potential cases, the international community needs to have a broader range of tools available to promote appropriate private sector involvement. The tools available to the international community should comprise the following:

a. Linking the provision of official support to efforts by the country to initiate discussions with its creditors to explain its policy program.

b. Linking the provision of official support to efforts by the country to seek voluntary commitments of support, as appropriate, and/or to commit to raise new funds from private markets.

c. Linking the provision of official support to the country's efforts to seek specific commitments by private creditors to maintain exposure levels.

d. Linking the provision of official support to the country's efforts to restructure or refinance outstanding obligations.
e. In cases where a country's official debt needs to be restructured in the Paris Club, the Paris Club principle of comparability of treatment applies to all categories of creditors other than the international financial institutions. The Paris Club should adopt a flexible approach to comparability, taking into account factors including the relative size and importance of different categories of claims.
f. Imposing a reserve floor that effectively ensures that the private sector makes an adequate contribution, such as through debt restructuring, alongside official resources in the resolution of crises.
g. In exceptional cases, it may not be possible for the country to avoid the accumulation of arrears. IMF lending into arrears may be appropriate if the country is seeking a cooperative solution to its payment difficulties with its creditors.
h. In exceptional cases, countries may impose capital or exchange controls as part of payments suspensions or standstills, in conjunction with IMF support for their policies and programmes, to provide time for an orderly debt restructuring.

51. We call on the IMF further to develop and define the legal and technical questions involved in implementing the specific approaches identified in the framework agreed here. We look forward to its conclusions by the autumn Annual Meetings.

52. In order to guide expectations more effectively, we agree that we will seek to provide a clear and timely explanation of the policy approaches, adopted in individual cases, in relation to the principles and considerations that we have laid out above.

F. Promoting Social Policies to Protect the Poor and Most Vulnerable

53. Recent events in the world economy have underlined the important link between economic and social issues; and that good economies depend both on stable relationships between governments and their citizens, and strong social cohesion. An efficient social system, by equipping people for change, builds trust and encourages people to take the risks which are a necessary part of a competitive modern market. This in turn helps to mitigate the risks and spread the benefits of globalization.

54. Effective social policy can in particular ease the task of adjustment during times of crisis, helping build support for necessary reforms and ensuring that the burden of adjustment does not fall disproportionately on the poorest and most vulnerable groups in society.

55. Action in these areas can be subject to a number of constraints. In general, the resources available for social programmes are limited, other priorities are pressing and institutional capacity can be stretched. In times of downturn, policy makers may face particularly difficult choices between safeguarding immediate social welfare, and ensuring the adjustment necessary to restore confidence and promote stable growth, which provides the best way of reducing poverty and supporting social welfare. We believe there are strong benefits for all countries and the IFIs in working together to develop and promote practices in social policies which most effectively support economic development.

56. Countries, each with their different culture and traditions, have developed their own systems and practices for addressing social issues. There is likely to be mutual benefit for countries in sharing experiences of policies which work best at different stages of development. Experiences were discussed at the seminar involving 33 economies held this spring in Washington. The seminar: a. considered the most important areas of social spending, the ways in which public expenditure can be effectively targeted to the neediest, and the trade-offs which are involved when levels of social spending are determined; b. underlined the importance of monitoring social developments and operating social policy in a transparent way, so that both governments and their populations can be more aware, at the earliest possible stage, of areas of particular need, and plan on that basis.

57. Moreover, since countries operating in the modern globalized economy are likely to face similar pressures, there is a case for identifying principles, policies and best practices, and for their promulgation through international organisations. We note with approval the principles of good practice in social policy which have been prepared by the World Bank, in collaboration with the United Nations. At the last meeting of the Development Committee, Ministers asked the World Bank to report back at the 1999 Annual Meetings on its work on policies and best practice to protect the poorest groups and maintain the momentum for development.

58. Further work is needed to identify and promulgate principles, policies and best practices in social policy. We call on:

a. the UN to make rapid progress in developing the basic social principles as part of the follow-up on the Copenhagen Declaration of the World Summit for Social Development;

b. the World Bank, with full participation from the IMF, to report back to the 1999 Annual Meetings on identifying policies and best practice to support the process of economic development. In times of crisis, these can be drawn upon in the design of adjustment programmes to ensure protection of the most vulnerable;

c. the IMF and the World Bank, in their work on transparency and good governance to consider more explicitly the way in which this can be geared to ensuring implementation of social programmes which minimises waste and maximises efficiency;

d. the World Bank and the IMF to strengthen collaboration in the preparation of public expenditure reviews of individual countries which analyse the composition and efficiency of public expenditure;

e. the IMF, in assisting countries to develop macroeconomic frameworks in times of crisis, to take into consideration the degree to which the adjustment programmes provide for adequate spending in the social sector;

f. the World Bank to work with countries, the Fund and Regional Development Banks on drawing up and monitoring implementation and follow up of social indicators;

g. the Fund and Bank to increase the attention they give to these issues in the design of adjustment and sector programmes, and to develop further their cooperation in this area. In addition, we call on all countries to consider what more can be done to encourage the pursuit of sound social policies both inside and outside of crisis situations.

59. Effective social policy will help provide a foundation for sustainable development, by ensuring that the benefits of globalization are widely shared, equipping people for change and ensuring that economies are more robust.

60. Sustainable development at a global level, enabling all countries to share the benefits of economic growth, also depends on measures to reduce the unsustainable debt burdens on the poorest countries and alleviate poverty. The

initiatives on social policy must therefore be taken forward together with initiatives on debt relief and poverty reduction, on which we have presented separate proposals to our Heads.

Bibliography

Aghion, Philippe, Philippe Bacchetta and Abhijit Banerjee (March 1999), "Capital Markets and the Instability of Open Economies", *Centre for Economic Policy Research, Discussion Paper No. 2083.*

Attali, J. (1995), *Verbatim III,* Fayard, Pads.

Bagehot, Walter (1910), *Lombard Street,* Smith, Elder, London.

Bank for International Settlements (1999), "Broadening Representation in the financial Stability Forum", Press Release 21, June, www.bis.org/press/index.htm.

Barro, R.J. (1999), "Let the Dollar Reign from Seattle to Santiago", *Wall Street Journal*, Midwest edition (March 8), p. A18.

Bartlett, Christopher A. and Ghoshal, Sumantra (1989) *Managing Across Borders: The Transnational Solution*, Harvard Business School Press, Boston.

Bartolini, L. and A. Prati (1998), *Soft Exchange Rates Bands and Speculative Attacks: Theory and Evidence from the ERM since August 1993*, IMF working Paper/98/156, International Monetary Fund, Washington DC.

Baxter, M. (1994), "Real Exchange Rates and Real Interest Differentials: Have We Missed the Business-Cycle Relationship?", *Journal of Monetary Economics*, Vol. 33.

Bayne, N. (1998), "Britain, the G8 and the Commonwealth; Lessons of the Birmingham Summit", *The Round Table,* No. 348, pp. 445-457.

Bayne, N. (1995), "The G7 Summit and the Reform of Global Institutions", *Government and Opposition,* 30(4), pp. 492-509.

Bayne, N. (1999), *Hanging In There: The G7 and G8 Summit in Maturity and Renewal,* Ashgate, Aldershot.

Bayne, N. (1999a), "Continuity and Leadership in an Age of Globalization", in Michael Hodges *et al.*, *The G8's Role in the New Millennium*, Ashgate, Aldershot.

Bayne, N., and R.D. Putnam (1995), "Introduction: The G7 Summit Comes of Age", in S. Ostry and G.R. Winham (eds.), *The Halifax G7 Summit: Issues on the Table,* Centre for Policy Studies, Dalhousie University, Halifax.

Bayne, N. (1997), "Globalisation and the Commonwealth", *The Round Table,* No. 344, pp. 473-484.

Bayne, N. (1992), "The Course of Summitry", *The World Today,* 48(2), pp. 27-29.

Bayne, N. (1997), "Impressions of the Denver Summit", at www.G7.utoronto.ca.

Bayne, N. (1999b), "Review of Andrew Cooper's Canadian Foreign Policy: Old Habits and New Directions", *The Round Table*, July.

Bergsten, F., O. Davanne and P. Jacquet (1999), "The Case for Joint Management of Exchange Rate Flexibility", Working Paper 99-9, Institute for International Economics, Washington DC.

Bergsten, C.F. and C.R. Henning (1996), *Global Economic Leadership and the Group of Seven,* Institute for International Economics, Washington DC.

Bhagwati, J. (1997), "Interview", *Times of India*, December 31.

Black, Conrad, (1997-98), "Taking Canada Seriously", *International Journal*, 53 (Winter): 1-16.

Blanchard, O. (1999), Comment on three reports to the French Conseil d'Analyse Economique, Report No. 18, Collection des Rapports du Conseil d'Analyse Economique, La Documentation Française, Paris.

Blanchard, O. (1997), *Macroeconomics*, Prentice Hall.

Blinder, Alan (1999), "Eight Steps to a New Financial Order", *Foreign Affairs* 78, September/October, pp. 50-63.

Block, Fred (1977), *The Origins of International Economic Disorder*, University of California Press, Berkeley.

Borowski, D. et C. Couharde (1999), "La Compétitivité Relative des Etats-Unis, du Japon et de la Zone Euro", annexe B, Report n° 18, Collection des Rapports du Conseil d'Analyse Economique, La Documentation Française, Paris.

Brown, G. (1999), "Toward a Strong World Financial System", *The Wall Street Journal*, April 30, p. A14.

Buiter, W. (1997), "The Economic Case for Monetary Union in the European Union", *Review of International Economics, Special Supplement*, 5(4), pp. 10-35.

Bullard, J. (1990), "Rethinking Rational Expectations", pp. 325-354 in G.M. von Furstenberg (ed.), *Acting Under Uncertainty: Multidisciplinary Conceptions*, Kluwer Academic Publishers, Boston.

Buria, A. (1999), "An Alternative Approach to Financial Crises", *Essays in International Finance*, No. 212, Princeton University.

Calomiris, Charles (1999), special issue editor, "Lessons from the Tequila Crisis for Successful Financial Liberalization", *Journal of Banking and Finance,* vol. 23, pp. 1457-1461.

Camdessus, M., and J.D. Wolfensohn (1998), "The Bretton Woods Institutions: Responding to the Asian Financial Crisis", in M. Fraser (ed.), *The G8 and the World Economy,* Strategems Publishing Ltd, London, pp. 6-8.

Camdessus, M. (1999), "Transparency and Improved Standards Are Key to Stable and Efficient Financial System", *IMF Survey*, 28(11), June 7, pp. 177-180.

Canada (1998c), Finance Canada, "Canada to Join Thailand Assistance Package", 15 April, Washington DC.

Canada (1998b), Finance Canada, "Minister Welcomes Declaration of G-7 Finance Ministers and Central Bank Governors", 30 October, Ottawa.

Canada (1998a), Finance Canada, "Remarks by the Honourable Paul Martin, Minister of Finance, to the Commonwealth Business Forum", 29 September, Ottawa.

Canada (1998d), Finance Canada, "International supervisory and surveillance initiative proposed", 15 April, Washington DC.

Caprio, Gerald and Patrick Honohan (1999), "Restoring Banking Stability: Beyond Supervised Capital Requirements", *Journal of Economic Perspectives,* 13(4), pp.

43-64.

Catte, P., G. Galli and S. Rebecchini (1994), "Concerted interventions and the Dollar: An Analysis of Daily Data", In P.Kenen, F. Papadia and F.Saccomani, eds., *The International Monetary System*, Cambridge University Press, Cambridge.

Choe, Hyuk, Bong-Chan Kho and René Stulz (1999), "Do Foreign Investors Destabilize Stock Markets? The Korean Experience in 1997", *Journal of Financial Economics,* vol. 54, pp. 227-264.

Coe, D. and S. Golub (1986), "Exchange Rates and Real Long-term Differentials: Evidence for Eighteen OECD Countries", Document de travail de l'OCDE, Organisation for Economic Co-operation and Development, Paris.

Coeuré, B. and J. Pisani-Ferry (1999), "The Case Against Benign Neglect of Exchange Rate Stability", *Finance and Development*, September 1999, 36(3).

Cohen, B.J. (1998), *The Geography of Money*, Cornell University Press, Ithaca NY.

Cooper, Andrew (1997), *Canadian Foreign Policy: Old Habits and New Directions*, Prentice Hall, Scarborough.

Cooper, R.N. (1999), "Should Capital Controls be Banished?", *Brookings Papers on Economic Activity*, No. 1, pp. 89-125.

Cooper, R.N. (1999), "A Tour of International Financial Reform: Interview with Richard Cooper", *Challenge*, pp. 5-28.

Cooper, R.N. (1995), "Reform of Multilateral Financial Institutions" in S. Ostry and C.R. Winham (eds.), *The Halifax G7 Summit: Issues on the Table,* Centre for Policy Studies, Dalhousie University, Halifax.

Council on Foreign Relations Task Force (1999), "The Future of the International Financial Architecture", *Foreign Affairs*, 78(6), pp. 169-184.

Crockett, Andrew (1997), "Why is Financial Stability a Goal of Public Policy?", in *Maintaining Financial Stability in a Global Economy: A Symposium Sponsored by the Federal Reserve Bank of Kansas City*, Jackson Hole, WY: Federal Reserve Bank of Kansas City, pp. 7-36.

Croome, J. (1995), *Reshaping the World Trading System: A History of the Uruguay Round,* World Trade Organization, Geneva.

Daniels, J. (1999), "Supervising the International Financial System", in M. Hodges, *et al.*, *The G8's Role in the New Millennium*, Ashgate, Aldershot, pp. 107-118.

Daniels, Joseph and David VanHoose (1999), *International Monetary and Financial Economics,* SouthWestern Publishing, Cincinnati.

Daniels, Joseph, Peter Toumanoff and Marc von der Ruhr (1999), "Optimal Basket Pegs for Developing and Emerging Economies", Working Paper, Marquette University.

Davanne, O. (1999b), "The Role of Transparency for a Better Pricing of Risks", mimeo.

Davanne, O. (1998), *L'instabilité du Sytème Financier International*, Report to the French Prime Minister, Collection des Rapports du Conseil d'Analyse Economique, La Documentation Française, Paris.

Davanne, O. (1990), "La Dynamique des Taux de Change", *Economie et Statistique*

No. 236.

Davanne, O. (1999a), "Transparency of Financial Portfolios and Control of Market Risks", available in French and English at www.finances.gouv.fr/pole_ecofin/politique_financiere.

Devenow, A. and I. Welch (1996), "Rational Herding in Financial Economics", *European Economic Review*, Vol 40.

Dewitt, David and John Kirton (1983), *Canada as a Principal Power*, John Wiley, Toronto.

Diaz, Miguel (2000), "Bringing Up Basel", *Latin Finance*, No. 113, pp. 44-46.

Dobson, Wendy (1999), "Fallout From the Global Financial Crisis: Should Capitalism be Curbed?", *International Journal*, vol. 54 (Summer), pp. 375-386.

Dobson, W. (1991), *Economic Policy Coordination: Requiem or Prologue?*, Institute for International Economics, Washington DC.

Dominguez, K. and J. Frankel (1993), *Does Foreign Exchange Intervention Work?*, Institute For International Economics, Washington DC.

Dominguez, K. (1990), "Market Responses to Coordinated Central Bank Intervention", *Carnegie-Rochester Series on Public Policy* 32, pp.121-64.

Doran, C. (1984), *Forgotten Partnership: U.S.-Canada Relations Today*, John Hopkins University Press, Baltimore.

Dornbusch, R. (1976), "Expectations and Exchange Rate Dynamics", *Journal of Political Economy*, 84.

Dornbusch, R. (1999), "The Euro: Implications for Latin America", paper prepared for a policy research project of the World Bank, available at web.mit.edu/rudi/www.

Eatwell, John and Lance Taylor (1998), "International Capital Markets and the Future of Economic Policy", CEPA Working Paper No. 9, Center for Economic Policy Analysis at www.newschool.edu/cepa.

The Economist (October 17, 1998), "Turmoil in Financial Markets: The Risk Business", p. 21.

The Economist (October 2, 1999), "Bail in, Bail Out", p. 19.

Edwards, Sebastian (1999), "How Effective are Capital Controls?", *Journal of Economic Perspectives*, 13(4), pp. 65-84.

Eichengreen, B. (1999), *Towards a New International Financial Architecture: A Practical Post-Asia Agenda*, Institute for International Economics, Washington DC.

Eichengreen, Barry, Paul Masson, Miguel Savastano and Sunil Sharma (1999), "Transition Strategies and Nominal Anchors on the Road to Greater Exchange-Rate Flexibility", *Princeton Essays in International Finance, No. 213.*

Eichengreen, B., A.K. Rose and C. Wyplosz (1995), "Exchange Market Mayhem: The Antecedents and Aftermath of Speculative Attacks", *Economic Policy*, vol. 21, October, pp. 251-312.

Eichengreen, Barry, Michael Mussa, Giovanni Dell' Ariccia, enrica Detragiache, Gian Maria Milesi-Ferretti and Andrew Tweedie (1999), "Liberalizing Capital

Movements: Some Analytical Issues", *International Monetary Fund Economic Issues*, 17.

Eichengreen, B., A. Rose and C. Wyplosz (1994), "Speculative Attacks on Pegged Exchange Rates: An Empirical Exploration with Special Reference to the European Monetary System", *NBER Working Paper, No. 4898.*

Evans, H. (1999), "Debt Relief for the Poorest Countries: Why Did It Take So Long?", Development Policy Review, 17(3), pp. 267-279, Overseas Development Institute, London.

Feldstein, M. (1998), "Refocusing the IMF", *Foreign Affairs,* 77(2), pp. 20-33.

Fischer, S. (1999), "The Financial Crisis in Emerging Markets: Some Lessons", Outline of comments prepared for delivery at the conference of the Economic Strategy Institute, Washington DC, (April 28), pp. 1-4.

Fischer, S. (1998), "In Defense of the IMF", *Foreign Affairs*, 77(4), pp. 103-106.

Fischer, Stanley (1999), "Reforming the International Financial System", *The Economic Journal,* 109(459), pp. F557-F576.

Fontagné, L. and M. Freudenberg (1999), "Endogenous Symmetry of Shocks in a Monetary Union", *Open Economies Review*, 10(3), pp. 263-288.

Frankel, Jeffrey A. (1999), "No Single Currency is Right for All Countries or At All Times", *Essays in International Finance*, No. 215.

Frankel, J. and K. Froot (1990), "Chartists, Fundamentalists and Trading in the Foreign Exchange Market", *American Economic Review*, 80.

Frankel, J.A. (1999), in International Monetary Fund Economic Forum, "Dollarization: Fad or Future for Latin America?", http://www.imf.org/external/np/tr/1999/TR990624.HTM, pp. 2-6.

Frankel, J.A. and A.K. Rose (1998), "The Endogeneity of the Optimum Currency Area Criteria", *Economic Journal*, vol. (449), pp. 1109-1025.

Frankel, J.A. (1997), *Regional Trading Blocs In the World Economic System*, Institute for International Economics, Washington DC.

French, K.R. and J.M. Poterba (1990), "Are Japanese Stock Prices Too High?", National Bureau of Economic Research Working Paper No. 3290, March.

Friedman, B.M. (1999), "The Power of the Electronic Herd", *The New York Review of Books*, 46(12), July 15, pp. 1-8.

Fry, Michael, John Kirton and Mitsuru Kurosawa, eds., (1998), *The North Pacific Triangle: The United States, Japan and Canada at Century's End*, University of Toronto Press, Toronto.

Fraser, M. (1998), ed., *The G8 and the World Economy,* Strategems Publishing Limited, London.

Fukuyama, Francis (1992), *The End of History and the Last Man*, Free Press, New York.

Funabashi, Y. (1988), *Managing the Dollar: From the Plaza to the Louvre*, Institute for International Economics, Washington DC.

Furman, J. and J.E. Stiglitz (1998), "Economic Crises: Evidence and Insights from East Asia", *Brookings Papers on Economic Activity*, No. 2, pp. 1-114.

G7 (1998a), *Statement by the G-7 Finance Ministers and Central Bank Governors*, Washington DC, 3 October, www.g7.utoronto.ca.

G7 Finance Ministers (1999), *Strengthening the International Financial Architecture: Report of G7 Finance Ministers to the Köln Economic Summit*, Cologne, 18-20 June.

G7 (1999), *G-7 Statement*, 18 June, www.g7.utoronto.ca.

G7 (1998b), *Leaders Statement on the World Economy*, 30 October, and *Statement by the G-7 Finance Ministers and Central Bank Governors*, (30 October), www.g7.utoronto.ca.

G8 (1999), G8 *Communiqué* Koln 1999, 20 June, www.g7.utoronto.ca.

Goldstein, M., (1998), *The Asian Financial Crisis: Causes, Cures, and Systemic Implications*, Institute for International Economics, Washington DC.

Goodhart, C, (1999), "Managing the Global Economy", in M. Hodges, *et al.*, *The G8's Role in the New Millennium*, Ashgate, Aldershot, pp. 135-140.

Gorbachev, M. (1987), *Perestroika: New Thinking for Our Country and the World*, Harper & Row, New York.

Gray, John (1998), *False Dawn: The Delusions of Global Capitalism*, Granta Books, London.

Hale, David (1998), "The IMF after Russia's Default", *Foreign Affairs* vol. 77, September/October.

Hajnal, P.I. (1999), *The G7/G8 System: Evolution, Role and Documentation*, Ashgate, Aldershot.

Hajnal, Peter (1989), *The Seven Power Summit: Documents from the Summits of Industrialized Countries*, 1975-1989, Kraus, Millwood, NY.

Hausmann, R. (1999), "Exchange Rate Debate" and other short articles, *Latin American Economic Policies*, vol. 7 (Second Quarter), pp. 1-2, 6-8.

Hausmann, R. (1999), "Should There Be Five Currencies or One Hundred and Five?", *Foreign Policy*, 65-79.

Hawes, Michael (1984), *Principal Power, Middle Power or Satellite? Competing Perspectives in the Study of Canadian Foreign Policy*, York Research Program in Strategic Studies, Toronto.

Hettne, Björn, András Inotai and Osvaldo Sunkel, eds. (1999), *Globalization and the New Regionalism*, Macmillan, London.

Hodges, Michael (1994), "More Efficiency, Less Dignity: British Perspectives on the Future Role and Working of the G7", *The International Spectator*, 29(2).

Hodges, Michael, John Kirton and Joseph Daniels, eds, *The G8's Role in the New Millennium*, Ashgate, Aldershot.

Holle, P. (1999), "Canadians Wonder Whether the Loonie is for the Birds", *Wall Street Journal*, August 6, p. A11.

Ikenberry, John (1993), "Salvaging the G7", *Foreign Affairs*, vol. 72 (Spring), pp. 132-139.

Institute of International Finance (1999), *Report of the Working Group on Transparency in Emerging Markets Finance*, Washington DC, March.

International Monetary Fund (1999), "IMF Takes Additional Steps to Enhance Transparency", *Public Information Notice No. 99/36*, April, pp. 1-3.

IMF (current URL), http://www.imf.org/external/standards/index.htm, source for data dissemination (http://dsbb.imf.org) and fiscal and monetary transparency standards and reports on country transparency practices.

IMF (1998), *World Economic Outlook*, International Monetary Fund, Washington, DC.

International Monetary Fund (1998), *World Economic Outlook, October 1998*, International Monetary Fund, Washington DC.

International Monetary Fund (1997), *Good Governance: The IMF's Role*, IMF, Washington DC.

Ize, A. and E. Levy-Yeyati (1998), "Dollarization of Financial Intermediation: Causes and Policy Implications", International Monetary Fund Working Paper, WP/98/28.

James, Harold (1999), "Is Liberalization Reversible?", International Monetary Fund, *Finance and Development*, 36(4), pp. 11-14.

James, H. (1996), *International Monetary Cooperation Since Bretton Woods*, International Monetary Fund, Washington DC.

James, Harold, 1999, "Is Liberalization Reversible?", International Monetary Fund, *Finance and Development*, pp. 11-14.

Jomo, K.S. (1999), "Financial Liberalization, Crises, and Malaysian Policy Responses", *World Development*, 26(8), pp.1563-1574.

Jurgensen Report (1983), *Report of the Working Group on Exchange Market Intervention*, US Treasury Department, March, Washington DC.

Kafka, A. (1973), "Optimum Currency Areas and Latin America", in H.G. Johnson and A.K. Swoboda, eds., *The Economics of Common Currencies*, George Allen & Unwin, London, pp. 210-218.

Kenen, P.B. (ed.), (1996), *From Halifax to Lyons: What Has Been Done About Crisis Management?*, Essays in International Finance no. 200, Princeton University, Princeton.

Kenen, P.B. (ed.), (1994), *Managing the World Economy: Fifty Years After Bretton Woods*, Institute for International Economics, Washington DC.

Keynes, J.M. (1936), *The General Theory of Employment, Interest and Money*, Macmillan.

Kindleberger, Charles (1988), *The International Economic Order: Essays on Financial Crisis and International Public Goods*, MIT Press, Cambridge MA.

Kirton, John (2000), "Deepening Integration and Global Governance: America as a Globalized Partner", in Tom Brewer and Gavin Boyd, eds., *Globalizing America: The USA in World Integration*, Edward Elgar, Cheltenham.

Kirton, John (1999a), "Explaining G8 Effectiveness", in M. Hodges, J. Kirton, and J. Daniels, eds., *The G8's Role in the New Millennium*, Ashgate, Aldershot, pp. 45-68.

Kirton, John (1999b), "Canada as a Principal Financial Power: G7 and IMF

Diplomacy in the Crisis of 1997-99", *International Journal*, vol. 54, pp. 603-624.

Kirton, John (1999c), "Canada and the Global Financial Crisis: G7 and APEC Diplomacy", *The Canadian Studies Journal*, vol. 3 (forthcoming).

Kirton, J. (1999d), "The G7, China and the International Financial System", Paper presented at an International Think Tank Forum on "China in the Twenty-First Century", China Development Institute, 10-12 November, Shenzen, China.

Kirton, John (1997), "Canada, the G-7 and the Denver Summit of the Eight:Iimplications for Asia and Taiwan", *Canadian Studies*, vol. 2, pp. 339-66.

Kirton, John (1997) "Le rôle du G-7 dans le couple intégration régionale-sécurité globale", *Etudes Internationales*, 28 Juin 1997, pp. 255-270.

Kirton, John (1995a) "The Diplomacy of Concert: Canada, the G-7 and the Halifax Summit", *Canadian Foreign Policy*, vol. 3 (Spring), pp. 63-80.

Kirton, John (1995b), "The G-7, the Halifax Summit and International Financial System Reform", *North American Outlook*, vol. 5 (June), pp. 43-66.

Kirton, John (1994), "Exercising Concerted Leadership: Canada's Approach to Summit Reform", *International Spectator* vol. 29 (April-June).

Kirton, John and Ella Kokotsis (1997-98), "Revitalizing the G-7: Prospects for the 1998 Birmingham Summit of the Eight", *International Journal,* vol. 53 (Winter), pp. 38-56.

Kirton, John J. and Joseph P. Daniels (1999), "The Role of the G8 in the New Millennium", in Michael R. Hodges, John J. Kirton and Joseph P. Daniels, eds., *The G8's Role in the New Millennium*, Ashgate Publishing Ltd., Aldershot, pp. 3-18.

Kokotsis, E., and J.P. Daniels (1999), "G8 Summits and Compliance", in M.J. Hodges, J.J. Kirton and J.P. Daniels (eds.), *The G8's Role in the New Millennium*, Ashgate, Aldershot, pp. 75-91.

Kokotsis, E. (1999), *Keeping International Commitments: Compliance, Credibility and the G7, 1988-1995*, Garland Publishing, Levittown.

Krugman, P. (1989), *Exchange Rate Instability*, MIT Press, Cambridge.

Lauridsen, Laurids (1999), "The Financial Crisis in Thailand: Causes, Conduct and Consequences?", *World Development*, 26(8), pp. 1575-1591.

Lewis, K.K. (1999), "Trying to Explain Home Bias in Equities and Consumption", *Journal of Economic Literature*, 37(2), June, pp. 571-608.

Lindgren, C. Gillian, G., and Saal, M. (1996), *Bank Soundness and Macroeconomic Policy*, International Monetary Fund, Washington DC.

Lockwood, M., E. Donlan, K. Joyner and A. Simms (1998), *Forever in Your Debt? Eight Poor Nations and the G8*, Christian Aid, London.

Mansfield, Edward and Helen Milner (1999), "The New Wave of Regionalism", *International Organization*, vol. 53 (Summer 1999), pp. 589-628.

Martin, Paul (1997), "Canada and the G-7", Notes for remarks by the Honourable Paul Martin, Minister of Finance, to the University of Toronto G-7 Research Group, (November), at www.G-7.utoronto.ca.

Mathieson, D.J. A. Richards, and S. Sharma (1998), "Financial Crises in Emerging

Markets", *Finance and Development*, 35(4), December, pp. 28-31.

McKinnon, R. (1998), "Exchange Rate Coordination for Surmounting the East Asian Currency Crisis", Paper presented at the Conference on *Financial Crises: Facts, Theories, and Policies*, International Monetary Fund, 18 November, Washington DC.

Meese, R. and K. Rogoff (1983),"Empirical Exchange Rate Models of the Seventies: Do They Fit Out of Sample?", *Journal of International Economics*, 14.

Meese, R. and K. Rogoff (1988), "Was It Real? The Exchange Rate-Interest Differential Relationship Over the Modern Floating-Rate Period", *The Journal of Finance*, 43.

Mishkin, Fredric S. (1999), "Global Financial Instability: Framework, Events, Issues", *Journal of Economic Perspectives*, 13(4), pp. 3-20.

Mundell, R. (1968), *International Economics*, Macmillan, New York.

Nossal, Kim Richard (1997), *The Politics of Canadian Foreign Policy*, 3rd ed., Prentice Hall, Scarborough.

Obstfeld, M. (1998) "The Global Capital Market: Benefactor or Menace?", *Journal of Economic Perspectives*, 12(4), pp. 9-30.

OECD (1999), *EMU Facts, Challenges and Policies*, Paris, Organisation for Economic Co-operation and Development.

Ohmae, Kenichi (1990), *The Borderless World*, Harper Collins, New York.

Ortiz, G. (1999), 6-10 in IMF Economic Forum, "Dollarization: Fad or Future for Latin America?", http://www.imf.org/external/np/tr/1999/TR990624.HTM.

Ostry, Sylvia (1997), *The Post-Cold War Trading System: Who's on First?*, University of Chicago Press, Chicago.

Pagano, Marco (1993), "Financial Markets and Growth: An Overview", *European Economic Review*, vol. 37, pp. 613-622.

Porter, Michael E. (1990), *The Competitive Advantage of Nations*, Free Press, New York.

Preeg, E.H. (1995), *Traders in a Brave New World: The Uruguay Round and the Future of the International Trading System*, University of Chicago Press, Chicago.

Putnam, R.D. and N. Bayne (1987), *Hanging Together: Cooperation and Conflict in the Seven-Power Summits,* SAGE, London.

Putnam, R. (1989), "Diplomacy and Domestic Politics: The Logic of Two Level Games", *International Organization*, vol. 42.

Putnam, Robert and Nicholas Bayne (1984), *Hanging Together: The Seven Power Summits*, Harvard University Press, Cambridge MA.

Putnam, Robert (1994), "Western Summitry in the 1990's: American Perspectives", *International Spectator*, vol. 29 (April-June 1994), pp. 81-94.

Radelet, S. and J. Sachs (1999), "What Have We Learned, So Far, from the Asian Financial Crisis?", Unpublished paper, (January 4), pp. 1-24.

Rajan, R.S. (1999), "The Brazilian and Other Currency Crises of the 1990s", *Claremont Policy Briefs* (99-02), May, pp. 1-4.

Rodrik, D. (1999), *The New Global Economy and Developing Countries: Making Openness Work*, Overseas Development Council, Washington DC.

Rogoff, Kenneth (1999), "International Institutions for Reducing Global Financial Instability", *Journal of Economic Perspectives, 13*(4), pp. 21-42.

Rowlands, Dane (1999), "High finance and low politics: Canada and the Asian Financial Crisis", in Fen Hampson, Michael Hart and Martin Rudner, eds., *A Big League Player: Canada Among Nations*, Oxford University Press, Toronto, pp. 113-36.

Rugman, Alan M., ed. (1994), *Foreign Investment and NAFTA*, University of South Carolina Press, Columbia, SC.

Rugman, Alan M. (1996), Selected Papers, *Volume 1: The Theory of Multinational Enterprises; Volume 2: Multinationals and Trade Policy*, Edward Elgar, Cheltenham.

Rugman, Alan M. and Joseph R. D'Cruz (1997), "The Theory of the Flagship Firm", *European Management Review*, 15(4), pp. 403-411.

Rugman, A. and John Kirton (1999), "NAFTA, Environmental Regulations and International Business Strategies", 11(4).

Rugman, Alan M. and Richard Hodgetts (1995), *International Business: A Strategic Management Approach*, McGraw-Hill, New York.

Rugman, A. (1999), "Negotiating Multilateral Rules to Promote Investment", in M. Hodges, J. Kirton and J. Daniels, eds., *The G8's Role in the New Millennium*, Ashgate, Aldershot, pp. 143-158.

Rugman, Alan M., John Kirton and Julie A. Soloway (1999), *Environmental Regulations and Corporate Strategy*, Oxford University Press, forthcoming, Oxford.

Sachs, J., A. Tornell and A. Velasco (1996), "The Collapse of the Mexican Peso: What Have We Learned?", *Economic Policy*, (22), pp. 15-56.

Sachs, J. and F. Larrain (1999), "Why Dollarization Is More Straitjacket than Salvation", *Foreign Policy*, Fall, 80-93.

Sachs, J. (1985), "The Dollar and the Policy Mix: 1985", *Brooking Papers on Economic Activity* 1.

Salyer, K.D. and S.M. Sheffrin. (1998), "Spotting Sunspots: Some Evidence in Support of Models with Self-Fulfilling Prophecies", *Journal of Monetary Economics*, 42(3), December, pp.511-523.

Serbin, Andres, Andres Stambouli, Jennifer McCoy and William Smith (1993), eds., *Venezuela: La Democracia bajo presion,* Editorial Nueva Sociedad, Caracas.

Shell, K. (1987), "Sunspot Equilibrium", pp. 549-551 in J. Eatwell, M. Milgate, and P. Newman (eds.), *The New Palgrave Dictionary of Economics, Vol. 4, Q to Z,* The Macmillan Press, London.

Shleifer A. and L. Summers (1990), "The Noise Trader Approach to Finance", *Journal of Economic Perspectives*, 4(2).

Snidal, Duncan (1985), "The Limits of Hegemonic Stability Theory", *International Organization*, 39(4), pp. 579-614.

Stein, E. (1999), "Financial Systems and Exchange Rates: Losing Interest in Flexibility", *Latin American Economic Policies*, vol. 7, pp. 2, 8.

Strange, Susan (1998), *Mad Money: When Markets Outgrow Governments*, University of Michigan Press, Ann Arbor.

Strange, Susan (1988), *States and Markets*, Pinter, London.

Strange, Susan (1996), *The Retreat of the State*, Cambridge University Press, Cambridge.

Summers, L.H. (1999), "Distinguished Lecture on Economics in Government: Reflections on Managing Global Integration", *The Journal of Economic Perspectives*, 13(2), (Spring), pp. 3-18.

Svensson, L.E.O. (1992), "An Interpretation of Recent Research on Exchange Rate Target Zones", *Journal of Economic Perspectives*, 6(4), pp. 119-144.

Tomlinson, John (1999), *Globalization and Culture*, Polity Press, Cambridge.

Transparency International (TI) (1998), 1998 Corruption Perceptions Index: A Joint Initiative Undertaken by TI and Göttingen University, Germany, http://www.gwdg.de/~uwvw/CPI1998.html.

Ulan, M.K. (2000), "Is a Chilean-Style Tax on Short-Term Capital Flows Stabilizing? A Review Essay", *Open Economies Review*, forthcoming.

United Nations Conference on Trade and Development (UNCTAD) (1997), *World Investment Report*, United Nations, New York.

U.S. Economics Analyst (1999), Goldman, Sachs & Co. Global Research, (99/23).

von Furstenberg, G.M. (1998), "From Worldwide Capital Mobility to International Financial Integration", *Open Economies Review*, 9(1), January, pp. 53-84.

von Furstenberg, George M. and Joseph P. Daniels (1992), "Economic Summit Declarations, 1975-1989: Examining the Written Record of International Cooperation", *Princeton Studies in International Finance, No. 72*.

Walter, N. (1999), "Prävention statt Krise. Zukunftsentwürfe für eine globale Finanzarchitektur", *Internationale Politik*, 54(12), p. 19-26.

Walter, N. (1999), "Again(st) the IMF", *Bulletins*, Deutsche Bank Research, No. 2, p. 3-4.

Watanabe, K. (1999), "Japan's Summit Contributions and Economic Challenges", in M. Hodges, J. Kirton and J. Daniels, eds., *The G8's Role in the New Millennium*, Ashgate, Aldershot, pp. 95-106.

Webb, Michael (1992), "Canada and the International Monetary Regime", in Claire Cutler and Mark Zacher, eds., *Canadian Foreign Policy and International Economic Regimes*, UBC Press, Vancouver, pp. 153-185.

Webb, Michael (1999), "The Group of Seven and Political Management of the Global Economy", University of Victoria (10 June).

Weintraub, S. and C. Sands, eds. (1998), *The North American Auto Industry Under NAFTA*, CSIS Press, Washington DC.

Williamson, John and Molly Mahar (1998), "A Survey of Financial Liberalization", *Essays in International Finance, No. 211*.

Williamson, J. (1998), "Crawling Bands or Monitoring Bands: How to Manage

Exchange Rates in a World of Capital Mobility", *International Finance*, October.
Williamson, J. (1994), *Estimating Equilibrium Exchange Rates*, Institute for International Economics, Washington DC.
Williamson, J. and M. Miller (1987), "Targets and Indicators: A Blueprint for the International Coordination of Economic Policy", *Policy Analyses in International Economics No. 22*, Institute for International Economics, Washington DC.
Wren-Lewis, S. and R. Driver (1998), *Real Exchange Rates for the Year 2000*, Institute for International Economics, Washington DC.

Index